Communications in Computer and Information Science   **561**

Commenced Publication in 2007
Founding and Former Series Editors:
Alfredo Cuzzocrea, Dominik Ślęzak, and Xiaokang Yang

More information about this series at http://www.springer.com/series/7899

Polina Eismont · Natalia Konstantinova (Eds.)

Language, Music, and Computing

First International Workshop, LMAC 2015
St. Petersburg, Russia, April 20–22, 2015
Revised Selected Papers

 Springer

Editors
Polina Eismont
Saint Petersburg State University
   of Aerospace Instrumentation
St. Petersburg
Russia

Natalia Konstantinova
University of Wolverhampton
Wolverhampton
UK

ISSN 1865-0929   ISSN 1865-0937   (electronic)
Communications in Computer and Information Science
ISBN 978-3-319-27497-3   ISBN 978-3-319-27498-0   (eBook)
DOI 10.1007/978-3-319-27498-0

Library of Congress Control Number: 2015956352

Printed on acid-free paper

This Springer imprint is published by SpringerNature
The registered company is Springer International Publishing AG Switzerland

Preface

This volume features the proceedings of the International Workshop on "Language, Music and Computing" that was held in St. Petersburg, Russia, during April 20–22, 2015. The workshop was organized by two leading universities of St. Petersburg– St. Petersburg State University of Aerospace Instrumentation and St. Petersburg State Conservatoire, named after N.A. Rimsky-Korsakov. The organizers intended to bring together scientists in different fields (linguistics, musicology, and computing) to discuss interdisciplinary problems. The workshop focused on such issues as language and music acquisition; influence of music skills on language acquisition and language processing; influence of linguistic skills on music acquisition; relationship between music and language training; linguistic and music knowledge, their structure and functioning; explicit and implicit knowledge of music and language; similarities and differences in understanding of music and language; automatic classification of linguistic and musical knowledge; formal models of linguistic and musical knowledge. This interdisciplinary (music/language/computing) workshop has become the first event of its kind in Russia.

The audience at the conference (about 70 participants from 18 countries) included researchers in the field of linguistics, music theory, and music history, computer science, mathematics, ethnography, performing arts, etc. The keynote speakers were distinguished specialists in these fields: Tatiana Bershadskaya (St. Petersburg State Conservatoire); David Pesetsky (Massachusetts Institute of Technologies, USA); Andrej A. Kibrik (The Institute of Linguistics, Russian Academy of Sciences, Moscow/Moscow State University); John Frederick Bailyn (Stony Brook University, New York, USA); Martin Rohrmeier (Dresden Technical University, Germany). In all, 23 submissions were chosen for oral presentations and 15 submissions were presented at the poster session. Each submission was reviewed by three reviewers who are well-known specialists in their field. The program of the workshop also included a concert of electronic music and a chamber concert of Russian romances. Only 13 full papers were selected for this volume.

The volume consists of five parts representing the variety of issues discussed at the conference. The papers in the first part briefly describe the state of the art in research on the relation between language and music in Russia. Tatiana Bershadskaya's article provides new arguments for the point that surface parallels in terminology reflect the structural analogies in syntax, morphology, and logic of subordination both in music and verbal language. The paper by Polina Eismont and Natalia Degtyareva reviews the main issues discussed in Russian studies examining the relation between language and music and discusses the experimental data of a sample case study that proves that the understanding of meaning in music depends on the listener's familiarity with the music and there is no evidence of any "innate" meaning.

Three papers in the second part represent a new view of the correlation of music and language in education. The first paper of the section by John Bailyn discusses the latest ideas of a critical period in music and language acquisition. The author argues that music skills are a form of advanced human accomplishment, which is not directly relevant to the issues of maturation and evolution of basic musical perception. Bijan Zelli's paper provides experimental data proving that focusing on the functions of *spatial, temporal, timbral,* and *dynamic* components of both music and language highlights hidden aspects of these similarities in semantic, syntactic, and pragmatic contexts that may become a helpful tool in music education. Caitlin Johnson explores pattern-thinking and reflective writing as the skills that may help composers in both synthesizing their ideas and arranging their patterns.

The third part describes corpus studies. Olga Mitrofanova's article deals with the problems of the Russian text corpus on musicology annotation. She suggests a new topic model based on latent Dirichlet allocation, which allows one to distinguish general and special topics. This new model helps to describe the conceptual structure of the corpus and to analyze paradigmatic and syntagmatic relations between lemmata within topics. The problem of Brazilian Portuguese pronominal verbs annotation is discussed in Aline Camila Lenharo's paper. The author proposes a way to formalize them based on the theoretical assumptions of functionalism (especially the Dutch current), with a view to treatment of linguistic knowledge into computational-linguistic contexts. The unique corpus of spoken Russian everyday speech containing regularly occurring singing fragments is examined in Tatiana Sherstinova's article. The analyzed data provide new information on people's singing behavior in everyday life. Among the results of the study, one of the most unexpected findings is the lack of singing by participants between the ages of 30 to 40 years, i.e., in the period that is usually considered to be the peak of a person's social maturity, normally characterized by active work and career development.

The main issue of the fourth part is the problem of music notation. María-Teresa Campos-Arcaraz suggests a basic set of new signs based on combinations of nine raised dots to modify Braille musicography, which is now insufficient for representing all the required musical signs. Indranil Roy's paper deals with the problem of communicating music across the boundaries, as different music cultures use different types of notation that need to be translated. The author proposes a new digital audio visual notation system for Indian music to reconcile them while addressing the limitations of printed sheet music through computer software solutions.

The final part of the volume includes three papers that propose new ways of applying linguistic theories and mechanisms in music research. Gregory Martynenko's paper discusses the results of a time series analysis of pitch and stress indices in Russian romances that show the differences in expressing intonation contrasts in a poetry-musical period (strophe). Maria Konoshenko and Olga Kuznetsova's paper suggests a new understanding of the interaction between tone and melody. Using songs in Guinean Kpelle and Guro as test cases, the authors prove that contour tones are less preserved in melody than level tones, and surface tones are reflected in melody rather than underlying tones. The last paper in the volume, by Oğuzhan Tuğral, presents a linguistic generative theory X-bar approach that is used to analyze "early music" repertoires and associates it with Foucault's archaeological approach to historical documents.

On behalf of the Program and Organizing Committees of the LMAC Workshop we would like to acknowledge the members of St. Petersburg State University of Aerospace Instrumentation and personally the head of the University, Prof. Yulia A. Antokhina, the vice-head, Prof. Konstantin V. Losev, the head of the Department of Foreign Languages, Prof. Marina A. Tchikhanova, and the members of St. Petersburg

State Conservatoire, named after N.A. Rimsky-Korsakov, and personally the head of the conservatoire, Prof. Mikhail K. Gantvarg, and the vice-head, Prof. Natalia I. Degtyareva, for their invaluable help and support. We would like to acknowledge all reviewers and especially Prof. Olga Mitrenina (St. Petersburg State University) and Prof. John Bailyn (Stony Brook University of New York) for their patience and helpful remarks. We would like to acknowledge the editors of Springer and especially Leonie Kunz for their help, support, and patience, which made this volume possible.

We would also like to thank the Russian Foundation for Basic Research for financial support of the event (project No. 15-06-20163).

October 2015

Polina Eismont
Natalia Konstantinova

Organization

Program Committee

Olga Mitrenina	Saint Petersburg State University, Russia (Chair)
John Frederick Bailyn	SUNY at Stony Brook, USA
Natalia Degtyareva	St. Petersburg State Conservatoire named after N.A. Rimsky-Korsakov, Russia
Polina Eismont	St. Petersburg State University of Aerospace Instrumentation, Russia
Sergey Krylov	Russian Academy of Science, Moscow, Russia
Maria Eskevich	EURECOM, France
Natalia Konstantinova	University of Wolverhampton, UK
Anton Tanonov	St. Petersburg State Conservatoire named after N.A. Rimsky-Korsakov, Russia
Nadezhda Solovyeva	St. Petersburg State University of Aerospace Instrumentation, Russia

Contents

Linguistic Studies of Music

General Questions

Analogies and Parallels in the Structure of Music and Verbal Languages

Tatiana Bershadskaya[✉]

Saint Petersburg State Conservatoire, Saint-Petersburg, Russia
chattepol@yahoo.com

Abstract. This paper is focused on the obvious similarities between verbal and music language, revealing their commonalities on a structural level while pointing out the similarities in their structural units, their hierarchy, laws of connection and development from smaller to larger constructions.

Keywords: Musical language · Verbal language · Terminology · Music theory

1 Introduction

In the article "Experience of novelistic composition analysis", A. Reformatsky states that "all sciences usually undergo three stages:

(1) chaotic accumulation of material
(2) classification and accumulation of the multiplicity of small laws (period of pluralism)
(3) synthesizing this collection into several general laws (tendency towards monism)" [1].

This statement is so wise and just, that its provisions can be attributed not only to science itself, but also increasingly to objects and phenomena which at first seem to be very different while at a deeper and more comprehensive study exhibiting many common features. Modern science is moving in this direction.

It would be strange if the situation were different, though the degree of manifestation of semantic-verbal subject specificity in verbal language and music were at opposite poles (A. Denisov writes about it in great detail and very convincingly; see [2]). The ways and means of expression, forms of information transmission embedded in a message are still closely connected.

Both verbal speech and music are *time* systems, which naturally implies similarity in form (mandatory division). Both verbal language and music encode their messages in sound. Bodies also similarly perform verbal speech and musical intonation, via our vocal apparatus and breathing. The role of speech apparatus components such as ligaments and breathing in the formation and implementation of musical tone apply not only to vocal music (which goes without saying), but also to instrumental music. Many experiments demonstrate that music written for an orchestra is intoned internally by both composer and listener in their minds and body; ligaments and breathing react to sound (reproduced or imagined). Therefore the existence of organic links cannot be doubted.

© Springer International Publishing Switzerland 2015
P. Eismont and N. Konstantinova (Eds.): LMAC 2015, CCIS 561, pp. 3–10, 2015.
DOI: 10.1007/978-3-319-27498-0_1

Both speech and music scientists, of course, have not overlooked these obvious phenomena. The analogy between verbal language and music has been studied very carefully by musicologists, especially on the issues of division, syntax (the structure of phrases), periods, sentences and larger forms. A. Reformatsky (a linguist) speaks about analogies between novels and sonata allegro [1]. The reflection of rhythmic-pitch parameters of verbal speech in the melodic line of vocal works has been studied broadly (B. Asafiev, V. Vasina-Grossman, E. Ruchyevskaya and others).

The role of intonation, as well as the role of music, in general, has become more prominent in many linguistic works. For example, Maslov argues that phrasal stress "is achieved by means of music - raising or lowering the pitch, dynamics, and so on." [3]. In my works I talk about it in great detail [4]. Here I can only say the following: a narrower, grammatical level has been much less studied by scientists (M. Aranovskiy. M. Bonfeld). In addition, the observed similarities and parallels are usually considered much more straightforward, often with the tendency to equate them.

Thus, for example, G. Riman tried to establish an identity of cadence with various punctuation marks. I would like to emphasize the fact that there is no similarity in those parallels. This distorts the essence of the problem and leads to vulgarization of the finest nuances of analogy. When drawing parallels and analogies between settings, one must remember that music and verbal languages significantly differ in many ways. The most important difference stems from the fact that verbal language is a system of *signs,* whereas music is a *non-sign* system. Verbal (non-artistic) speech enables the separation of expression and content. As for music, *what* is said is always equal to *how* it is said. Any change in *how* implies a change in *what.* As we shall see, many of the differences in the functioning of the individual units of verbal language and music are due to this circumstance.

I divide my report into 3 items:

(1) parallels in terminology
(2) parallels in morphology
(3) parallels in logic of subordination

2 Parallels in Terminology

Why pay so much attention to the coincidences in terminology of musicology and linguistics? Because if a term is really a *term,* it is certainly a part of a *terminology system,* which reflects some existing concept. Thus, the matching of a certain term in different sciences may indicate the analogy of the subject studied. Here I make a rough "dictionary of terminology concurrence", divided into two main groups:

(1) term and meaning are similar
(2) one term - different meaning (Table 1)

Many similarities are found during the process of cognition, throughout the formation of the term and the complexities which arise when science tries to specify some

Table 1. Parallels in linguistic and music terminology

Terms	
Musicology	Linguistics
Accent (Lat. accentus – stress)	
The meaning of the term is almost identical in both sciences	
Dialect (Gr. dialektos – parlance)	
The term is commonly used in Folklore studies. It is primarily studied as a regional phenomenon, especially strong on phonological level	The term defines a variety of the language in question. Regional and social dialects are distinguished
Inversion (Lat. inversion – turning upside down)	
Refers to any change in ordering of tones in the initial musical structure	Any deviance in word order of a sentence from the canonical
Intonation (Lat. intonio – pronouncing loudly)	
The meanings of the term coincide in both musical and verbal language theory	
Context (Lat. contextus – connection, joining together)	
This notion is widely applied in both musicology and linguistics. "Context is a system of relations between the words used to determine the function of an element in a text" [5]	
Melodics	
A generic term for a number of melodic phenomena. The term *melody* is of more specific meaning	The term *melodics* has an almost identical meaning to the notion of *melody* in musicology
Orthography (Gr. orthos – correct, grapho – to write)	
In both music and verbal language it presents a conventional system of unified spelling used in written speech	
Raising/lowering the pitch	
The notion is used in similar fashion in both musical and verbal systems	
Period, sentence	
The analogy in functioning of these terms is only distant. In both musicology and linguistics they denote structural units of speech. Structural characteristics of those units and their correlation in a given context, however, are not quite identical. However, this requires additional consideration	
Syntagm (Gr. sintagma – put together in order, connected)	
In music this presents a segment within a text, separated with rest symbols, as well as breath marks, caesurae, occurring when phrase repetition takes place (e.g. in sequences)	Tone and sense unit consisting of a word, word group, or even a sentence. The primary way to divide a sentence into segments or syntagms is a pause, acting as an integral element of speech melody
Syntax (Gr. syntaxis – construction, order)	
All forms, features and principles of segmentation; structural hierarchy of the units in a text; principles of combining small parts to form larger structures	Grammar in connected speech, grammar of units of a higher level than words. It studies processes of speech production: compatibility of words and word order within a sentence, in addition to general properties of a sentence

(Continued)

Table 1. (*Continued*)

Terms	
Musicology	Linguistics
Subordination	
Generally, denoting a hierarchical pattern in coupling the parts of a whole	
Text (Lat. texus – a thing woven, connection)	
In both 'word' and 'music', sounds are represented in written form, different in the method applied, but consistent with the intended meaning. This appears another substantial indicator of similarity between the two systems	
Ellipsis (Gr. elleipsis – omission)	
Denotes omission of a resolving chord, especially within melodic and harmonic modulations, as well as in dissonant chord progressions	Omission of the intended linguistic unit in speech or text. E.g. *'Another helping, please!'* (Ivan Krylov's *Demian's Fish*)
Same terms denoting different phenomena	
Arrangement (Fr. arranger – to place things in order)	
Adaptation of an original composition for a different instrument and performing ensembles	Used to indicate the word order
Complement	
A complementary phrase affirming the tonality which follows the period ended in cadence (a structural unit)	A subordinate part of the sentence (a functional unit).
Consonance, consonantism	
Consonance is defined by the degree of acoustic tonal fusion of the notes	Refers to a consonant system in a given language. Ratio of consonants to vowels.
Modality (Lat. modus – measure, manner)	
A way to organize the elements based on the use of particular modes – melodic idioms, rhythmical formulas, rules to build an integral structure, fixed scales	Functional and semantic category reflecting a certain kind of attitude of a speaker towards reality expressed in speech; subjectivity of a speaker's message.
Forte (Ital. forte – strongly, loudly)	
It is used to denote the degree of loudness and sound intensity	Denotes the force of exhaling (aspiration) when articulating voiceless consonants

phenomena and structures. Notable is the fact that difficulties arise when dealing with structures that are similar in verbal language and in music. A few examples follow.

Tune/motive (in music) and word (verbal) cannot be totally identical especially in their semantic volume. Nevertheless, they are often compared; this is not a coincidence. Structurally, they have much in common. They are both the smallest separated elements of the text which possess individual meaningfulness. Tune/motive is determined from the point of view of rhythm, structurally, as a thematic element, and there is still no united position on it. The definition of the category of "words" is also quite vague in linguistics. Here are two statements: "The concept of word is clear, but in reality it is one of the most ambiguous concepts that occur in linguistics" [6]. "It is very difficult to give a precise definition of a word. Many linguists were ready to abandon this concept" [7].

Similar problems arise in determining period, sentence, phrase, statement and construction. None of these have received a clear definition in linguistics, nor in music. From the points mentioned above, it is seen how close the parallels are that exist between these phenomena in verbal language and in music. Those parallels are reflected even in the difficulties of the terminology establishment.

3   Parallels in Morphology

Morphology is word structure. Morphology studies the structure of a language's meaningful units and, in particular, the rules of constructing lexical items and words, as well as their context variation. In short, it covers the hierarchy of *phoneme - morpheme - word* and the preservation of the word's original meaning in any transformations. Particularly interesting is the process of transformation of insignificant ("unilateral") sound units - phonemes into meaningful ("bilateral") morphs and words. There seems a close analogy to the processes which occur in music. I chose such units, as a *word* in verbal language and *motive/tune* (also structurally similar *-popevka (melody))* in music. At the same time I should emphasize on the fact that I do not claim their identity, especially on a semantic level. *Motive/tune* will never be identical to words for the simple reason that a word is a *sign,* which retains its meaning for all the texts where it is used. Music is fundamentally a *non-sign* system. Therefore *motive/tune* retains its inner meaning and thematic significance only for a particular text. However, as structural units, these two elements are quite comparable. Both *motive/tune* and *words,* as mentioned above, are the smallest detachable particles of a text that preserve their recognizability at a distance even when being converted. Therefore, it seems to me scientifically correct to compare them from a formally-structural point of view.

How are bilateral units of language formed? Phonemes form morphemes, morphemes – words. At the same time, there are no absolute boundaries. In some cases, a phoneme can be equal to a morpheme (e.g. *a* as an article), a morph as an indivisible particle can become a significant word (meaningful), a word can become a sentence (Fire!). The same can be seen in music. The motive tune consists of tones. At the same time a motive can consist of only one tone (Waltz-Scherzo by Tchaikovsky, the first sound of the main role of the first part of Beethoven's First Symphony). A word can consist of a different number of phonemes, like as a motive can consist of a different number of tones. A word implies a certain order of phonemes. Changing of the order changes the word *(name – mane).* The same process may be found in music (compare the main melody of the folk song "Goodbye Joy" to "Nocturne in G Minor" by Chopin).

The same phoneme in some cases is only a part of a word/morpheme, in some other cases it can become the morpheme itself (see the same example). Similarly, this happens in music. In some cases tone is just a part of motive; in others, it becomes the motive itself (the same example). Changes in the phoneme result in a change in the word *(cat-cut, mate-mat).* In music, any changes in one tone can affect the essence of the motive, turning, for example, a major theme into a minor one, and so on (cf. Beethoven's Fifth Symphony, part II).

At this point, it is worth paying attention to such verbal language phenomenon as *allophone,* which, in my opinion, also has analogies in music language. It is known that the essence of one phoneme can correspond to its several specific manifestations, depending on various positional conditions of pronunciation. This is similar to what N. Garbuzov defined as "the zone nature of sound", that is our understanding of tone as the same pitch within six oscillations. The analogy seems quite fitting.

Heaving considered, in my opinion, unquestionable analogies in the structural actions of phoneme and tone, it is necessary to emphasize the considerable difference in roles which appear at a juncture of units in linguistic terminology, expression of function, and function's content. The phoneme in verbal language is a completely insignificant unit. In music, the function of tone coincides with the function of phoneme, but only partially, if we consider tone as a representative of only definite absolute pitch. However, when a tone gets into tune, this tone is immediately filled with modal function (stability - instability), i.e. it stops being completely insignificant. It can no longer be a *toneme* representative. In another motive the same tone gets a different modal value and is therefore seen in a completely different quality.

In other words, even though analogies in the structures of verbal language and music are undoubted, it is necessary to consider their significant differences, which appear while going from the level of expression to the level of content.

Let us consider some similarities in the structures of bilateral units. Since these units are not only related to the level of expression but also to the level of content, the problem becomes more complex. I will try to stay closer to the issues of structural analogies.

A motive-tune (as a word) is recognizable and stands out not only in the expositional parts of the text, but also in developing areas. Here its changes (intonational, modal, tonal, sometimes rhythmic) can contribute significant adjustments to the nature of the emotional impact it produces (and that is the very essence of music); (cf. Tchaikovsky, the Fifth Symphony, part II). Such changes of a recognizable motive/tune are similar to the change of words in different cases, tenses and voice (this is not identity, only an analogy!) I find this analogy referring to the element's form of existence in a system quite convincing.

4   Parallels in Logic of Subordination

Leaving aside the question of the role of intonation, one can proceed to a fundamentally different level - the level of logical subordination. Focusing on analogies between the modal system of music and the phenomenon which is known in linguistics as *predication* (the connection between independent objects of thought, what makes a series of individual words a *sentence*). Predication is expressed by accrediting words (material units) with functions of a sentence's parts (the ideal category, which is a characteristic of *the highest level of abstraction).*

The same can be said about *mode.* It is the result of such musical intonation characteristics as the ability to give an impression of tone differentiation. This is due to pitch, as well as psychological effect (the impression of calming down, ability to stop, or anxiety, the necessity to continue the movement).This is what has been defined as *stability – instability* by musicologists.

So, here we are talking about the transition from material level to the level of psychology and cognition. It is particularly important to consider two points:

(1) The impression of this differentiation is formed as an *overscript* (though based on a specific text, exists separately).
(2) Functional differentiation of tones occurs regardless of their absolute pitch: the same tone in one tune will sound as a steady tone: in another - as a flutter tone, and so on. This was discussed while comparing the roles of phoneme and tone.

This could lead to some objections: the elements of the systems in consideration belong to different levels: *words* (bilateral units) in a sentence and *tones* in a system of mode.

Firstly, recall how flexible and mobile the boundary between the statuses of units in verbal language is. As for duality of a tone status, it has already been mentioned before. Secondly, the question under discussion is about more general and deeper processes - the processes of transitioning from a material substance into an ideal substance. Thus the parallels seem quite legitimate.

Analogies can be observed in the forms and methods of detection of subordinate systems. The ideal modal function system can only be found through its material incarnation. One cannot "play" or "sing" a keynote without voicing (virtually or in the mind) at least a brief (but tonally meaningful) motive or phrase. This is true for verbal language. It is possible to "show the subject" without voicing (or imagining) the whole phrase. As a result, we can see the necessity of some kind of material layer in order to reach an ideal essence.

Sentence constituent function can be detected in different ways: morphologically, by order, by intonation, and so on. An analogy can be seen in music.

In stereotypical modes (major and minor), certain structures are fixed for certain functions, which allow one to recognize the element's function by its structure (major seventh as an undeniable dominant). This is comparable to the morphological features by which a word in a verbal system is detected. However, there are also effective modes, which, in each case, have different structures. In this case, as well as in some verbal language sentences, tone function will depend on context (its position in the motive, order of appearance, connection with the caesura breath mark, accents, and so on). All this is very reminiscent of non-morphological ways of sentence function detection.

Also one cannot forget about such verbal forms of mode expression as "systems without keynote" (systems without framed key note), so typical of modern music. They are often, and incorrectly, termed *atonal*. There are some analogies in verbal language. Here is the text where all the main parts of a sentence are absent, while subordinate parts of the sentence manage the text:

"On the hills - round and tan,
Under the ray - dusty and strong,
With a boot - meek and mild -
After the cloak - reddened and torn"
(Marina Tsvetaeva, "The Student" (translated by Ilya Shambat))

There are no subjects, no predicates, and thus the text makes one feel *suspended*. It is deprived of support, but nevertheless the system of subordination is expressed quite definitely by coordination of subordinate sentence parts.

5 Conclusion

This report is just a fragmentary draft of the large problem, which awaits research at the deepest level and from numerous angles. Only then will the affinity of music and verbal text be confirmed and scientifically demonstrated with appropriate completeness.

References

1. Reformatsky, A.A.: Opyt analiza novellisticheskoy kompozicii (Experience of novelistic composition Analysis), Opoyaz, Moscow (1922). (in Russian)
2. Denisov, A.: Muzykalny yazyk: structura i funkcii (Musical language: structure and functions). Nauka, Saint-Petersburg (2003). (in Russian)
3. Maslov Y.S.: Vvedenie v yazykoznanie (Introduction to linguistics). Vysshaya shkola, Moscow (1975). (in Russian)
4. Bershadskaya, T.S.: Stat'I raznykh let (Selected papers of different years). Soyuz khudozhnikov, Saint-Petersburg (2004). (in Russian)
5. Aranovsky, M.: Muzykalny tekst: struktura i svoystva (Musical text: Structure and characteristics). Kompozitor, Moscow (1998). (in Russian)
6. Bally, C.: Linguistique générale et linguistique française. E. Leroux, Paris (1932)
7. Reformatsky, A.A.: Vvedenie v yazykovedenie (Introduction to linguistics). Prosveshchenie, Moscow (1967). (in Russian)

In Search of Meaning: Study on Relation of Language and Music in Works of Russian Scientists

Polina Eismont[1(✉)] and Natalia Degtyareva[2]

[1] Saint Petersburg State University of Aerospace Instrumentation,
Saint Petersburg, Russia
polina272@hotmail.com
[2] Saint Petersburg State Conservatoire, Saint Petersburg, Russia
natad-49@mail.ru

Abstract. The article explores the problem of meaning perception in music. It gives a short review of the main issues discussed in Russian studies on relation of language and music. The paper deals with the experimental data of a sample case study. The data of associative and semantic differential experiment shows that understanding of the meaning of music depends on how familiar listener is with the music. A well-known melody is a part of the world's image, having a specific place in the conceptual system, thus, the meaning of its cognitive frame [30] is used. On the other hand, if the musical fragment does not belong to a frame, its perception is limited to its emotional impact which is perceived as its meaning.

Keywords: Music · Language · Speech · Semantics · Semiotics · Emotions · Three orders of information

1 Introduction

All existing studies on expression of the musical meaning may be divided into two groups. Adepts of the first group believe that some elements of the musical text have an absolutely clear meaning which may migrate from one piece to another, forming kind of an intertext; it is possible to trace its development (etymology) from one piece to another, from one epoch to another [14]. The correlation between the musical phrase and the meaning is so tight, that it is possible to propose a dictionary where each melody will have a meaning or a set of meanings. Thus, we may suggest semiotics of the musical phrase, similar to the bilateral structure of language.

Adepts of another point of view, on the contrary, believe that in music we deal with a unilateral text which is not a sign system since in a new context tones and melodies have individual meanings, which cannot be derived from their previous use, thus preventing us from unifying all these elements into a dictionary (Bershadskaya, in this volume).

Another difference which is crucial for defining whether the musical text has a constant meaning or not, refers to an idea of universality of the musical language. It is widely known that to understand the meaning of the text in any language it is necessary

P. Eismont and N. Konstantinova (Eds.): LMAC 2015, CCIS 561, pp. 11–23, 2015.
DOI: 10.1007/978-3-319-27498-0_2

first to learn this language. Otherwise, the speech would be a senseless flow of inarticulate sounds[1].

Furthermore, it is clear that the musical text may be perceived without any special musical background. Any person, regardless of his/her hearing, musical background[2], origins and native language is able to hear (and listen to) the music. Of course, some people prefer classic music, jazz, while others love chanson songs, but regardless of their preferences they all listen to the musical texts and distinguish them from each other.

The paper reviews all existing theories of understanding of musical meaning in Russian musicology (Sect. 2), introduces the notion of *informativity* of music text and discusses the results of a sample case study of music understanding by naïve listeners (Sect. 3) and comes to the conclusion that understanding of the meaning of music depends on how familiar listener is with the music which proves the absence of any determined initial meaning of musical fragments (Sect. 4).

2 Studies of Meaning in Russian Musicology

Studies of the relation between language and music in Russia were started by Boris Asafiev, prominent Soviet scientist, who published its "Speech Intonation" in 1925. Boris Asafiev suggested that musical and speech intonations have common origin, and proposed a special system for developing hearing which is based on the idea of a single background of musical and speech intonation [1]. In "Musical Form as a Process", Boris Asafiev expanded his idea about common origins of music and speech onto other properties of both speech and musical phrases ([2]; see more detailed discussion in [3]).

For a long period of time, ideas about the relation of music and language were developed by Russian scientists, however they were on the periphery of music and linguistic sciences. Interest in studying analogies between language and music resumed in the 2nd half of 20th century. Search of common properties of speech and musical phrases and applicability of the provisions developed and used by the language science to the theory of music were among the main research areas. First of all, they had common terminology (see Bershadskaya, in this volume), covering both general principles and separate fields of linguistics (such concepts as text, dialect, syntax, accent, context etc.).

Scientists got interested in studying the semantics of musical text in early 1970s. Maurice Bonfeld stressed the importance of drawing terminology parallels between the theory of music and linguistics and considered it necessary, first of all, to identify the dichotomy of language and speech in music [4]. In linguistics, the language is a tool comprising the dictionary of units and the rules of text generation to make up speech [5, 6]. Therefore, the language is a sustainable element, universal for all speakers, thus ensuring mutual understanding during communication. On the contrary, speech is

---

[1] Furthermore, studies of intonation structure of different languages show that perception of phrase intonation of the unknown language is different from that of native speakers [26].

[2] Hereinafter by musical background we mean not only attending special educational institutions or learning how to play a musical instrument, but a habit to listen to the music from the very childhood.

individual, changeable, flexible. Identification of these two substances in music presents special difficulty since there is no tool which would be universal for all speakers and would comprise a dictionary of units and the rules. If talking about the set of rules, we may refer to the laws of harmony, polyphony, form generation, stylistic principles of the musical text, however, the existence of the dictionary of units is quite dubious (see in detail further).

Therefore, identification of the meaning-bearing components in music is under question, in other words, it is under question whether the musical text and its components are bilateral signs with expression and content planes. M. Bonfeld mentioned non-discreteness of the musical text as the main reason of failure to identify any musical units with meaningful nuclear area, independent of the context [4]. Referencing the works of Yu. M. Lotman who stressed that the poetic text could not be divided into verbal units [7], Bonfeld made the same conclusion for music: "Any independent artistic (and thus, musical) piece is a single undividable sign" [4: 39].

Not all scientists share the described point of view. In particular, it was suggested that music is a "non-sign semiotic system" [8], that it has special signs with only connotative meaning without any denotatum [9]. There were studies of music as a functional multilevel system with both bilateral syntax and morphological structures and unilateral structures – tones [10, 11]. Following the theory of M. Aranovsky, I. Pyatnitskaya-Pozdnyakova identifies two levels of semantics in music — intramusical (meanings arising from the text interaction within the context) and extramusical (additional connotations to the intramusical semantics) [12].

Some scientists share opposite point of view, giving reasons for identification of various-size musical bilateral signs. For instance, V. Kholopova introduces a new structural and semantic unit – *musical lexeme*, which is an "expressive and meaningful unity which has non-verbal or oral expression and is related to musical experience and non-musical associations" [13: 58]. This approach has been further developed in the Laboratory of semantics of music in the Ufa State Conservatoire, where the theory of musical meaning is developed. This theory assumes that "the musical language has sustainable meaning structures of musical texts, i.e. intonation expressions with defined meanings — lexemes, semantic figures, altogether forming intonation vocabulary representing the inventory and art images" [14: 33]. Among them are so called migrating intonation formulas, which are migrating from one piece to another and may slightly change depending on the stylistic context, generating new meanings under influence of other formulas, thus helping to trace the developmental history of intonation formulas. The Laboratory is working on a dictionary of intonation formulas and studies their origins and functioning of the direct and metaphorical meanings[3].

Discussion about the meaning of musical signs is closely related to the universality of music. Almost all scientists agree that unlike natural language, musical sign is universal, clear to everyone and does not need translation [16]. Nevertheless, transparency of the meaning of the musical text is under the question. Some scientists

---

[3] First tries to create such dictionaries date back to XVII–XVIII, when rhetoric figures and affects expression dictionaries were created, for example: Musurgia universalis by A. Kircher (1650), Musikalisches Lexikon by I.G. Valter (1732) [15].

believe that consistent perception of musical text is impossible without special education [14] and the musical text cannot be generated without special skills and knowledge of appropriate laws [17]. However, many scientists believe that music is a universal communication tool since the main function of the musical text (unlike the verbal text) is communication of aesthetic information, emotional impact on the listener [18–21]. Music is a cultural product reflecting musical image of the world [22] which is unique for every culture.

Investigation of interaction of literature and musical texts gives interesting results for studies of the music semantics. N. Khruscheva is investigating structural interaction of musical and literature texts and is considering such properties of music and literature cross-influence, as particular structural properties (universal formulas, such as repetition, symmetry, etc.; structural analogies: retrograde — palindrome, double canon perpetuus – pantum) and conceptual parallels (methods and approaches for communication of aesthetic meaning) [16]. This cross-influence results in development of a complex system with non-linear relations, a multilevel musical-literature unity, with new means of expression, clear structural logic, multidimensionality — non-reducibility to a single paradigm [16]. The same effect can be traced in interaction of music and words in vocal pieces ([23, 24], articles by Martynenko, Konoshenko and Kuznetsova in this volume). Words and music enrich each other: verbal speech helps to identify the meaning of the musical speech, while musical text underlines emotional properties of the words [23].

3   In Search of Meaning

3.1   Objectives and Methodology

The musical background influences the capability to perceive the texts having various orders of informativity. The concept of the text informativity introduced in the linguistics of text may be applied for the theory of music as well. Beaugrande and Dressler introduced the main principles for defining the orders of informativity in the text (three orders of informativity) [25]. The texts of the first order of informativity fully comply with the communicated information, thus there are no multiple interpretations of such texts. To understand the texts of the second order it is important to identify the relations between the components of the situation. The texts of the third order are specific since the situation described in these texts does not correspond to knowledge of the perceivers, thus they need to realize why the information received does not meet the expectations. Therefore, the texts of the first order are close to the prototypic texts, and they form a basis for the texts of the second and third order, however it is more difficult to interpret such texts, since one may stay at the second order of informativity or may achieve the third order.

In music, the first order of text informativity covers the genre of musical materials (so called primary genres: march, song, dance, etc.). Identification of the genre does not require any knowledge of musical theory. It is a prototypical concept which is a basis of the musical piece and allows almost no diverse interpretations[4]. It is one of the first concepts the children learn in the course of their musical studies. The second order of the text informativity is the emotional meaning, mood expressed by music. No special musical education is needed for its perception; however, it is necessary to listen to the music attentively, define its emotional properties and nuances.

The third order of text informativity is the deepest level of the musical text structure and means perception of the author's (composer's) intention, understanding of the musical meaning, overall meaning of the musical text. To be able to achive this level, the listener needs at least many years of experience of attentive listening to a large number of musical texts and being familiar with various musical pieces belonging to different cultural traditions.

To identify interaction of three orders of informativity in the musical texts and perception of the meaning of the musical texts by naïve (unprepared) listener, a sample case study was carried out. The initial hypothesis was that if the music is universal any person who does not have any special musical background may understand the meaning of the musical text without preliminary deep knowledge of this music. If the musical phrase has a clear, well-defined meaning, all listeners will understand this meaning without errors.

For the study, two methodologies were selected: free associative experiment and semantic differential.

The method of free associative experiment was selected to check understanding of the musical text meaning by listeners. To avoid influencing the perception of musical pieces, the instructions were as follows: "Please write down at least two associations (words, ideas, etc.) which first come to your mind while listening to the music". We intentionally did not include the direct questions ("What is this music about?" "How will you call this melody?", etc.), since associations may reveal subconscious deep understanding of texts. On the contrary, direct questions would, first of all, reveal objectives of the study and could somehow influence the received associations, and secondly would reduce the spontaneity of replies. The associations methodology may clarify both properties of perception of the first order information (genre properties of music) and of the third order information at deep subconscious level.

The method of semantic differential [27] was used to identify the second order information, and study perception of aesthetic meaning of musical pieces by listeners. The listeners were proposed to assess the pieces using three scales: *bad – good*, *week – strong*, *cold – warm*, and seven grades — from −3 to +3, including neutral mark (0). These scales do not fully correspond to those proposed by Osgood and al., however the recent studies have shown that when using this method for analysis of perception of musical stimuli it is better to pay more attention to valence scales [28], thus, the potence scale (*passive – active*) was replaced by the valence scale (*cold – warm*). The instructions were as follows: "Listen to the melodies and evaluate them using the scales (from −3 to +3). For instance, using the valence scale: −3 — *very bad*; −2 — *bad*;

---

[4] Cf. the concept *musical-communication archetypes*, which are "some basic forms of musical meaning related to protointonation form of music, which represent the initial level of musical meaning perception which is based on a range of non-special non-discrete musical means" [22: 123].

−1 — *rather bad, than good*; 0 — *neutral*; +1 — *rather good than bad*; +2 — *good*; +3 — *very good*". It was assumed that while identifying perception of the second order information, among other properties (rhythm, beat, colour etc.) there will be tonality structure of the musical piece (major, minor and complex tonality systems).

The following results were expected. If the initial theory is correct, than the number of associations belonging to the nuclear of the association field, will exceed 50 % of total associations and these associations will correspond to the meaning of the musical piece commonly accepted in the history of music. Besides, everyone will identify the first order information, and grades of three scales will coincide as well, correlating with the tonality structure of the musical piece.

If the initial hypothesis is not correct, and the meaning of the musical piece is not subject to accurate identification and is not universally perceived, then the associations received will show a significant diversity, being mostly single and individual reactions. The grades of three scales will show this diversity of perception, however, there will be certain correlation with the initial musical tonality.

An additional result to be received is a correlation between the information perceived with different orders of the text informativity. Even if the initial theory is not correct, the nuclear of each association field shall have associations of the first order of informativity along with large diversity of associations referred to the third order of informativity. Correlation between received grades and tonality structure of the musical piece will show the perception rate of the second order of informativity by naïve listeners.

3.2   Data

Twelve popular classic pieces by both Russian and European composers of XVIII–XX centuries were selected. Eleven pieces were instrumental (orchestra, piano, and violin) and one piece was presented by chorus with an orchestra:

1. P.I. Tchaikovsky "Neapolitan Dance" from "Album pour enfants", Op. 39
2. J.S. Bach "Toccata and fugue in d minor", BWV 565
3. L. van Beethoven "Symphony 5", op. 67, part 1
4. I.F. Stravinsky "Sacrificial Dance" (the Chosen One) from "The Rite of Spring"
5. V.A. Mozart "Symphony No. 40", K 550, Part 1
6. M.I. Glinka "Patriotic Song"
7. N. Paganini "Caprice No. 24 in a minor" from the cycle of 24 caprices for violin, op. 1
8. L. van Beethoven "Symphony 9", op. 125, Part 4 (theme to the text of Schiller's Ode to Joy)
9. G. Gershwin "Summertime" lullaby from "Porgy and Bess"
10. R. Wagner "Ride of the Valkyries" from "Die Walküre"
11. F. Chopin "Waltz", op. 64 No. 1, A flat major
12. P.I. Tchaikovsky "Waltz of the flowers" from "The Nutcracker"

Five of these musical pieces have major tonality (No. 1, 6, 8, 11, 12), and six pieces have minor tonality (2, 3, 5, 7, 9, 10), the piece No. 4 is a sample of complex tonality structure. Well-structured, finished thematic abstracts were selected for the study.

The listeners received a questionnaire with instructions (see above) and 12 questions as follows:

Associations:		
Scale:		
Bad	−3 | −2 | −1| 0 | +1 | +2 | +3	Good
Weak	−3 | −2 | −1| 0 | +1 | +2 | +3	Strong
Cold	−3 | −2 | −1| 0 | +1 | +2 | +3	Warm

for each musical piece.

The length of each musical piece did not exceed one minute with a 10-second pause between pieces to complete analysis of the musical piece and get prepared to the next one. Every musical piece is presented only once, and it is not possible to return to the previous music after its completion.

30 Russian-speaking adults aged from 18 to 53 took part in the study (M_{age} = 33.2, SD = 8,56), including 18 women and 12 men. All of them did not have special musical background (two women used to attend the musical classes however it was 10–12 years before the study took place).

3.3   Results and Discussion

All associations received were divided into two groups – *semantic* (meaning-bearing) associations and *general musical* associations not related to emotional or meaning properties of the music (names of instrument, genre, etc.). The later associations also included associations related to *recognition* of the presented music, such as the composer's name or title of the melody. Semantic associations were also divided into two groups – *individual* and *thematic* associations, depending on their frequency and coincidence with the traditional common understanding of the melody used in the history of music.

Frequencies of associations were used to generate the associative-semantic field of each musical piece by dividing the received associations into nuclear and peripheral ones (nuclear associations accounted for at least 10 % of cases).

The predominance of nuclear general musical and peripheral original associations was considered as an absence of any clear and easy-perceivable meanings identified by the naïve listeners. On the other hand, the predominance of nuclear thematic associations means the possibility to identify the universal meaning of the melody, and, thus, presence of the meaning available for identification and verbalization by the naïve listener.

During the experiment 640 associations and 12 rejections were received. The largest number of associations was for the melodies from Tchaikovsky's Nutcracker's ballet and Glinka's Patriotic Song (66 and 63 associations correspondingly). Large number of associations for these melodies may be explained by the fact that these pieces are well-known to the listeners: in 1990–2000 "Patriotic song" was an official hymn of Russia, and the music from the Nutcracker's ballet is broadcast on radio and TV during New Year's holidays every year. The smallest number of associations was received to Wagner's opera "Die Walküre" — only 37 associations. Average number of associations received amounted to 53.

In all responses to 12 stimuli, semantic associations prevailed. Maximum number of general musical associations was received to melodies from Paganini's Caprice No. 24 and Chopin's Waltz (46 % and 43 % of associations correspondingly). These are mono-instrument pieces. Semantic associations to these pieces have shown large variety of associations with mostly original and peripheral associations prevailing. The smallest number of general musical associations was for the melodies with semantic associations coinciding with traditional understanding of these melodies. These were, first of all, melodies No. 6, 3, 10, 4, and 2 (14 %, 15 %, 16 %, 17 %, and 19 % correspondingly).

These results suggest that the number of general musical associations depends on the listener's understanding of meaning of the melody. If the meaning is unclear, the perception will be superficial, and the listener will be limited to the first order information as the associations show. If the meaning of the melody is clear, the associations mostly include the semantic ones, and the listeners show absolute or thematic coincidence in their associations.

Among *semantic* associations, the *thematic* associations prevail. However, only once this predominance was really significant – in associations related to PATRIOTISM for the melody No.6 "Patriotic Song" by M.I. Glinka (89 % of the total number of semantic associations). In other cases, the number of thematic associations did not exceed 76 % from the total number of semantic associations. However, among the associations to the melody No. 7 (Caprice No. 24 by N. Paganini), the number of thematic associations was significantly lower than the number of individual associations (33 % and 67 % correspondingly). This might be explained by the form of this melody, which is a theme with variations (the melody presented during the study had the theme and 2 variations).

Interesting results were received during the analysis of associations for melodies No. 6, 3, 10, 4, and 2 that showed the largest numbers of semantic associations. All melodies, except for the discussed above melody No. 6, have shown thematic associations related to the following thematic groups: "WAR" — musical pieces No. 4 (Stravinsky) and 10 (Wagner), "SUPREME FORCES" — musical pieces No. 2 (Bach), 3 (Beethoven's Symphony 5), 4 (Stravinsky), "DEATH" — musical piece No. 2 (Bach), "QUICK MOVEMENT" — musical pieces No. 3 (Beethoven's Symphony 5), 4 (Stravinsky), 10 (Wagner)[5]. Furthermore, the melodies with mostly positive, cheerful properties and emotions did not reveal predominance of thematic associations over individual ones. It

---

[5] The associations of thematic group PATRIOTISM for the melody No. 6 - *victory, parade*, etc. – are also connected with thematic group WAR, but they refer to the positive emotions, while the associations for the pieces No. 4 and 10 – *fight, attack*, etc. – are aggressive and negative.

might be explained by the fact that the negative emotions are much more vivid than positive ones (73 out of 116 emotions in Russian account for negative emotions; cf. also [29]).

In all musical pieces, nuclear themes can be identified (Table 1).

Table 1. Nuclear associations (in %)

Piece	Thematic group	% of total reactions
1	Light, joy	20
2	Death	34
3	Supreme forces	33
4	War	23
5	Joy	23
6	Festival	43
	Patriotism	34
7	Positive emotions	14
8	Religion	20
	Joy	18
9	Peace	35
10	Movement	30
	War	24
11	Grace, legerity	27
12	Ball	30

As it is shown, in many cases, the identified thematic groups coincide with the figurative meanings of the melodies used in the theory of music. However, do these results confirm bilateralism of musical sign and the presence of clear universal meaning of the melody perceivable by any listener? We believe, they do not. Though the associations related to traditional meaning of melodies under consideration, account for at least 20 %, these figures only confirm that the traditional meaning is present in these melodies along with all other possible meanings, which can be identified in the musical text by a naïve listener.

To illustrate this variety of perceived meanings, let us consider the associations received for the melody from Beethoven's Symphony No. 9 (theme of the Ode to Joy). Associations received may be classified as follows: RELIGION (20 %), JOY (18 %), DEATH (8 %). Therefore, the musical text has a meaning, a sense, but this meaning is not uniform and is not universally perceived by all naïve listeners. Listening to the melody in a specific situation continuously generates sustainable associations between the music and the situation, thus incorporating the melody into the world model (cf. associations to the melodies 6 (*hymn, parade, victory*) and 12 (*ball, magic, festival*). The listener perceives the meaning of the melody as an element of the concept which has no (or almost no) relation to the initial author's intention. This may also partly explain a large number of Symphony No. 9's associations related to RELIGION: in Beethoven's music the listeners were able to hear the chorus and the orchestra which resulted in associations with church and church service (general-music associations included: *theatre, opera, performance*).

Thus, the results show that the musical text is an element of declarative knowledge, i.e. a slot in a multi-modal cognitive structure – a frame which is generated by the individual and modified during his/her life [30]. The meaning of the frame, the musical text belongs to, is perceived by the listener as a meaning of this text (cf. study of music conceptualization in [31]). Furthermore, the unknown or insufficiently known musical texts may belong to different frames, mostly related to emotions or memories, which confirms the fact that aesthetic function is the main function of music (unlike the verbal text).

Perception of emotional music properties may be identified by analyzing the semantic differential allocations, shown below (Fig. 1).

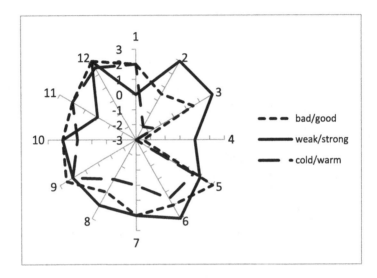

Fig. 1. Semantic differential results.

Surprisingly, no evident relation was identified between the grades and mode of music. Assessment of the major melodies (No. 1, 6, 8, 11, 12) using the scale *bad — good* and *cold — warm* does not show any significant difference with that of minor melodies (No. 2, 3, 5, 7, 9, 10). However, the major and the minor are clear in modes of grades allocation: the grades of pieces 1, 11, 12 show clear mode — +3, and only pieces 5 and 9 of the minor show the same mode and only for the scale *bad – good*.

Assessment of the fragment No. 4 from Stravinsky's ballet "The Rite of Spring" shall be mentioned, since this melody was characterized as the coldest one (median value — -3, mode — -3) and the worst one (median value — -2,5, with no clear mode). This negative assessment suggests that though no direct relation between the tonality and emotional perception of music was identified, nevertheless, the mode seems to be one of the main properties which influences perception of the musical text, while the complexity of the mode structure prevents understanding of the melody by a naïve listener.

Comparison of these results with those of the tonality perception study by Korsakova-Kreyn and Dowling shows that if individual cadences and modulations are presented to the listener, the listener defines major elements as positive and warm ones, and minor elements as negative and cold ones [28]. If whole melodies are presented, no relation is identified. These grades correlate well with the associations received (see *strength* grades of pieces 2, 3, and 4 with clear modes +3), therefore we may suggest that the musical text is actually perceived at some emotional meaning level which is not subject to division into two separate components. However, it is also possible that the listeners were subconsciously assessing not the music itself, but the associations, however this suggestion needs separate study using the said two methodologies.

4 Conclusion

This sample case study shows that the musical text, surely, has some meaning perceivable by naïve listeners. However, this meaning is not uniform and clear to everyone. Identification of the first order information in the melody – which is prototypical information about the genre of music – presented almost no difficulties, which was proved by quite a large number of general musical associations to the melodies with unclear semantics. It was further found that such melodies (No. 1, 7, and 11) are perceived only as a source of aesthetic information giving rise to some emotions. While perceiving the music without well-defined meaning, the listeners generally keep to the first and second order information. Furthermore, the analysis of semantic differential did not identify any dependency between grades and mode of music, but has shown the tendency of assessing not the melody as a whole, but its meaning.

Therefore, the results of the analysis suggest that naïve listeners perceive the musical text as follows:

- First of all, the listener identifies whether (s)he knows the melody or not. If the answer is positive, the melody is a part of a cognitive frame, and the listener assigns to this musical text the meaning of the whole frame. Furthermore, the listener does not have any problems with defining all three orders of text informativity;
- If the musical piece is unknown or insufficiently known, the listener is limited to the first and second order information, perceiving only the aesthetic value of the musical text. Such melody does not belong to any frame, however, its comparison with existing frames results in assigning some non-attributable, but possible properties (cf. assessment of the melody No. 8).

All in all, it should be noted that perception of the musical text is two-valued depending on the listener's familiarity with the music. The melody is a part of the world image, having a specific place in the conceptual system, thus, the meaning of its frame is used. Emotional perception of the melody depends on the emotional assessment of the frame, and not of the properties of the musical text. Or, if the musical text does not belong to a frame, its perception is limited to its emotional impact which is perceived as its meaning.

Finally, it is impossible to discuss these ideas without resort to the listener, because the meaning of any message, both general-purpose and artistic, verbal and musical – is addressed to the recipient, and is aiming to modify his/her world image. Eliminating any element of the main communication triad *author – melody – recipient* will make the communication meaningless and will result in the communicative failure.

References

1. Asafiev, B.V.: Izbrannye stat'i o muzykalnom prosveshchenii i obrazovanii (Selected Works About Musical Education) (in Russian). Muzyka, Leningrad (1965)
2. Asafiev, B.V.: Muzykalnaya forma kak process (Musical Form as a Process) (in Russian). Muzyka, Leningrad (1971)
3. Polshikova L.D.: "Intonacionny fond" i "Intonacionny slovar" (M.M. Bakhtin I B.V. Asafiev) ("The found of intonations" and "the vocabulary of intonations" ((M.M. Bakhtin I B.V. Asafiev) (in Russian). J. New Philol. J. **3**, 5–14 (2006)
4. Bonfeld, M.S.: Muzyka: jazyk ili rec'? (Music: is it a language or a speech?) (in Russian). J. Muzykalnaya kommunikaciya **8**, 15–39 (1996) (RIII, Saint-Petersburg)
5. Saussure Ferdinand de (préf. et éd. de Charles Bally et Albert Sechehaye, avec la collaboration d'Albert Riedlinger; éd. critique préparée par Tullio De Mauro; postface de Louis-Jean Calvet), Cours de linguistique générale, Paris, Payot, coll. « Grande bibliothèque Payot », 1995 (1re éd. 1916), 21 cm, XVIII-520
6. Shcherba, L.V.: Yazykovaya sistema i rehcevaya deyatelnost' (The Language System and Speech Activity) (in Russian). Nauka, Moscow (1974)
7. Lotman, Y.M.: O soderzhanii i structure ponyatiya "khudozhestvennaya literature" (About the meaning of the term "fiction") (in Russian). In: Selected Works, vol. 1, Tallinn, pp. 203–216 (1992)
8. Aranovsky, M.: Muzykalny tekst: struktura i svojstvva (Music Text: Structure and Characteristics) (in Russian). Moscow, Kompozitor (1998)
9. Kozarenko, O.: Ukraiska nacionalna muzichna mova: geneza ta suchasni tendencii rozvitku (Ukrainian national musical language: genesis and modern development) (in Ukrainian). Dissertation. Kiev (2001)
10. Ship, S.V.: Znakova funkciya ta movna organizaciya muzychnogo movlennya (Sign function and speech organization of music utterance) (in Ukrainian). Dissertation. Odessa State Conservatoire, Odessa (2002)
11. Nazaykinsky, E.V.: Logika muzykalnoy kompozicii (Logic of Music Composition) (in Russian). Muzyka, Moscow (1982)
12. Pyatniskaya-Pozdnyakova, I.: Muzichne movlennya v diskursi movno-znakovykh teorij (Musical Speech in the Discourse of Signs and Speech Theories) (in Ukrainian). J. Ukrainske muzykoznavstno **39**, 31–44 (2013) (Centr muzychnoy ukrainistiki, Kiev)
13. Kholopova, V.N.: Muzyka kak vid iskusstva (Music as an Art) (in Russian). Lan', Saint-Petersburg (2002)
14. Shaymukhametova, L.N.: Semantichesky analiz muzykalnogo teksta (o razrabotkakh problemnoj nauchno-issledovatel'skoy laboratorii muzykalnoy semantiki (Semantic analysis of musical text (about the work of a scientific laboratory of music semantics)) (in Russian). J. Problemy muzykalnoy nauki. **1**, 31–43 (2007)
15. Baranovskaya, T.G.: Muzykalnaya estetika (Music Aesthetics) (in Russian). GrGU, Grodno (2012)

16. Khrushcheva N.A.: Vzaimodejstvie muzyki i literatury v tvorchestve P. Buleza, L. Berio, J. Joyce (Interrelation of music and language in the works of Pierre Boulez, Luciano Berio, James Joyce) (in Russian). Dissertation. Saint Petersburg State Conservatoire, Saint-Petersburg (2014)

17. Bonfeld, M.S.: Muzyka: Jazyk. Rec'. Myshlenie. Opyt sistemnogo issledovanija muzykalnogo iskusstva (Music: Language. Speech. Thinking. A Sample of Systematic Study of Music Art) (in Russian). Kompozitor, Saint-Petersburg (2006)

18. Medushevsky, V.V.: O zakonomernostiakh i sredstvakh khudozhestvennogo vozdejstvija muzyki (About tendencies and means of aesthetic influence of music) (in Russian). Muzyka, Moscow (1976)

19. Zhukova, G.K.: Muzykalnyj smysl: jazyk, rec', myshlenie, diskurs (Music meaning: language, speech, thinking, discourse) (in Russian). J. IZVESTIA: Herzen Univ. J. Humanit. Sci. **120**, pp. 96–101 (2010)

20. Kozhenkova, A.S.: Znakovaya pripoda muzyki (A sign nature of music) (in Russian). J. Young Researcher **1**(2), 159–162 (2012)

21. Lazutina, T.V.: Jazyk muzyki v ontologicheskom aspect (Language of music from ontological point of view) (in Russian). J. Vestnik Samara State Univ. **5/2**(55), 15–23 (2007)

22. Lazutina, T.V.: Simvolichnost' muzykalnogo zhanra (Symbolism of music genre) (in Russian). J. Tomsk State Univ. **324**, 123–126 (2009)

23. Ruchyevskaya, E.A.: Slovo i muzyka (Word and Music) (in Russian). Muzgiz, Leningrad (1960)

24. Spist, E.A.: Dramaturgiya muzykalnogo cikla kak otrazhenie vzaimodejstvija Muzyki i Slova (na primere "6 stikhotvoreny dla golosa s fortepiano", op. 38 Sergeya Rakhmaninova) (The Dramaturgy of a suite as a reflection of music and word relation (based on "6 Songs" by Sergey Rakhmaninoff)) (in Russian). J. Philos. Humanit. Inf. Soc. **2**(8), 77–85 (2015)

25. De Beaugrande, R.A., Dressler, W.U.: Introduction to Text Linguistics. Longman, London. (De Beaugrande, R., Dressler, W.U.: Introduction to text linguistics/Robert-Alain de Beaugrande, Wolfgang Ulrich Dressler Longman, London, New York 1981)

26. Leed Richard, L.: A contrastive analysis of Russian and English intonation contours. Slavic East Eur. J. **9**(1), 62–75 (Spring, 1965)

27. Osgood, C.E., Suci, G., Tannenbaum, P.: The Measurement of Meaning. University of Illinois Press, Champaign (1957)

28. Korsakova-Kreyn, M., Dowling, W.: Jay Emotional processing in music: study in affective responses to tonal modulation in controlled harmonic progressions and real music. Psychomusicology: Music Mind Brain **24**(1), 4–20 (2014)

29. Ortony, A., Clore, G.L., Collins, A.: The Cognitive Structure of Emotions. Cambridge University Press, Cambridge (1988)

30. Minsky, Marvin: A framework for representing knowledge. In: Winston, P. (ed.) The Psychology of Computer Vision, pp. 211–277. McGraw Hill, New York (1975)

31. Zbikowski, L.: Conceptualizing Music: Cognitive Structure, Theory, and Analysis, AMS Studies in Music. Oxford University Press, New York (2002)

Music and Language in Education

Language, Music, Fire, and Chess: Remarks on Music Evolution and Acquisition

John Frederick Bailyn[(✉)]

Department of Linguistics, Stony Brook University, New York, USA
john.bailyn@stonybrook.edu

Abstract. There is considerable debate about the evolution of both language and music cognition in human beings (see [10, 13, 24, 25] for the former, and [6, 11, 21, 33] for the latter). However, the two debates have distinct characters. In the case of language, most agree that there exists a significant biological component to the underlying cognitive system that modern humans enjoy, which in some form was either the direct or indirect product of evolutionary changes in biology. In the case of music, however, human ability in this domain has recently been compared to mastery of fire (an obvious cultural invention) [21] and specifically dismissed as not arising through evolutionary forces, understood in the standard Darwinian sense. Patel's primary arguments [21] for this relate to childhood acquisition, which he argues occurs quite differently for language and music. In particular, he claims that there is no critical period for acquisition of music perception. I examine his arguments here, coming to quite different conclusions.

1 Introduction

In this article, I first review and reject Patel's [21] arguments against music as having developed along familiar evolutionary lines, arguing that the reasoning is at best inconclusive, at worst contradictory or simply irrelevant to the core issues of the evolution of musical perception. Through the prism of well-known diagnostics, some taken from the early philosophy of mind literature ([7] a.o.), and some from Patel [21], we will see that musical perception, like basic linguistic competence, and as opposed to mastery of fire, comprises a cognitive *module*, in the sense of [8, 12], and as such is acquired developmentally much as language is. Children go through an important critical period and, if healthy with normal exposure to a local idiom, develop a steady state of musical competence in music perception of that native idiom, which requires no explicit instruction, training or study. It is as much a part of our cognitive biology as language is, and therefore just as much a product of biological evolution.

I then turn to a brief presentation of a plausible account of music evolution, based on [19], which relies on the archeological record to make the case for the evolution of music as a biological development and not a cultural invention. In conclusion, I show that some of the confusion in Patel's presentation [21] concerns the status of the mastery of musical *output* in humans, in the form of (often brilliant) facility with

© Springer International Publishing Switzerland 2015
P. Eismont and N. Konstantinova (Eds.): LMAC 2015, CCIS 561, pp. 27–44, 2015.
DOI: 10.1007/978-3-319-27498-0_3

instrument, voice, or with musical composition. In this area, I argue that we are dealing with something much more similar to advanced mastery of chess, a form of human accomplishment which, though fascinating in its own right, is not directly relevant to the issues of maturation and evolution of basic musical perception.

2 Patel's Basic Claim

The human ability to create and manage fire distinguishes us from all other species and appears to be universal across human cultures. However, as Patel points out [21], the universality of a human competency does not necessarily entail its biological foundation:

> The ability to make and control fire is also universal in human cultures... Yet few would dispute that the control of fire was an invention based on human ingenuity, not something that was itself a target of evolutionary forces [21: 356].

Fire is clearly a cultural invention that proved so useful that it was then taught to every succeeding generation as a matter of basic cultural knowledge. Importantly, Patel claims that the null hypothesis should be that a certain human ability not be considered part of basic human biology unless there is strong evidence to that effect:

> ... the example of fire making teaches us that when we see a universal and unique human trait, we cannot simply assume that it has been a direct target of selection. In fact, from a scientific perspective it is better (because it assumes less) to take the null hypothesis that the trait in question has not been a direct target of selection. One can then ask if there is enough evidence to reject this hypothesis [21: 356].

This presupposition about which null hypothesis is more scientific could be objected to, as it considerably weakens the burden for the case against the biological nature of musical abilities. However, I will accept Patel's assumption about the null hypothesis, and show that the evidence is nevertheless strong enough to conclude about musical perception what Patel agrees we must conclude about language abilities, namely that they are unlike mastery of fire, a true cultural invention. Music, like language, has all the major hallmarks of a biological system and a mental module, under Fodor's diagnostics for the latter and under Patel's for the former. In the next section, I briefly review and apply those diagnostics to music perception.

First, however, a brief note on my assumptions about the nature of musical perception. I assume that human beings process music on a multitude of levels simultaneously (for a possible description, see *A Generative Theory of Tonal Music* [17]). These levels can include, at very least, hierarchical representations of metrical and grouping structure, tonal pitch structure and, where applicable, harmonic structure. It is important to note that Patel [21] describes musical abilities in similar terms, so that any disagreement here concerns only the evolution of these abilities, not their essentially hierarchical and representational nature.

3 Is Music Perception a Mental Module? Fodor's 1973 Diagnostics Applied

Fodor [7] provides a series of now well-known diagnostics for independent mental modules, though he does not discuss music. I will not engage in a lengthy review of the motivation for this list versus any other, but will assume that some list or other, of similar content, must be correct in identifying mental modules.

1. Characteristics of mental modules [7]

- rapidity
- automaticity
- informational encapsulation
- domain-specificity
- neural specificity
- innateness

Patel [21] does not directly address Fodor's diagnostics, though some of them clearly overlap with his own (see below). In this section I will briefly review how Fodor's diagnostics might be applied to human music perception.

3.1 Rapidity and Automaticity

It is uncontroversial that music is processed every bit as rapidly as language, under similar circumstances.[1] Experimental research clearly confirms that "this capacity rests on *fast acting* and *irrepressible processes* that enable us to extract subtle musical structures from short musical pieces" [2: 119, emphasis mine]. On this diagnostic, music processing clearly represents a unique mental module.

3.2 Informational Encapsulation

Here, Fodor has in mind the irrelevance of signals not involved in the given module's domain to perception within that domain. That is, other auditory signals, so long as they do not obscure the physical perception of the acoustic signal (by drowning it out to the ear, let us say), should not interfere with or change the organization of perceived musical signals. And indeed, what we see, smell, touch, and even hear in other domains does not affect our cognitive representation of the music. On this diagnostic, then, we have evidence of a distinct mental module at work.[2]

---

[1] From here on, I will assume "music" to mean familiar music within one's native musical "idiom", such as Western tonal music for presumably most, if not all, readers of this article. This is not to trivialize the significance of research into musical universals, non-tonal systems, polyphonic music and so on. See [17] for important discussion of this same assumption.

[2] Signals from other domains might, of course, combine in our *emotional* reaction to perceived music, but I contend that such interactions involve cognitive connections *across* domains, and they certainly do not affect the basic workings of the independent modules.

There is another important sense in which musical perception is informationally encapsulated. Memory, even of the identical piece of music, does not impinge on internally constructed musical expectations, in the sense of [17]. As Lerdahl [16] points out, "the unconscious processing of music continues blindly, no matter how well our conscious mind knows the music in question. To the internal processor, the musical input is always new" [16: 173].

3.3   Domain-Specificity

If there is a level of cognitive organization within a postulated module that involves principles specific to that module, not attested in other modules and not resulting from general principles of cognition, or from requirements of the cognitive interfaces, then it represents an instance of domain-specificity. The existence of entirely linguistic principles of organization, for example, is a common argument for the independence of the language module – certain purely syntactic constraints constitute such a case, and there are many more on the various linguistic levels. In musical perception, tonal pitch relations [16], constitute an equally domain-specific realm of psychological reality. Neither mathematical [9] nor psycho-physical principles can explain (even Western) tonal organization [17] in either the significance of the tonal center ("tonic") or the abstract organization of "distances" around that tone; these cognitive notions of distance do not relate to physical/acoustic distance in any measureable sense: "The general picture emerges of a theory whose ... underlying constructs are constant, reflecting permanent features of musical understanding" [17: 5]. Such domain-specificity is more evidence in favor of a distinct mental module for musical representations.[3]

3.4   Neural Specificity

Can brain damage affect musical perception alone, without impacting other cognitive systems? If so, then we have an argument for neural specificity – similar to that involving aphasia in language. There is abundant evidence that such musical impairments exist. Peretz [22] and Peretz and Colheart [23] provide extensive physical evidence for "acquired selective amusia" – that is, for specific impairments that affect ONLY the musical module and in fact only certain musical sub-modules:

Patel acknowledges the existence of music-specific impairments, though he denies that this implicates natural selection, arguing that "the modularity of music processing in adults is orthogonal to the issue of selection for musical abilities. This is because modules can be a product of *development*, rather than reflecting innately specified brain specialization" [21: 357, emphasis mine]. He goes on to compare amusia with "orthographic alexia" – a reading deficit caused by brain damage. In particular, these deficits show that "there are areas in the occipitotemporal region of the left hemisphere

---

[3] That tonal pitch space is unique to human music in its basic abstract properties is not denied by Patel. Rather, Patel sidesteps the issue of domain specificity by arguing that modularity itself is not evidence of an evolutionary adaptation (see next section).

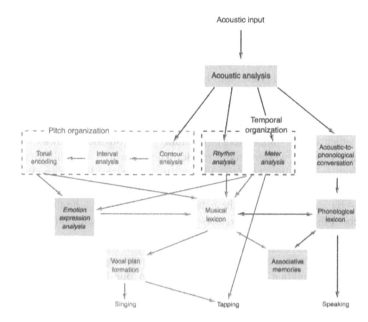

Fig. 1. Musical sub-modules showing impairments ([23] - music-specific impairments in green/light grey) (Color figure online)

that are specialized for recognizing alphabetic letters in literate individuals." Since reading is a recent human innovation, and is not universal or innate, "we can be confident that specific brain areas have not been shaped [for reading] by natural selection" [21: 357]. The argument takes the following form: if there are neurally-specific deficits attested for an ability we don't think was naturally selected for (such as alexia), we should be skeptical that we have evidence for biological evolution in other cases of neurally-specific deficits (such as amusia). However, the argument appears flawed: Patel does report findings that orthographic alexia is related to brain centers that surely *are* part of human biology, namely those involved in object recognition. Thus alexia *does* in fact reflect evidence of evolution of a neutrally specific system, one for object recognition, which is called upon in reading as well. If each of Peretz' identified cases of amusia could also be so attributed to deficits in other cognitive systems, then perhaps the argument for natural selection is weakened. But as Fig. 1 clearly shows, many of the attested deficits involve musical abilities alone (the green/light grey ones), and thus exactly resist association with other cognitive abilities. Therefore, for these cases the argument remains strong that we are dealing with evidence of musical modularity, in exactly the same sense Patel himself argues for modularity in language, and hence for natural selection.

In general, modularity arguments remain problematic for Patel's anti-evolutionary story for music. However, because his primary arguments against music as an evolved system rely on somewhat different diagnostics, I address those now separately.

3.5   Existence of Universals

The argument typically runs that for an ability to represent the product of biological evolution, we should expect it to show significant universals across idioms/dialects, that is, without significant variation. Here, then, to support the anti-evolutionary argument for music perception, we would expect Patel to deny the validity of claims of musical universals. To do so would not be unreasonable, since we have so little familiarity with distant musical idioms unrelated to our native idiom (western tonal music), and much of our music theory (including, as is obvious from its title, GTTM itself), restricts itself to western tonal music. Therefore it is difficult to substantiate claims of universals with so few idioms to compare. However, Patel tacitly acknowledges the existence of musical universals by appealing to a different strategy in this section – by casting doubt on the nature of the diagnostic – he expresses extreme skepticism about the existence of *linguistic* universals, while maintaining the biological viability of languages as a selected for system:

> grammatical universals are the focus of an interesting controversy, with some researchers arguing that these are not built into our brains but result from the convergence of a number of forces, including human limits on sequential learning, and the semiotic constraints that govern complex communication systems [21: 367]

So *linguistic* universals are in doubt for Patel. His logic appears to be as follows: If system A is biological, yet possibly shows no universals, then the presence of acknowledged universals in system B does not add to its viability as a biological system. I will leave it to the reader to decide if they find this kind of argument effective. Regardless, there are many well-known, generally accepted, musical universals, some of which are listed here (see [17] for discussion):

- All music consists of organized rhythms with organized melodies/harmonies
- Discrete perception of tones pervades all musical systems
- Melodies are perceived in terms of *motion* with regard to a tonic
- Octaves are perceived as equivalent in all musical cultures
- Octaves in all musical cultures are divided into scales consisting of 4–7 scale pitches selected from between 10 and 15 small steps

One could discuss each of these in a separate article. Taken together, though, they constitute a fairly strong case for the existence of some musical universals. Perhaps that does not seal the case in favor of natural section, but it certainly undermines the arguments against it, on this particular (and well-known) diagnostic.

4   Is Music Perception a Biological System? Patel's 2008 Diagnostics Revisited

4.1   Biological Cost of Failure

Patel argues that with any naturally selected-for system, we should expect to find a biological cost for 'failure'. That is, the giraffes that did not happen to develop long necks would have more difficulty passing their genes along, and the trait is thus selected for over evolutionary time. One unambiguously physical deficit in musical processing is tone-deafness. Patel therefore focuses his attention on that deficit, and argues as follows:

> such [musically tone-deaf] individuals appear to bear no biological cost for their deficit, and there is no evidence that they are less successful reproducers than musically gifted individuals. This is consistent with the view that natural selection has not shaped our bodies and brain for specifically musical purposes [21: 377]

However, this argument seems to entirely ignore the role of human technological manipulation of our own environment and its effect on natural selection. All that matters to an argument in favor of evolution is that there *was* a stage when people without musical perception ability *were* "less successful reproducers than musically gifted individuals" (and such a stage is presupposed by any adaptionist story, such as that of [19], discussed below). At very least, the *modern* absence of biological cost of people with such deficits (that is, absence of evidence of less successful reproduction), tells us nothing about the relevance of the trait *at the time in human evolution when it was selected for*. After all, there are humans without language, or without any of a multitude of clearly biological subsystems, who are perfectly successful reproducers in modern societies, where we have the technological ability to compensate in individual cases for quite a wide range of deficits. This is a great human achievement in many cases but clearly obscures the use of modern reproductive survival as indicative of being the product of natural selection in the original sense. I therefore contend that this argument is inconclusive and should be removed from the criteria, except to say that any adaptionist story must have such a component embedded in it to be viable, as Mithen's does (see below).

4.2   Babbling and Specialized Anatomy

The vocal tract is well adapted for both music and speech. Furthermore, children go through a babbling period for both music and language. Patel acknowledges that

> babbling... and the anatomy of the vocal tract could all reflect adaptations for an acoustic communication system that originally supported *both* language and vocal music. It is ... ambiguous which domain (music or language) provided the relevant selective pressures for these features of human biology" [21: 371-2, emphasis mine]

This is a remarkable statement, if the purpose is to argue *against* adaptive pressures for music, since it simply says that it is indeterminate whether musical or linguistic adaptive pressures (if the two can be distinguished) underlie the existence of a babbling stage of acquisition and of the development of specialized anatomy. If we cannot tell what the source of the selective pressure was, then these features of human biology simply cannot be used to differentiate music from language in terms of evolution! (Not to mention that it is being admitted at the outset that music *can*, in principle, provide selective pressures). At very least, these diagnostics do not speak *against* a possible evolutionary story for musical processing abilities (and possibly speak in favor of one). Again, at best (for Patel) inconclusive.

In the next sections I turn to Patel's central arguments against natural selection of music– that humans do not show a robust predisposition for music and do not go through a critical period for music acquisition as we do for language.

4.3   Predisposition and Precocious Learning

One of the points of contention here is the speed and regularity of the early childhood acquisition process. The implicit comparison is with language, where it is generally accepted that there is a strong predisposition and a robust critical period ([3, 4, 6, 27], a.o.). Patel [21] reports studies that show relatively slow acquisition of the musical notion of key membership, a central piece of knowledge of tonality in western tonal music. Primarily, this is based on his reading of Trehub and Trainor's studies [29, 30] comparing infant vs adult perception of in-key vs out-of-key changes in tones. The experiments work as follows: infants and older children are presented with tonal changes, some of which maintain key membership and some of which do not. Various behavioral measures determine the extent to which the children are more aware of the in-key changes than the not-in-key changes. Patel summarizes: "[there is] evidence that implicit knowledge of key membership is not in place by 8 months of age... [but] somewhere [before] 5 years, children develop a sense of key membership..." [21: 372]. He then reasons as follows:

> if musical pitch abilities had been the target of natural selection, one would expect accurate perception and production of musical pitch patterns to be learned far more quickly [than these studies show]. The slow development is especially striking given that *the music children hear* (e.g. nursery songs) *is especially strong in its tonal structure*, with few out-of-key notes [21: 372, emphasis mine]

First, a comment on the last point (that the nature of nursery songs should influence the speed of acquisition). It is perfectly possible that nursery songs share analogous characteristics with *motherese*, the exaggerated intonational patterns and lexical sim- plification used in child-directed speech, but there is no evidence that these impact the *speed* of the acquisition process with language [20]. It is also inaccurate to claim these songs have "stronger tonal structure" than other input music – that's akin to saying certain linguistic input is "more grammatical" than other input. We know that complex linguistic structures are simply not perceived at certain early stages (see [18] as well as [26] for discussion of "zero level" triggers accessing main clause information only in setting linguistic parameters). Presumably the same would apply to more complex musical structures –basic relations would be attended to, more complex ones not. At very least, the existence of simplified infant-directed song does not in any theory of acquisition entail that things should be different than with language, where we also find infant-directed speech.

More important, however, is Patel's claim that the music acquisition process is, in fact, relatively slow, in developmental terms. In actuality, the observed rate for acquisition of key membership looks quite similar to the trajectory for learning certain linguistic distinctions *in one's native language*, which (western) tonal relations are analogous to (specific tonality systems are of course not universal). That is, we know that although tonality as a cognitive notion may well be universal (see above), its particular instantiation has to be learned, like one's native lexicon in language, a process that continues throughout childhood and beyond, or like complex syntactic relationships, some of which do not fall into place until late in the acquisition period, such as the development of A-chains, which have been shown not to be correctly handled until past age 8 ([1], see also [26]). So if key membership is in place by age 5, then mastery of one's native musical idiom, in all it idiosyncrasies, does not seem to be any slower in acquisition terms than many analogous aspects of linguistic competence.

Crucially, in the studies reported by Patel, 8 month old infants "detected both kinds of changes" (that is, both in- and out-of-key changes). This shows exactly a strong early predisposition to one of the central aspects of musical perception – differences in scalar tones. One could imagine the distinctions not even being attended to at all until a much later age – this might well be what we expect if music were simply a cultural invention, as Patel claims.

Patel also reports on foot-tapping studies (where subjects are asked to tap their feet to the metrical beat of a piece of music) in which non-musicians fare worse than musicians, and claims that "humans appear far more uniform in their linguistic than in their musical abilities. Although some normal people are certainly more fluent speakers or have keener ears for speech than do others, these variations seem minor compared to the range of musical abilities in normal people" [21: 375]. It is entirely unclear on what basis Patel is able to draw this conclusion, other than the obvious distinctions between trained musicians and ordinary healthy music perceivers – clearly the former can have abilities the latter do not have, such as being able to read music, play an instrument, analyze musical relationships, compose music and so on. With language, however, one could also identity a huge range of differences among humans, if we included in the picture literacy (or even degrees of literacy), public speaking ability, the kind of creativity expressed through literature, poetry and so on. Patel is confounding musical *creativity* and *output* skills with the basic human musical competence of Lerdahl and Jackendoff's "experienced listeners" where there seems to be very little variation. The fact that trained musicians perform better on foot-tapping experiments than non-trained individuals is beside the point – it shows merely that training helps one succeed at such exercises just as explicit linguistic training would help one explicitly identify, say, syllable boundaries in one's native language. But even those who cannot explicitly identify syllable boundaries, or even know what a syllable is, still apply internalized phonological rules requiring knowledge of syllable boundaries in exactly the same way as trained linguists. Analogously, all listeners perceive the metrical structure of a piece equally accurately, and create the same representations for it, even if some cannot perform output tasks such as foot-tapping as accurately.

The overall conclusion is that the studies cited by Patel do not in fact show that acquisition of basic music processing abilities proceeds more slowly than language acquisition does. Nor does Patel present evidence for lack of strong predisposition with regard to music. This, combined with the evidence summarized in [31], leaves us with a comparable situation with music and language acquisition. Critical period effects, which I turn to next, reinforce this conclusion.

4.4   Critical Period

For Patel, the existence of a critical period in acquisition of a cognitive function (such as language or music), is practically synonymous with it having undergone a process of natural selection. Recall that his null hypothesis is that any ability should be considered a cultural invention unless and until there is strong empirical evidence to the contrary, which for language he claims there is, in particular with regard to a critical period. "Until good evidence appears showing rapid development of musical skills *that are not related to language* or to general principles of auditory function, there is no reason to reject the null hypothesis that music has not been a target of natural selection" [21: 374].

This is not an unreasonable way to proceed. By most accounts, however, this leads to the exact opposite conclusion from what Patel proposes. Specialists in child acquisition of basic music processing abilities (again, not to be confused with musical output skills), agree that a critical period is clearly present (see [22, 31, 28] among many others).

> studies of genetics, behavior, and brain structure and function in conjunction with the experiences of auditory deprivation and musical enrichment, ... conclude that *there is more supporting evidence for critical periods for basic than for more complex aspects of musical pitch acquisition...* [28: 262-4]

Remarkably, Patel does not directly engage with the existing literature on musical acquisition. Rather, he hypothesizes that experimental results can be ignored in the face of a larger theoretical point. Consider carefully the following selection from [21] (for ease of reference, I have numbered the assertions here):

(1) *even without doing ... experiments, it seems that even if a critical period effect for music is found, the effect will be rather weak compared to language.*
(2) One reason to suspect this is that some highly accomplished musicians did not start playing their instrument until after the age of 10. (To take just one example, George Gershwin was introduced to the piano at 13.)

First, with regard to (1), clearly we do not want to promote an anti-experimentalist approach to the issues at hand. The questions are empirical, and there is extensive experimental work reported in the literature, though clearly much more remains to be done. But to argue that that "even if a critical period effect for music is found, the effect will be rather weak compared to language" is to presuppose an empirical result on the basis of ones biases, rather than to trust the scientific method. This clearly contradicts Patel's general stance on experimental work, evident in successful discussion throughout the rest of his important book, and must be viewed with extreme skepticism, unless the theoretical argument against the hypothetical experimental results is overwhelming. However, as (2) and (3) show, this is far from the case.

(2) implies that we are discussing the existence of a critical period for *trained* musicians, rather than for typical human 'experienced listeners' without musical training.[4] However, that is not the appropriate subject matter for discussion of a critical

---

[4] This is not to deny the importance of understanding technical musical skills, musical creativity, output abilities and so on. I return to those issues in the conclusion.

period for basic music processing abilities. The issue is not the status of trained musicians, or anything about "output", but rather the status of basic human competence. To be clear: "the experienced listener" is *not* a trained musician, s/he is simply a healthy human being who was exposed to some kind of musical input as a child and who processes musical signals into complex and uniform representations, about which s/he has strong intuitive knowledge.

Naturally, we might wonder about experimental results comparing the brains of trained musicians vs. those with nothing beyond basic musical exposure. Here, again, one must listen to the experts:

> Given the current stage of research, the differences found between the brains of musicians and nonmusicians remain rather weak in light of the considerable difference in musical training that exists between the two groups. ... To our view, *these differences are negligible in front of the large overlap in brain activities found in musically trained and untrained listeners* [2: 124, emphasis mine].

That is, training is irrelevant to the basic cognitive ability in question.

The example of George Gershwin (3), is misleading in the same way. Gershwin can be studied as an example of musical genius, a brilliant composer, and wonderful cultural producer. And yes, his formal musical training began after the end of the traditionally understood critical period. But this is beside the point. If Gershwin had not been exposed to any music at all *of any kind* before age 13, then surely his successes (or indeed any normal human's success in acquiring the complex system of processing one's native musical idiom) could be taken as a problematic case for the critical period hypothesis. But his basic cognitive musical processing abilities were surely in place, just as anyone else's are, when his musical training began. If by musical abilities one means ability to perform, produce, compose and analyze music, then of course the question of a critical period changes to one of a possible critical period for this and many other aspects of human creativity, genius, acquired technical skill and so on. Much of Patel's reasoning confounds the two distinct kinds of musical ability, and could in the end be attributed to a kind of terminological confusion, rather than a deep misunderstanding of the importance of a critical period for acquisition of basic musical processing ability. Experimental work needs to therefore be consulted, and on this the Trainor/Trehub results seem quite clear: basic human music processing abilities are subject to a clear critical period.

4.5   Existence of Alternate Modalities

Patel appeals to the fact that language emerges in distinct modalities – it is not only spoken, but also signed, and sign-language research has clearly shown us that the level of complexity is similar across the modalities. He points to the fact that there does not seem to exist anything like "signed music" which could utilize a visual rather than auditory modality but which shares the same mental representations as usual music. This is an interesting argument that requires careful attention. Cognitive studies of dance, for example, may prove an interesting realm in which to search for alternate musical modalities. However, because basic musical cognition is a form of processing (just as visual processing does not have an output component), the issues are difficult to evaluate. At this stage, I do not find anything conclusive in the existence of both aural and visual modalities for languages that suggests that music is merely a cultural invention. I leave the empirical issues here to further research.

4.6 Summary

In Sect. 3, we found strong evidence for the independent modularity of music, in the sense of Fodor [7] and Jackendoff [12], using 5 well-known characteristics, only one of which Patel makes different claims about (#5 below). In Sect. 4, we looked at 7 of Patel's own diagnostics for music vs language, which start from his comparison of music to fire, rather than language. For 3 of his 7 diagnostics (#s 9, 10, 11), we have seen strong reason to doubt Patel's claims that music and language differ in any significant way (predisposition, robustness of acquisition and the critical period). For the other 4 properties, Patel in fact concedes music has the same properties as language, and that either language or music could have provided the selectional pressures to create the current situation. The following chart summarizes the findings (making some uncontroversial assumptions about the nature of fire as a 'cognitive' system) (Fig. 2.)

	Language	Fire	Music (P)	Music (JFB)
0. (Universality)	✓	✓	✓	✓
• Modularity:				
1. Rapidity and automaticity	✓	*	✓	✓
2. Informational encapsulation	✓	*	✓	✓
3. Domain specificity	✓	*	✓	✓
4. Neural specificity (biological defects)	✓	*	✓	✓
5. Existence of universals	✓ /*	*	*	✓
• Predisposition:				
6. Biological cost of failure to acquire	✓	??	*	NA
7. Babbling	✓	*	✓	✓
8. Specialized anatomy	✓	*	✓	✓
9. Predisposition	✓	*	*	✓
10. Precocious learning	✓	*	*	✓
11. A critical period for acquisition	✓	*	*	✓
12. Existence of alternate modalities	✓	*	✓	??

Fig. 2. Summary of 5 of Fodor's [7] and 7 of Patel's [21] diagnostics for language, fire and music

Nothing we have seen supports Patel's assertions of a radical difference between music and language.[5] If this article is on the right track about the four diagnostics shaded dark grey above, where I differ from Patel, then we find no significant distinctions between language and music, either in the modularity literature, or based on the diagnostics taken from Patel's own chapter on music evolution. Patel's conclusions about music evolution are all the more paradoxical given his own work, and that of [15] on shared linguistic and musical resources (the "shared syntactic integration resource hypothesis" - SSIRH) also presented in [21] (mostly in Chap. 5; the evolution claims are in Chap. 7). "Cross-domain interference effects show that although the two domains have distinct syntactic representations (e.g., chords vs. words), *they share neural resources for ... integrating these representations during ... processing*" [21]. The SSIRH specifically claims a common resource center in the brain for language and music, something unlikely, though not impossible, to be found if one of the abilities were a biological development and the other a cultural invention. This, along with the diagnostics above that were rejected as being indistinguishable between linguistic and musical pressures on evolution (such as development of human vocal tract anatomy) compel us to take seriously stories of music/language co-evolution. A co-evolution story allows early human *musical properties* to be associated with *communicative and expressive functions*, without implicating speech itself. In the next section I turn to one such story.

5   A Plausible Story of Music Evolution

As noted above, Patel's work on shared music/language resources, the common development of various physical traits that support both language and musical abilities, as well as a host of theoretical work showing a strong parallelism between the combinatoric system of both modules (esp. [14]) support the "musi-language" model of language evolution schematized below, from [33] (Fig. 3):

It is not the purpose of this article to promote a particular view of music evolution – I have not studied the complex issues of language or music evolution enough to be qualified to do so. However, because I am convinced as a cognitive scientist that the claim that music is purely a cultural invention cannot be maintained, it is worthwhile in this context to point to a plausible evolution story, one that is consistent with what we know about both the similarities and the differences between music and language. For that purpose, I turn to Mithen [19].

5.1   Mithen's HMMMMM

Mithen [19] argues that early humans had a common vocalization system with elements of both music and language, which he calls "Hmmmmm" (Holistic, manipulative,

---

[5] Perhaps his claim stems from the difficult task of determining what adaptionist pressure might have helped music develop in human evolution. However, Patel does not enter into the debate over language evolution, and to conclude that some sort of evolutionary pressures were involved in the development of human musical processing ability would not commit him to a particular story.

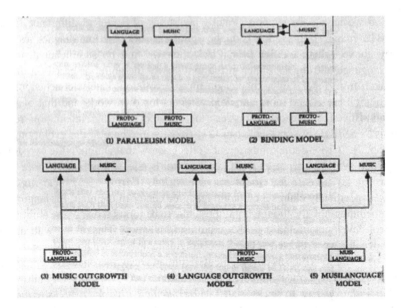

Fig. 3. Possible language and music evolution stories [33]. The musi-language model that best describes Mithen's proposal [19] is shown in the bottom right of the figure.

multi-modal, musical, mimetic). The Hmmmmm system, active around 2 million years ago, is fully consistent with the archeological record, and what is known about human cognition and group interaction at that time. Its primary function was connected with social cooperation and establishment of trust within groups, allowing longer term group-beneficial decisions to prevail over shorter-term individualistic goals. The time-frame is given in Fig. 4 on the next page.

The Hmmmmm system had the following characteristics:

- **Each utterance was** *holistic* **- it carried a single meaning** - there was no semantic compositionality, explaining why there was little or no change from 3 M to .75 M years ago. (They had fire and tools, but no fireplaces)
- **Each utterance was** *manipulative* - it was an attempt to achieve a resulting interaction or reaction; appropriate to the level of theory of mind known at the time
- **Each utterance was** *multi-modal* - it contained rhythm, pitch, tone, melodic contour, accompanying gesture, etc.
- **Each utterance was** *musical* - the elements listed under multi-modality comprise the basic building blocks of all human music
- **Each utterance was** *mimetic* - it imitated or mimicked (almost, but not quite 'referred to') something in the surrounding environment, be it hunting parties, food opportunities, social interactions, emotional expression, group bonding, sexual attraction and so on

The Hmmmm story is consistent with the most successful adaptive narrative of music evolution: as a way to 'coordinate coalitions' (group activity). Mithen describes it as follows:

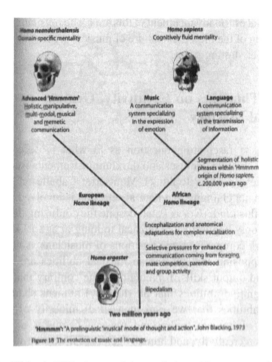

Fig. 4. Mithen's [19] picture of the evolution of language and music

Hominids would have frequently and meticulously examined the likely intentions, beliefs, desires and feelings of others members of a group before deciding whether to cooperate with them. But on other occasions simply trusting them would have been more effective, especially if quick decisions were necessary. As a consequence, those individuals who suppressed their own self-identity and instead forged a group identity by shared "Hmmmmm" vocalizations and movements, with high emotional and hence musical content, would have prospered.

Joint music-making served to facilitate cooperative behaviour by advertising one's willingness to cooperate, and by creating shared emotional states leading to "boundary loss"/"we-ness"/"coupling"/"in-group bias" With the evolution of *Homo ergaster* and full bipedalism, 'Hmmmmm' gained additional musical qualities, while further selective pressures for its evolution arose from the need to transmit information about the natural world, to compete for mates and to care for infants [19: 217-8].

Later, language and music divided, each becoming associated with modern human abilities, as we know them, while retaining certain cognitive points of similarity. Thus the shared resources of [21] and the syntactic identity identified in [14] find a natural source – their common history (claimed, I should certainly point out, by none of them).

Cognitive archeology is a growing field, and we can one day expect to understand far better than we do now how human cognitive evolution proceeded, especially once we have a better understanding of its neural instantiation. But that day may be some time off, and we owe it to those working then to be sure we are now asking the right questions, and looking in the right places for advancement in this area. The musilanguage approach, and a strong understanding of the biological nature of musical processing abilities in modern humans, are the proper starting point.

6 Conclusion: Thoughts on Creativity, Genius, and Technical Mastery

Of course it remains a fascinating question as to what is different about brilliant musicians, especially creative geniuses and dazzling instrumentalists such as Mozart or Bernstein or Prokofiev or Janis Joplin or Montserrat Caballé or Lang Lang. To be absolutely clear; I am not claiming that natural selection is involved in the development of musical genius of this kind. (Nor is Patel, despite the confusing discussion of Goerge Gershwin as having only begun formal musical training at age 13.) However, some of the experimental work comparing brain reactions of musicians vs non-musicians bears this character, presupposing that all human musical abilities are a reduced form of musical creativity and output skills. I maintain on the contrary that it is imperative to distinguish basic cognitive abilities that all (healthy) humans share from learned (or innately enhanced) abilities that we find in a small minority of gifted individuals. Surely the question of how to understand musical genius is a subset of a larger questions about human creativity, and human "genius", which are so poorly understood by cognitive scientists (though see [32] for a recent attempt).

Here, we are at a loss similar to what we encounter in trying to describe what is different about the mind of chess masters. A game invented for human entertainment now captivates the world of cognitive and computer science because of its intense complexity, and the facility with which some human minds grasp it to a degree that cannot be matched by computers, by description, by discussion etc. Little is known about genius of this sort, except that it is, in addition to everything else, the product of intense study and hard work (even for those most gifted). Gobet and Campitelli [8], for example, found a strong correlation between the number of hours chess players have dedicated to chess (deliberate practice) and their current rating:

i. Unrated players reported an average of 8,303 h of dedication to chess; rated players reported 11,715 h; Fide Masters reported 19,618 h and International Masters reported 27,929 h
ii. Stronger players tend to own more chess books (and read them) than weaker players. As an individual activity, *reading chess books is the most important predictor of chess skill.*

So what does it take to become an expert-a chess master, a concert pianist, or a tennis champion? Studies of expertise … show some consistent parallels across domains. One needs a certain amount of time; …. In music, for instance, *reaching a professional level of expertise appears to take 10.000 h*, with a further 25,000 h of added exposure to music-related activities (listening to pieces, reading scores, taking relevant classes, etc.), (see Ericsson 1996). Similar times hold for gaining expertise in complex games like chess … [5, emphasis mine]

Of course if the training takes place at a young age, the results may be more impressive; that depends on the nature of a critical period for learning in general. At very least we know that no study at all is required to achieve complex mastery of basic musical processing, and that the human mind is endowed with the unique modular ability to organize musical input into complex hierarchical representations.

References

1. Babyonyshev, M., Ganger, J., Pesetsky, D., Wexler, K.: The maturation of grammatical principles: evidence from Russian unaccusatives. J. Linguist. Inq. **32**(1), 1–44 (2001)
2. Bigand, E., Poulin-Charronnat, B.: Are we "experienced listeners"? A review of the musical capacities that do not depend on formal musical training. J. Cogn. **100**, 100–130 (2006)
3. Brown, R., Hanlon, C.: Derivational complexity and order of acquisition in child speech. In: Hayes, J.R. (ed.) Cognition and the Development of Language, pp. 155–207. Wiley, New York (1970)
4. Crain, S., Lillo-Martin, D.: Linguistic Theory and Language Acquisition. Blackwell, Cambridge (1999)
5. Clark, E.: Critical Periods, Time, and Practice. U Penn Working Papers in Linguistics, vol. 9.2 (2003)
6. Fitch, W.T.: The biology and evolution of music: a comparative perspective. J. Cogn. **100**, 173–215 (2006)
7. Fodor, J.: Modularity of Mind: An Essay on Faculty Psychology. MIT Press, Cambridge (1983)
8. Gobet, F., Campitelli, G.: The role of domain-specific practice, handedness, and starting age in chess. J. Dev. Psychol. **43**(1), 159–172 (2007)
9. Harkleroad, L.: The Math Behind the Music. Cambridge University Press, Cambridge (2006)
10. Hauser, M.D., Chomsky, N., Fitch, T.: The faculty of language: what is it, who has it, and how did it evolve? J. Sci. **298**, 1569–1579 (2002)
11. Huron, D.: Is music an evolutionary adaptation? In: Wallin, N.L., et al. (eds.) The Origins of Music, pp. 57–75. MIT Press, Cambridge (2001)
12. Jackendoff, R.: Consciousness and the Computational Mind. MIT Press, Cambridge (1987)
13. Jackendoff, R.: Foundations of Language. Oxford University Press, New York (2002)
14. Katz, J., Pesetsky, D.: The Identity Thesis for Music and Language. LingBuzz (2011)
15. Koelsch, S., Gunter, T.C., Wittfoth, M., Sammler, D.: Interaction between syntax processing in language and in music: an ERP study. J. Cogn. Neurosci. **17**(10), 1565–1577 (2005)
16. Lerdahl, F.: Tonal Pitch Space. Oxford University Press, Oxford (2001)
17. Lerdahl, F., Jackendoff, R.: A Generative Theory of Tonal Music. MIT Press, Cambridge (1983)
18. Lightfoot, D.: Why UG needs a learning theory: triggering verb movement. In: Jones, C. (ed.) Historical Linguistics: Problems and Perspectives, pp. 190–214. Longman, London (1993)
19. Mithen, S.: The Singing Neanderthals: The Origins of Music, Language, Mind and Body. Weidenfeld & Nicolson, London (2006)
20. Nelson, D.G.K., Hirsh-Pasek, K., Jusczyk, P.W., Cassidy, K.W.: How the prosodic cues in motherese might assist language learning. J. Child Lang. **16**(01), 55–68 (1989)
21. Patel, A.D.: Language, Music and the Brain. Oxford University Press, Oxford (2008)

22. Peretz, I.: The nature of music from a biological perspective. J. Cogn. **100**, 1–32 (2006)
23. Peretz, I., Coltheart, M.: Modularity of music processing. J. Nat. Neurosci. **6**(7), 688–691 (2003)
24. Pinker, S., Bloom, P.: Natural language and natural selection. J. Beha. Brain Sci. **13**, 707–784 (1990)
25. Pinker, S., Jackendoff, R.: The faculty of language: what's special about it? J. Cogn. **95**, 201–236 (2005)
26. Snyder, W.: Child Language: The Parametric Approach. Oxford University Press, Oxford (2007)
27. Snyder, W., Lillo-Martin, D.: Principles and parameters theory and language acquisition. In: Hogan, P. (ed.) The Cambridge Encyclopedia of Language Sciences. Cambridge University Press, Cambbridge (2011)
28. Trainor, L.J.: Are there critical periods for music development? J. Dev. Psychobiol. **46**, 262–278 (2005)
29. Trainor, L.J., Trehub, S.E.: A comparison of infants' and adults' sensitivity to western musical structure. J. Exp. Psychol. Hum. Percept. Perform. **18**, 394–402 (1992)
30. Trainor, L.J., Trehub, S.E.: Key membership and implied harmony in western tonal music: developmental perspectives. J. Percept. Psychophys. **56**, 125–132 (1994)
31. Trehub, S.E.: Musical predispositions in infancy: An update. In: Peretz, I., Zatorre, R. (eds.) The Cognitive Neuroscience of Music, pp. 3–20. Oxford University Press, New York (2003)
32. Turner, M.: The Artful Mind: Cognitive Science and the Riddle of Human Creativity. Oxford University Press, Oxford (2006)
33. Wallin, N.L., Merker, B., Brown, S. (eds.): The Origins of Music. MIT Press, Cambridge (2001)

Constructive Interrelationship Between Structural Components in Early Music and Language Learning

Bijan Zelli[(✉)]

Independent Researcher, San Diego, USA
bijanzelli@gmail.com

Abstract. This paper explores the similarities between music and language in communicating meaning, and considers the advantages of using these similarities to enhance language acquisition in a school curriculum. Comparing music (as a sonic, non-verbal, and inter-human medium with cross-domain connotations according to particular socio-cultural conventions) with language (as a verbal, cognitive medium, demonstrating denotation and a direct pathway from an object/idea to an interpreter) reveals common structures inherent to both. This study relies on both recent research in the overlapping fields of language and music and personal data collected while teaching language and music over the last six years to address the following question: how can music education ease language acquisition in schools? Although the positive influence of music on language acquisition is well established, the current research will elaborate the dynamism of this influence.

Keywords: Musical language · Verbal language · Terminology · Music theory

1 Introduction

The influences of music on language are explored here based on recent research and data gathered while teaching K-8 music classes at Darnall Charter School in San Diego, California, USA during the 2013–14 school year. The aim and purpose of this research was to determine the ways in which music education might ease and speed language acquisition and subsequently the integration of English learners in the classroom. Although this research is specifically focused on English learners, the results are applicable to any other language as there is no direct relationship between music and a specific language like English.

The central hypothesis is, of course, that music education can be a great help in this process. The long-standing concept of music and language as independent and totally different disciplines has been abandoned in the modern research. Patel [1] and others have shown that these activities rely on similar data processing and underlying neural mechanisms. Indeed, the modern awareness of similarities between music and language has been central to many studies and conferences in this area and has led to increased curiosity and redefinitions of concepts. Significant conferences have included "Language and

© Springer International Publishing Switzerland 2015
P. Eismont and N. Konstantinova (Eds.): LMAC 2015, CCIS 561, pp. 45–58, 2015.
DOI: 10.1007/978-3-319-27498-0_4

Music as Cognitive Systems" in Cambridge (2007) and "Music, Language, and the Mind" in Boston (2008); major studies have been published by [2–4].

The convergence of different views on music and language as communicative tools, along with a better understanding of musical and lingual components, has paved the way for new research about the reciprocal impact of the two disciplines in child development. Patel, for example, suggests that the most important commonality between music and language is their shared mechanism for the learning of sound categories, which he formulates under the *Shared Sound Category Learning Mechanism Hypothesis* (SSCLMH) [1: 72].

Although these similarities are striking, we should not forget the differences. As Patel emphasizes, and as is readily apparent from daily experience, human lingual capabilities are more uniform than our musical capacities. Music, contrary to the opinion of some researchers who believe that musical skills are a result of natural selection, is primarily a cultural invention. On the other hand, language has evolved over time due to the need to convey information to others [5].

The similarities and differences between music and language and their relationship in learning are described by several models introduced by Brown, including *parallelism, binding, music outgrowth,* and *language outgrowth.* His *musilanguage* model, emphasizing a creative interference of music and language in the early years of learning, is especially useful [6]. One of the most important similarities between music and language is the capacity of the brain for hierarchical grouping, introduced by, among others, Lehrdal and Jackendorff in their *Generative Theory of Tonal Music* (GTTM, 1983 [7]), Selkirk [8], and Nespor and Vogel [9] in modern linguistics. These theories express the capacity of the brain to construct concepts and meanings beyond their constitutive components. Although musical and lingual meanings convey imagination and cognition, respectively, the brain's capacity for hierarchical grouping is fundamental to the communicative functions of both music and language.

Without trying to construct an artificial and unreal parallelism between music and language in all areas, it is obvious that this relationship can be seen in a wide weak-to-strong spectrum, highlighting difference just as strongly as similarity. As an example, timbre, or sound color, is a component of both music and language. Distinguishing between a melody played on a violin and on a flute is a matter of sound color, which in music has a cultural and expressional function. The invention of many different instruments and the creation of chamber ensembles, bands, and orchestras are signs of a need for sound color differentiation. In language, sound structure is not a matter of choice. The sounds of a child, a woman, and a man are different, and vary by age. While we generally do not choose how to produce our consonants and vowels in terms of timbre, the presence of timbre in language has a decisive role in our social lives. Recognizing the gender or the age of a speaker is sometimes of great significance in our communications. Although there are similarities here, the degrees to which we can choose sound colors and their functions in music and language are extremely different.

Taking advantage of the similarities between music and language, a parallel modeling method could be used effectively in improving the lingual skills of young learners. This is of course not the only method for supporting early language acquisition. Cross-lingual parallelism is a more established method in this respect, taking advantage of similarities between the first language and the target language of the learners. The benefit of music here is its ease of acquisition and its entertaining nature. Parallel components of music and language will be compared and discussed here to show how the two work in similar ways to build communicative structures.

The biggest advantage of music education in supporting language acquisition is in providing an appropriate *zone of proximal development* (ZPD, Vigotsky) for young learners. Group activities inherent to musicianship provide a safe, directed, and scaffolded working area [10] from which children are able to advance to more sophisticated personal achievements.

2   Musical versus Lingual Components

Music and language could be discussed and compared at length through the lenses of history, neurology, sociology, education, and philosophy. To relate this comparison to the topic at hand, i.e. the impact of music education on language acquisition, it will be limited to a study of four important components of music and language: *spatialization, temporality, tonality,* and *dynamics.*

2.1   Spatialization

The extensive use of space in music of the second half of the twentieth century has thrown light on the importance and function of space in musical composition. Karlheinz Stockhausen, Pierre Boulez, John Cage, and many others emphasized this hidden aspect of music in numerous compositions and stressed the fact that music occurs both in time and space. Although composed space in music belongs to the twentieth century and after, space as an important musical dimension has always been present both in composition and performance. From early antiphonal performance practices like *call and response* to sixteenth-century vocal music at San Marco Basilica in Venice, from Berlioz' *Tuba Mirum* to Stockhausen's *Helicopter String Quarter*, there has long been a curiosity and interest in understanding and using musical space. With musicians having reached a sophisticated theory and application of space in music after World War II, many questions arose to address the similarities and differences between space in music and in other fields such as visual arts, sociology, cultural studies, and language.

Musical space is dependent upon important components like distance, direction, and the placement of sound sources in the physical performing context. Influenced by theories of space in the arts, the psychological concept of *localization* has also become central to the study of musical space. Although the placement of sound sources in the performance space is an important starting point in creating spatial music, the spatial perception of the listener – their localization – plays a decisive role in their interpretation and understanding of space. In this respect, spatialization and localization reflect the physical and the psychological mode of spatial music, respectively.

Similarly, space has both an inherent as well as socio-cultural relationship to language. Both music and language are registered in space (Coslett), something that has been largely ignored throughout history. As in music, distance and direction are essential parameters of linguistic communication. However, language has unique access to some other components. Many words like locative prepositions (here, there) and deixes (close, far, spiral, wave, etc.) include spatial hints at a conceptual level. Language can also exist spatially through various sign languages or languages with hand gestures (such as Italian).

Accepting the fact that the main function of language is to transfer meaning – "language is the organ that shapes thought" – spatial factors can have an effective impact on the purpose, mood, and intention of such a meaning [11: 53]. Neurological studies show that the neuroanatomies of language and space are different. Although the left hemisphere is dominant in our lingual perceptions, the right hemisphere is responsible for the recognition of spatial topography in communication. Coslett [12], Coslett and Lie [13], and Talmy [14] show how space can influence language. The *Simon Effect* is a clear illustration of the degree to which our multi-modal perceptions are affected by spatial factors. Chatterjee, after an interesting study of interactions between space and language, clearly shows the differences between spatial and lingual perception and assigns categorical adjectives to each of them, with space being sensorial, perceptual, and geometrical, and language being conceptual, algebraic, and amodal. He concludes:

> Despite reasons to think that mental representations of language and space are likely to be segregated, these cognitive domains make contact at critical junctures. These points of contact are evident in both the communication and the representation of language. The interactions reviewed here suggest that language and space are not modular cognitive systems in the strong sense of being informationally encapsulated from each other. Rather, at certain points the information from one domain bleeds into the other [15: 60].

2.2 Temporality

Peretz and Coltheart recognize pitch and temporal organization as two fundamental sub-modules of musical perception [16]. Despite an older understanding of music and language as having ontological distinctions (linearity versus non-linearity in time), these two phenomena share many elements in the realm of temporality. Although it is the most intrinsic component of music, temporality is also essential in understanding and producing language. Temporality here will refer to all time-related components of music and language, i.e. rhythm, meter, and tempo. These components will be considered and compared to understand how they might influence each other in an educational context.

Recent research has recognized several temporal categories among languages. Although the idea dates back at least to Steele's 1775 work *Prosodia Rationalis* and was developed through Saussure (*synchronic description*) at the end of the nineteenth century, it is only recently that a serious effort has been made to understand the function of time in lingual communications. Pike, working in the 1940s, cast new light on the temporality of languages. Although it is impossible to strictly categorize languages in terms of temporality, attempts have been made since then to recognize and define *syllable-timed* (French, Turkish, and Spanish), *mora-timed* (Japanese and Ganda), and *stress-timed* (English, German, and Russian) languages. Ignoring the serious challenges in such an approach to languages, one thing is obvious: temporality affects, to a great extent, the expression and meaning of lingual communication.

Temporality is inherent to both music and language. While our conception of language has developed over time from a lexical/static to a temporal/dynamic phenomenon, serious efforts must be made to gain insight into this new dimension of language. In the history of modern linguistics, the temporalization of language is almost as recent as the spatialization of music.

Temporality in language is bound to larger units of words combined under a single coherent contour [17] in speech or reading [18]. As in music, temporality in language is bound to other components like tempo, dynamics, space, syntax, semantics, and intonation. Tempo is primarily significant to language in direct communicative action, and its relationship with additional components of language is stressed by Fraisse [19], Fenk-Oczlon and Fenk [17], and other researchers. Further, temporal components of music like rhythm and meter have direct equivalents in language. Although meter is more relevant in poetry, it and rhythm, in the sense of the temporal length of tones or words, have similar functions in both music and language. Patel discusses rhythm as systematic temporal, accent, and grouping patterns of sound, and stresses the non-periodic character of lingual rhythm [1]. The manipulation of rhythm in music and language leads to substantial changes in our modes of expression and communicated meanings.

2.3   Tonality

Pitch is another inherent component of music; linear pitch changes lead to melodies and vertical pitch changes lead to harmony. We do not know when and where melodies started to form, but with all certainty we may state that melody, after rhythm, is the oldest component of music. The presence of melody in most musical cultures around the world hints at the importance of melody in organizing musical thought throughout history. Melodies in music as sequential organizations of pitches are directly linked to meaning.

Pitch changes in languages lead to what we call intonation. Similar to melody, intonation is linked to meaning in many cases and lexicality in some specific cases as well. Intonation also has a grammatical function in placing boundaries between phrases, clauses and sentences, questions and statements, etc. Tonal languages including Scandinavian languages, Chinese, and some African languages such as Hausa are widely known. In these, as in music, intonation contours work together with spatialization, temporality, and dynamics to build semantic and syntactic blocks on both phonemic and global scales.

Comparing the universality of melody in music and intonation in language, there are vast varieties in both, although melody benefits from more uniformity or commonality. Although the pre- and post-common practice periods of music history approach melody with a relaxed and loose attitude, melodies follow certain specific patterns in the common practice era. Intonation, on the other hand, shows a much freer pattern throughout the history of language. Having less universality than melodies, the intonation contours described as rising, falling, and reaching peaks and bottoms are the most commonly applied (with some exceptions in their meanings). Wells [20] and Couper-Kuhlen [21] categorize six functions of intonation in languages: attitudinal, grammatical, focusing, discourse, psychological, and indexical. These categories are of cognitive, emotional, structural, and social character, as opposed to the typically connotational function of melody.

Finally, the structural and cognitive blocks built on accuracy and relativeness have different functions in music and language. Pitch is an important factor for forming musical tones and is highly dependent on accuracy. The perception of difference in pitch, and thus the basis of both melody and harmony, requires a variation of as little as 3.6 Hz. On the contrary, rather than relying on individual pitches in the domain of utterance, language is dependent on the contour of intonation [22] based on relative pitch that is definable as low, middle, high, and very-high [23].

2.4   Dynamics

Dynamics, referring to changes in loudness, are a strong expressional tool in music. They create contrast and emphasis, distinguish between different musical layers in a polyphonic texture, contribute to spatialization, and, perhaps most important of all, work together with harmony and melody in building musical sentences, especially during the common practice period. Although musical dynamics first appeared in the musical score in the eighteenth century, they have always existed as an important component in musical expression. Gregorian chant, early call-and-response, and many ancient religious hymns reveal an embedded dynamic flow. Sometimes the implementation of dynamics in music has been inevitable. Transitions from choir to solo song or from full orchestra to only a few instruments create an unavoidable change of dynamics. This type of integrated dynamics is featured in the Baroque *concerto grosso* as *terraced dynamics* (dynamic changes without transitions), which played an important role in the musical language of that period. In that same period, dynamics in music experienced a turning point. The need for richer dynamic nuances in musical composition gave birth to the piano (*forte-piano*), which, compared to its predecessor, the harpsichord, had a greater capacity for dynamic contrast. Myriad dynamic terms entered the musical vocabulary, which in turn enforced the increasing role of the musical score in composition and interpretation. The role of dynamics in musical expression intensified during the twentieth century, as they became a central element of serial music. Arnold Schönberg in his dodecaphony, Olivier Messiaen in his *parametrisation* of musical elements, and finally composers like Karlheinz Stockhausen and Pierre Boulez in serial music paid special attention to dynamics and used them extensively in their compositions. Electroacoustic music met the challenges and benefits of dynamics in its own way in the 1950s. Controlling the level of unwanted noise in early electronic music was a challenge, and raising its volume to the pain threshold is found in later examples of the genre.

In comparison, dynamics in language convey almost the same functionality, but with a more limited scope. Dynamics are used in language to create emphasis, much like syntactical ordering strategies including anaphora and epistrophe. Dynamics work on two fronts: bringing chosen words to attention in a sentence by making them louder, and allowing a listener to distinguish between multiple sources by leveling dynamics to systematically map partial information. Space and dynamics are also closely related in language. Loudness is automatically linked to closeness and quietness to distance. Although spatialization in music is a compositional tool (at least in the modern era), it is embedded naturally in languages. The localization of a speaker talking to us from different directions or distances is a natural human ability. Spatialization through dynamics affects the phonology and subsequently the pragmatics of the language, meaning that the manipulation of dynamics could involve variations in intentions and utterances. Dynamics in language have both a pragmatic and psychological aspect. Fletcher and Munson stress that loudness is a subjective psychological construct that is related to the estimated magnitude of an auditory sensation [24]. The perception of loudness depends on many factors including body language, word selection, intonation, and of course the acoustical loudness of the sound. Lehiste and Peterson distinguish between speech and non-speech sounds and mention that the perception of these sounds can be different [25], and studies by Orr, Montgomery, Healy, and Dubno, show differences in perceived loudness of consonants and vowels [26].

3   Workshops

3.1   Musical Melody versus Lingual Intonation

In the training phase of this research, organized around workshops, students listened to and sang standard four-measure melodies with one turning point (tonic-dominant-tonic) and then tried to build the same type of melodies (Vigotsky's *internalization*). Students also constructed sentences requiring more than seven words and having one turning point (a comma), similar to the music. Additionally, monitored readings with a focus on intonation helped students to focus on the tonal structure of language. Students in this workshop could understand how meaning in music and language is related to pitch and intonation, respectively. In many cases, students even adopted a personal form and contour for their melodies (Vigotsky's *appropriation*), often in conflict with the common practice routines or cultural-conventional intonations. In these instances, the main goal – arousing sensitivity about the relationship between intonation/melody and meaning – was reached (Fig. 1).

Fig. 1. Typical four-measure melody

(1) Typical sentence with a turning point:
      I went to school today, although it was raining.

The results during the pre-testing period revealed a noticeable percentage of students with difficulty using proper intonation in reading a grade-level text. As shown below, 60 % of students demonstrated a poor understanding of how meaning and intonation are linked in the English language. The post-testing phase showed better results, particularly for this area, but saw an increase in incorrect performance from 10 % to 15 %. This increase indicates that manipulating intonation can confuse some students who are still unfamiliar with a new language (Figs. 2 and 3).

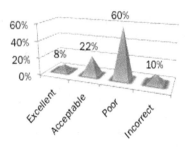

Fig. 2. Results from testing the understanding of the impact of intonation on meaning: Pre-testing results

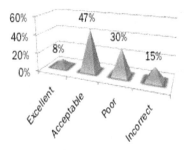

Fig. 3. Results from testing the understanding of the impact of intonation on meaning: Post-testing results

3.2   Musical versus Lingual Dynamics

Despite the importance of dynamics in verbal language, many language learners showed deficiencies in using correct accentuation while reading. This is closely linked to a misunderstanding of the intent of the writer. The pre-testing phase demonstrated a direct connection between vocabulary and English learners' reading abilities. The workshop was focused first on understanding the text and then on rereading the text with the right dynamic. Music was a great help in this process; students learned how to use rhythmical patterns with different accentuations. As stated earlier, music of the common practice period has certain dynamic patterns, which even today are used in many popular songs. Students were easily able to notice how emphasizing the second beat of a common time metrical pattern can ruin the flow of this type of music. This can be replicated in language, when unnecessary parts of a sentence are accentuated without having anything to do with the purpose of the writer or the communicated meaning. Results from the pre-testing period showed 35 % acceptable and 30 % poor understanding of dynamics in reading. These numbers improved to 55 % acceptable and 20 % poor after the workshop. Even the weakest section improved in this workshop, from 20 % to 10 % (Figs. 4 and 5).

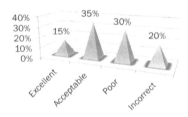

Fig. 4. Results from testing the understanding of the impact of dynamics on meaning: Pre-testing results

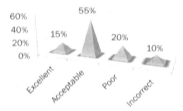

Fig. 5. Results from testing the understanding of the impact of dynamics on meaning: Post-testing results

3.3   Breathing Technique

Although breathing technique is not critically important in communication, it can greatly influence the fluency of spoken language. Most English learners experiencing difficulty with their breathing technique also have issues with linguistic fluency. Therefore the focus of the research here has been those learners having decent fluency but poor breathing technique. Although correct breathing in spoken language could improve with time and most of the immigrants to any host society with a different language do not have any significant issue, music education can speed up this process noticeably. To address this, the workshop used vocal music to improve the breathing technique for sentence building in music. Students learned how to follow a breathing pattern while singing a song. Different articulation patterns like legato, staccato, and portato were introduced to English learners to improve their sensibilities regarding breathing. The same focus was applied to reading standard texts to gauge the potential negative impact of breaking down a sentence with incorrect breathing on fluency of the language. Pre-testing results showed 30 % poor and 10 % incorrect breathing technique in reading, which fell to 8 % poor and 7 % incorrect after the workshop (Figs. 6 and 7).

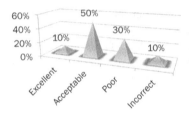

Fig. 6. Results from testing proper breathing technique in spoken English: Pret-testing results

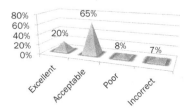

Fig. 7. Results from testing proper breathing technique in spoken English: Post-testing results

3.4   Concentration

It is absolutely clear that many students today suffer a lack of focus and concentration. Phones, iPads, gaming devices, and other convenient distractions are a major part of students' daily lives and challenge the ability to focus on class assignments. This is the reality in many developed countries, where advanced technology is readily available. Having access to different audio-visual sources and not having enough maturity to isolate or discriminate one or more of the sources to focus on one task is called multi-sensory stimulation, which, most of the time, distracts young learners. Even for many adults, it is challenging to read a newspaper or a book in a noisy environment like an airport or a park. Car accidents caused by distracted drivers talking on a hands-free phone are an extreme example of auditory distraction. As a matter of fact, multi-tasking is not a reality. Research shows that the brain is not dealing with two or more tasks at the same time, but switching between tasks rapidly. Our selection, processing of data, encoding, and storing of information can be greatly affected and slowed down by multi-tasking.

Anxious and distracted students who feel the need to check their emails every five minutes or engage with highly attractive virtual games present big challenges for many educators. Being able to differentiate simultaneous audiovisual events and make a selection to optimize learning is something that can be trained from an early age. Getting easily distracted by a speaker, music, or noise while reading a text is quite common among school students. Music education can effectively improve the multi-sensory abilities of individuals through the use of polyphonic music. The workshop intending to improve this ability sought to train students to sing polyphonic vocal music, from easy rounds to three- or four-voice textures. Vocal music is not just another modality of lingual communication [1]; in its polyphonic form, it aids in discriminating, differentiating, and selecting a desired input among multi-layered auditory stimuli. The results of the workshop were better than expected. The poor group, at 50 % during pre-testing phase, shrank to 10 % and the acceptable group grew from 40 % to 70 % (Figs. 8 and 9).

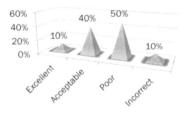

Fig. 8. Results from testing the ability to concentrate on in-class tasks: Pre-testing results

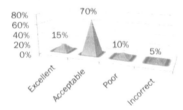

Fig. 9. Results from testing the ability to concentrate on in-class tasks: Post-testing results

3.5   Communication/Self-esteem

Self-esteem plays a decisive role in musical and lingual communication. Many encounter the stressful, out-of-control, and irrepressible nervousness of musicians, who in some cases need to step off the stage before completing their performance, or individuals who are unable to maintain eye contact, speak clearly, or use a convincing and logical semantic/syntactic verbal structure. Group music activities, due to their slightly less personal nature, help to develop students' self-esteem in an entertaining environment. Self-esteem in this respect is related more to the individual's social skills than their lingual development and has a major impact on their personal and social appearances. Although school performances are not mandatory in many educational systems around the world, those schools with early, organized music programs show satisfactory results in building up students' self-esteem. Issues around this are revealed when students in later grades have little or no experience being the target of focus and attention. Attempting to address this lack of background consumes time and energy with no guarantee of success. Thinking of music performance as self-esteem enforcement rather than simply as the development of musical skills is an important aspect of this type of activity. Consistency in music education and support for performing arts in schools, with the goal of extending participation and engagement in these programs, can overcome the ephemeral impact of such an education. In this respect even investment in speaking or reading a poem in front of an audience provides similar benefits to self-esteem and communication abilities.

In this workshop, students learned to perform songs or short instrumental pieces in a group in front of their class. Effective background instruction was provided through group performances with guidance and modeling, providing technical resources and positive feedback in the process of reaching autonomous learning in solo performances. This workshop culminated in school events in the form of group and solo performances, revealing the other major advantage of this activity: vigorous emotional support from parents, friends, and the social environment (*reciprocal scaffolding*), providing further support towards an established, functioning self-esteem. Being the target of focus or judgment is not an easy task, neither for adults nor for school students. Many students refused, during the pre-testing period, to perform on stage. Even group performances were a challenge for some. On the other hand, there were students who met the challenge of performing solo in school performances, a sign of sound self-esteem. As seen below, the high rate – 60 % – of poor self-esteem fell to 50 % and the acceptable percentage improved from 20 % to 30 %. These results show an improvement in students' self-esteem, despite working against years of habit and tendency (Figs. 10 and 11).

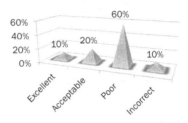

Fig. 10. Results from testing students' self-esteem in group and solo performances: Pre-testing results

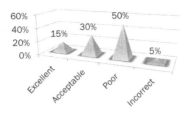

Fig. 11. Results from testing students' self-esteem in group and solo performances: Post-testing results

4   Conclusion

Different components inherent to music, language, or both were introduced and compared in this study to illustrate that many challenges in language acquisition could be addressed indirectly through a well-planned music curriculum. Migrant students in a

California middle school showed improved results in language acquisition through support from music education. This paper concludes with the following results: (1) different lingual and musical components present clear relationships to the communication of meaning; (2) great ease and convenience in music acquisition in early learning could be of great help in supporting language acquisition; (3) as learners age, the positive influence of music on language acquisition, well-established by case studies, is followed by concept-building abilities, and language in its turn will assume a decisive role in in-depth musical understanding in adulthood.

References

1. Patel, A.D.: Music, Language, and the Brain. Oxford University Press, New York (2008)
2. Besson, M., Schön, D., Moreno, S., Santos, A., Magne, C.: Influence of musical expertise and musical training on pitch processing in music and language. J. Restorative Neurol. Neurosci. **25**(3–4), 399–410 (2007)
3. Patel, A.D., Iversen, J.R.: The evolutionary neuroscience of musical beat perception: the action simulation for auditory prediction (ASAP) hypothesis. J. Frontiers Syst. Neurosci. **8**(57), 1–31 (2014)
4. Schellenberg, E.G., Peretz, I.: Music, language and cognition: unresolved issues. J. Trends Cogn. Sci. **12**(2), 45–46 (2008)
5. Pinker, S., Bloom, P.: Natural language and natural selection. J. Behav. Brain Sci. **13**(4), 707–784 (1990)
6. Brown, S.: Characteristic of Successful Speaking Activities. Cambridge University Press, New York (2001)
7. Lerdahl, F., Jackendoff, R.: A Generative Theory of Tonal Music. MIT Press, Cambridge (1983)
8. Selkirk, E.O.: English compounding and the theory of word structure. In: Moortgat, M., van der Hulst, H., Hoekstra, T. (eds.) The Scope of Lexical Rules. Foris, Dordrecht (1981)
9. Nespor, M., Vogel, I.: Prosodic structure above the word. In: Cutler, A., Ladd, D.R. (eds.) Prosody: Models and Measurements, pp. 123–140. Springer, Berlin (1983)
10. Silliman, E.R., Wilkinson, L.C.: Discourse scaffolds for classroom intervention. In: Wallach, G.P., Butler, K.G. (eds.) Language Learning Disabilities in School-Age Children and Adolescents, pp. 27–52. Allyn and Bacon, Boston (1994)
11. von Humboldt, W.: Gesammelte Schriften: Ausgabe Der Preussischen Akademie Der Wissenschaften, Berlin, vol. 7, pp. 1903–1936
12. Coslett, H.B.: Spatial influences on motor and language function. J. Neuropsychol. **37**, 695–706 (1999)
13. Coslett, H.B., Lie, E.: Spatial influences on language performance. In: Proctor, R., Reeve, T. (eds.) Stimulus–Response Compatibility, vol. 1990, pp. 331–350. Elsevier (Suppl) (2000)
14. Talmy, L.: Fictive motion in language and 'Ception'. In: Bloom, P. (ed.) Language and Space, pp. 211–276. MIT Press, Cambridge (1996)
15. Chatterjee, A.: Language and space: some interactions. J. Trends Cogn. Sci. **5**(2), 55–61 (2001)
16. Peretz, I., Coltheart, M.: Modularity of music processing. J. Nat. Neurosci. **6**(7), 688–691 (2003)
17. Fenk-Oczlon, G., Fenk, A.: Measuring basic tempo across languages and some implications for speech rhythm. In: Interspeech, pp. 1537–1540 (2010)

18. Klein, W., Perdue, C. (eds.): Utterance Structure: Developing Grammars Again. Benjamins, Amsterdam (1992)
19. Fraisse, P.: Rhythm and Tempo. In: Deutsch, D. (ed.) The Psychology of Music, pp. 149–180. Academic Press, San Diego (1982)
20. Wells, J.C.: English Intonation: An Introduction. Cambridge University Press, Cambridge (2006)
21. Cooper-Kuhlen, E.: Introduction to English Prosody. Edward Arnold, London (1986)
22. Bolinger, D.: Intonation – levels versus configurations. J. Word 7, 199–200 (1951)
23. Trager, G.: The intonation system of American english. In: Abercrombie, D. (ed.) In Honour of Daniel Jones. Longmans, London (1964)
24. Fletcher, H., Munson, W.A., Loudness, : Its definition, measurement, and calculation. J. Acoust. Soc. Am. 5(2), 85–94 (1933)
25. Lehiste, I., Peterson, G.E.: Vowel amplitude and phonemic stress in American english. J. Acoust. Soc. Am. 31, 428–435 (1959)
26. Orr, S.B., Montgomery, A.A., Healy, E.W., Dubno, J.R.: Effects of consonant-vowel intensity ratio on loudness of monosyllabic words. J. Acoust. Soc. Am. 128(5), 3105–3113 (2010)

Inverting the Mozart Effect: Discovering What Composers Can Learn from Writing

Caitlin R. Johnson[✉]

Brigham Young University, Provo, UT, USA
crj1227@gmail.com

Abstract. According to the Mozart Effect, listening to Mozart can briefly increase IQ's in certain circumstances. Today, we generally accept that studying classical music benefits us in other areas. This paper investigates an unnoticed connection with the opposite phenomenon: if studying music can help us learn other subjects, can studying other subjects help us learn music? Specifically, how can composers improve their compositional skills through writing?

I explore two approaches: pattern-thinking and reflective writing. Composers and writers both employ patterns, and composers can transfer skills of assembling building blocks to their music. I consider innovative, non-traditional patterns in composing and writing. Composers can also use reflective writing to synthesize their ideas and decide how to arrange their patterns. Whereas manipulating patterns is a mental shift, reflective writing is a physical action to accomplish the shift. Composers can use reflective writing to capture and interpret moments of real learning.

Keywords: Mozart effect · Composing · Writing

The last few decades have seen a surge in pregnant women who listen to classical music. Before becoming pregnant, some mothers had never been fans of 18th-century oratorios or orchestral works. Now some women listen over speakers at home, crank it in the car, and even put headphones on their bellies. Specifically, there has been an increased interest in the music of Wolfgang Mozart, the Austrian composer. What fueled this demographic's sudden interest in the powdered-wig prodigy? Expectant mothers believe that listening to Mozart will make their child smarter.

This phenomenon is based on the Mozart Effect, which emerged in 1993. According to the research of Frances Rauscher and her colleagues, listening to Mozart's music can enhance spatial-temporal reasoning. The study's subjects were college students. After the students listened to Mozart's Sonata for Two Pianos in D Major (K448), their spatial IQ's rose about eight points for no longer than fifteen minutes [7]. The general public may have oversimplified the study's findings, thinking that just listening to Mozart for a few minutes raises IQ's dramatically. This oversimplification helps explains the spike in sales of Mozart tapes for babies and the headphones on Mom's belly.

Further research in the more than twenty years since the Mozart Effect was named confirms that it's not as simple as we may think. Through the years, scientists have continued to study the Mozart Effect and the benefits of exposure to classical music. A recent article in the Journal of Neuroscience, one of the most prominent neuroscience

P. Eismont and N. Konstantinova (Eds.): LMAC 2015, CCIS 561, pp. 59–66, 2015.
DOI: 10.1007/978-3-319-27498-0_5

publications, reports that the brains of those who are musically trained respond faster and better to other sounds than do the brains of those who are not musically trained. In fact, adults who studied music only when they were young still showed this increased response [6]. Though the Mozart Effect has become more controversial as researchers have discovered nuances that change the data, this study and others report positive effects of classical music on intelligence and learning. Based on research and people's experience, we generally accept the notion today that studying classical music helps students succeed in other subject areas.

This statement makes me wonder about possible connections between music and other subjects. The Mozart Effect says that music increases brain activity. So spending time with classical music makes us, in some ways and for some amount of time, more intelligent or more adept at conquering new concepts. Can the Mozart Effect be inverted? If studying classical music teaches us to be better students, can studying other subjects teach us to be better musicians? I want to identify and understand the unnoticed connection between music and other subject areas. Specifically, is there something about learning writing that helps composers develop and refine their composing skills? What can we learn from the act of writing, or composing words, that we can translate to composing music? In this paper, I will explore how we can reverse engineer the Mozart Effect. That is, I will investigate what musical composers can learn from writing.

In considering the idea of inverting the Mozart Effect, I looked for sources that showed that people are not talking about using other subjects to improve music skills. I read Kariuki and Honeycutt's study, "An investigation of the effects of music on two emotionally disturbed students' writing motivations and writing skills." The researchers investigated listening to music as a tool to improve writing skills, and the subjects were two fourth-grade, special education students in Tennessee who struggled to write [5] (11). The researchers hypothesized that listening to music—movie soundtracks, instrumental music, and classical music—would help the students to write (12). The results showed that music helped students develop positive attitudes toward writing, write more, write more creatively, and write better (15–16).

Kariuki and Honeycutt acknowledge that further research needs to be conducted on how to use music to help writing (3). They suggest, "Perhaps music could be associated with writing in such a way as to stimulate their imagination and provide the motivational boost necessary to enhance their writing skills and give them some measure of appreciation of their ability to write" (4). Among the possibilities for further studies is testing the reverse of this study's findings. Few if any studies consider how writing can be used as a tool to improve music-making, specifically composition. Following Kariuki and Honeycutt's research, future studies could test how writing can be used to help composers improve their attitudes toward their work, compose more, compose more creatively, and compose better.

Next, I found an article linking music and literacy. In "Music and Literacy: Strategies Using 'Comprehension Connections' by Tanny McGregor," Kathleen Frasher discusses the skills that music and literacy have in common. She cites a 2007 study that states that both studying music and learning to read utilize "oral, aural, and print communication" [3]. She further explains that music and reading share "parallel skills," such as "phonological awareness, phonemic awareness, sight identification, orthographic awareness, cueing systems awareness and fluency." For example, when we read music notes and when we read words, we identify them by sight; we recognize them as symbols with certain meanings attached. Because of the similarities, it is natural to use music to teach reading. Frasher suggests specific ways that educators can use music to help young kids learn to read, including displaying lyrics to age-appropriate songs while playing the music.

Frasher reports her own classroom success using music to teach kids to read. She also cites studies that report more focus and motivation, better listening skills, and more effective communication in preschool students when music is incorporated in teaching reading. Frasher's analysis connects music and literacy, but it focuses on reading, not writing.

I next consulted Dee Hansen's article "Writing in the Music Classroom." Like Frasher, Hansen draws a connection between music and literacy [4] (28–29). In this article, Hansen discusses how writing can fit in the music-making process. She describes how making music involves three aspects: creating, performing, and responding. She says that students become musically literate by music-making, not music-reacting. She asks, "Then how do we encourage students to respond to music through writing yet preserve high-quality music learning and performance?" Hansen's answer is to prioritize (28). She suggests making time for students to respond to music by writing in order to promote music literacy and encourage a lasting love of music (28–29). In other words, Hansen sees writing as fitting in with the bigger picture. She says the purpose of writing about music is not to help improve a single performance or overall skill level, but to improve understanding and love of music. Hansen links music and writing by considering how to use writing to foster music appreciation, but she does not consider how to use writing to help improve music composition.

June Countryman discusses a concept similar to Frasher's in her article "Learning posts: A pedagogical experiment with undergraduate music education majors." Countryman, a university music education professor, added reflective writing elements to coursework called "Learning Posts." Every week of the semester, students wrote a Post, a narrative exploring and analyzing something they learned while attending or teaching a class [2] (2). Countryman hoped that this writing component would help students experience "significant learning," or "some kind of lasting change that is important in terms of the learner's life" (3).

She describes what her Posts are trying to capture: "Young adult students need complex learning experiences followed by intentional reflection, experiences that enable them to 'consider knowledge as complex and their own role in constructing it as critical'" (15). Countryman wanted her students to actively take steps to learn and recognize what they learned, setting aside time and energy to verbalize their purposeful learning.

Countryman was surprised by some of the results, especially her discovery that students found the reflective writing assignments unfamiliar and even uncomfortable (7). She asserts that the actual writing process was not hard for students, but rather, "This development from external to internal authority is cyclical, complex, highly individual and often uncomfortable" (14). Countryman calls this shift progress toward self-authorship. She argues that moving toward self-authorship is essential because doing so is how we make meaning rather than just go through the motions of school or learning (12–13).

Countryman's study of using writing to help teachers recognize and achieve significant learning is not exhaustive. She outlines possibilities for future inquiry and acknowledges that her research is an "on-going conversation" (2). Her experiences encouraging and enhancing real learning could extend beyond music teachers to include composers. A future article could address composers achieving greater learning of their craft through writing.

This body of literature addresses different connections between music and writing. The authors discuss how listening to music can improve writing performance, how music can be used to help young children learn to read, how writing about music can promote lifelong appreciation of music, and how music teachers can use writing to learn more effectively. However, further sources are needed on how writing can help musicians improve their music-making. We need to discover parallels between the processes of composing and writing. Specifically, further research is needed on how composers can improve their composing by transferring their writing skills.

My literature review guided my thinking in brainstorming how we can expand the Mozart Effect, or the concept that music helps us succeed in other subject areas, including writing. In searching for solutions, I considered Kariuki and Honeycutt's statement, "Other research has suggested that the spontaneous disposition students have toward rhythm and melody makes music an ideal tool for assisting them with the interwoven facets of language: listening, speaking, reading, and writing (Kolb, 1996)" [5] (8). Kariuki and Honeycutt essentially reaffirm the Mozart Effect by identifying that being skilled with the rhythm and melody in music leads to greater skill with the processes of communicating in language. This statement reminded me of Frasher's study of "parallel skills" and fueled my thinking about the similarities between components of music and of language.

One similarity I considered is the terminology common to music and writing. For instance, both disciplines use the term "composition," but in different contexts. Both mean a piece of work created, but composers refer to a composite of notes, rhythms, and dynamics to create phrases, sections, and entire pieces. Writers refer to an aggregate of words and punctuation to create sentences, paragraphs, chapters, and books. Connecting music and writing in such a way that helps composers requires a mental shift, as Countryman described significant learning. This mental shift is thinking in terms of patterns. Rather than considering composing and writing as two separate tasks, composers can think of composing and writing as both using the same skill of recognizing and arranging patterns.

I relate the linguistic process of composing to the musical process of composing. One uses words; one uses notes. Both words and notes are associated with symbols that we can construct and deconstruct. If being a musician makes us better students, what is it about music that helps us understand math better, for example? Math uses formulas—predictable patterns. Writing is the same. It uses syntactical patterns that writers manipulate. These patterns are our building blocks. For example, writers learn to write a thesis statement, or a sentence that encapsulates the paper's controlling idea [8] (16). But a thesis is more than a summary. A thesis acts as an agreement between the reader and writer. A thesis sets up an expectation. In other words, the reader is not bound to continue reading if the paper does not follow the pattern set forth in the thesis statement.

The thesis is often in the introduction, but it can also appear later in an essay near the conclusion. But no matter the thesis's placement, readers rely on the thesis as a guide.

Music, too, has these agreements between the composer and the listener, especially in musical form. For example, when listening to early Romantic concertos, we expect to hear a sonata form. The exposition has a primary theme, a transition, a secondary theme, and a closing theme. A development follows the exposition then leads to a recapitulation that has the same four elements as the exposition. Listeners can rely on this predictable pattern. Some Romantic composers occasionally make small alterations —for example, they might omit the secondary theme—but this is the exception rather than the rule, and the overall form remains intact.

Learning the structures of writing helps us put patterns together. I think we can translate this skill to then learn how to put patterns together in music; learning writing teaches rhetorical, cognitive moves that help a musician learn music. Using patterns is one way that writing can make better composers. However, I see some limitations with pattern-thinking. Following patterns does not guarantee the quality of content. I'm not focusing on the linguistic meaning of writing; I'm focusing on the power of learning structures.

Another limitation is that pattern-thinking does not guarantee that listeners will automatically accept or embrace a composer's music. This limitation is evident when composers use patterns that aren't recognizable to listeners. I think of Stravinsky's The Rite of Spring. The ballet tells the story of a girl who dances herself to death as a sacrifice to the gods. The performance was so controversial that riots broke out at the premiere, but the storyline wasn't the only shocking part. Stravinsky's use of patterns was innovative. He wrote in new, strange, compound meters with accents on unexpected beats. His complex patterns weren't always readily recognizable or predictable to his audience, but he did use patterns. The Rite of Spring was controversial at first, but now scholars call the 1913 composition the most influential piece of music of the twentieth century.

With The Rite of Spring in mind, that's not to say that by studying writing, composers will all assemble and use patterns in the same way. Composers today don't all follow the same form. Within the twentieth century, Arnold Schoenberg used patterns in his twelve-tone-row compositions. He invented the twelve-tone method of composing, wherein all twelve pitches must be used once before repeating any note. At first, Schoenberg's compositions may sound chaotic, but they are in reality tightly organized, repetitive patterns. Another modern composer who uses patterns masterfully is Philip Glass. Often called a minimalist, Glass composes with repetitive configurations of short segments. Both Schoenberg and Glass used patterns, just not the same patterns and not in the same way.

Celebrated writers, too, have used patterns masterfully. Ernest Hemingway is known for packing powerful meaning into short, blunt sentences. I think of the entire story he famously wrote in six words: "For sale: baby shoes, never worn." The poet e.e. cummings consistently did not capitalize words. He made and followed his own rules of punctuation and grammar, too. Even James Joyce, known for his stream-of-consciousness writing, was following a pattern by not following established patterns. Like Schoenberg, Glass, and other composers, writers don't always follow the same patterns, but they do follow patterns.

By recognizing the patterns needed to write, composers can transfer this skill to composing. Some people may think that using patterns would restrict the possibilities, but really it would expand composers' sets of tools. Schoenberg and Glass used different patterns and assembled them differently, but they followed the same concept of pattern-thinking. Translating pattern-thinking from writing to composing will help composers assemble patterns creatively and innovatively.

Whereas my first solution involves a shift in thinking, my second solution involves physical action to accomplish a shift in thinking. Composers can write to explore and improve their musicianship and to experience "significant learning." My idea stems from Countryman's article, especially her purpose in creating Learning Posts. "I sought vivid snapshots of personal learning, followed by reflective meaning-making" [2] (7). She discusses how music educators can use writing to strengthen their music teaching, but I will apply the same ideas to how composers can use writing to improve their composing. Put simply, writing helps people learn. Music helps people learn. And writing can help musicians learn. Reflective writing is one way to help musicians, especially composers, better learn their craft.

Composers can use reflective writing to capture moments of real learning and then discover and preserve the new knowledge in prose. In defining what type of writing composers could use in these exercises, we run the risk of confining their creativity. But I think some basic definitions of reflective writing are helpful here. One purpose of reflective writing is "thinking about and critically analyzing one's actions with the goal of improving one's professional practice." Another description of reflective writing is a "challenging, focused, and critical assessment of one's own behavior as a means toward the development of one's own craftsmanship" [1] (59).

When musicians hear about writing and music, they might think of a practice log. The kind of writing I am discussing is not a record of how musicians spend their work time and what they do. I mean writing that helps narrow ideas, identify thought processes, put vague concepts into words, and focus creative efforts. Writing about composing could be as simple as documenting struggles and brainstorming solutions. Composers may find creative expression and motivation through this other medium. I am not suggesting that writing detract from composing time. In fact, I'm not suggesting that composers always devote a certain amount of time to writing. Finding this balance of time spent composing and writing will depend on the individual.

In her article on why teachers should use writing in the music classroom, Hansen writes, "By allowing time for students to cognitively and metacognitively react to music through writing, we will encourage music literacy and lifelong music appreciation. Responding, then, becomes a means to the end" [4] (28–29). I think we can apply this concept to composers. Reflective writing is the means to the end, and the end could be a finished composition. But the goal of writing in this context isn't just one composition that is better than it would have otherwise been. On a larger scale, the end is improved composing skills overall.

One limitation of this approach is that it is hard to determine how good a composition is. Do we measure a composition's success by the decibel level of applause at the premiere or at subsequent performances? Do we measure success by how many people enjoy the music or find meaning in it? Do we consider the personal satisfaction that composers find in creating the work or the lessons they learn while composing?

Do we consider if a composition withstands the test of time? It is possible that there is no universal way to decide if a composer or a composition is successful. Furthermore, it's hard to measure progress, or what a composition would have been like if the composer had not utilized reflective writing.

Building on the idea that writing can be a vehicle for improving composition skills, I apply a concept from Frasher's article. Frasher discusses how young children learn to read. "Students take what the author has to say (text) and add it to what's going on in their head (thinking), which results in real reading." In other words, "text + thinking = real reading" [3]. In the context of composing, composers can use their tools (patterns) plus their own thinking (including writing) to achieve "real" composing. The thinking component is when composers figure out what they want to say with patterns. This process is where reflective writing could be invaluable. Composers can use writing to synthesize their ideas and decide how to arrange their patterns.

A limitation of reflective writing as a composing tool is the process of writing itself. Some musicians are drawn to composing because music expresses what words cannot say; they feel that music transcends words. In this case, composers may find it difficult to verbalize their thoughts and work in this other medium.

My goal was to explore the unnoticed connection between music and writing. I wanted to do this by answering the question of how we can invert the Mozart Effect, or how we can use writing to improve compositional skills. These two ideas to think in patterns and use reflective writing as a compositional tool are possible solutions, but they are by no means the only options. Furthermore, these solutions also present some limitations. Just as the Mozart Effect is not as simple as general knowledge suggests, neither is its reversal. Using writing to improve compositional skills is a multifaceted concept that probably does not happen in one step.

Further studies are needed to discover how composers can facilitate a shift to thinking in patterns and how pattern-thinking in this context is beneficial. Further studies are also needed to understand the details of how reflective writing may help composers. On a larger scale, we need more information on how studying other subjects besides writing can help musicians generally and composers specifically. Another research idea is to consider how studying other areas within music—performance practice and pedagogy, for example—could help composers. Most composers already are familiar with these other aspects of music, but we may not understand the best way to incorporate lessons learned with composing. The great limitation of all these proposed studies is that it may be difficult for researchers to evaluate composing skills, so progress or success may be hard to measure. In the end, we can conclude that writing can be used to improve composing skills, but more research is needed to define how.

References

1. Bush, J.E.: The effects of gender and classification on university music education students' attitudes toward electronic journal writing as a reflective practice. J. Contrib. Music Educ. **30** (2), 59–74 (2003)

2. Countryman, J.: Learning posts: a pedagogical experiment with undergraduate music education majors. Int. J. Educ. Arts **13**(7), 1–21 (2012)
3. Frasher, K.D.: Music and literacy: strategies using 'Comprehension Connections' by Tanny McGregor. J. Gen. Music Today **27**(3), 6–9 (2014)
4. Hansen, D.: Lectern: writing in the music classroom. J. Teach. Music **16**(4), 28–30 (2009)
5. Kariuki, P., Honeycutt, C.: An investigation of the effects of music on two emotionally disturbed students' writing motivations and writing skills. Paper presented at the Annual Conference of the Mid-South Research Association, New Orleans, Louisiana, 4–5 November 1998
6. Parbery-Clark, A., Strait, D.L., Hittner, E., Kraus, N.: Musical training enhances neural processing of binaural sounds. J. Neurosci. **33**(42), 16741–16747 (2013)
7. Rauscher, F., Shaw, G.L., Ky, K.N.: Music and spatial task performance. J. Nat. **365**(6447), 611 (1993)
8. Rosen, L.J.: The Academic Writer's Handbook. Bentley College, New York (2006)

Corpus studies of Language and Music

Probabilistic Topic Modeling of the Russian Text Corpus on Musicology

Olga Mitrofanova[(✉)]

Faculty of Philology, Department of Mathematical Linguistics,
Saint Petersburg State University, Universitetskaya embankment,
Saint Petersburg 199034, Russia
oa-mitrofanova@yandex.ru

Abstract. The paper describes the results of experiments on the development of a statistical model of the Russian text corpus on musicology. We construct a topic model based on Latent Dirichlet Allocation and process corpus data with the help of the GenSim statistical toolkit. Results achieved in course of experiments allow us to distinguish general and special topics which describe conceptual structure of the corpus in question and to analyze paradigmatic and syntagmatic relations between lemmata within topics.

Keywords: Musicology · Corpus linguistics · Text corpora · Probabilistic topic modeling

1 Introduction

It has been proved that language and music reveal similar structure which admits reasonable treatment in symbolic and statistical models: phenomena occurring in natural language and in musical texts can be properly explained in terms of statistically enriched grammatical formalisms [1, 2].

Evidently there is considerable overlap between natural language and music which appears in the study of prosody, tonal languages, verse in vocal pieces, etc. This overlap also manifests itself in musicology.

Musicology is a peculiar field of knowledge which attracts much attention of linguists as it has a regular and well-structured terminological system [3]. Although the conceptual core of musicology is extremely complex, it springs up from heterogeneous sources and is extremely rich in emotionally coloured terms [4, 5]. At the same time it has seldom been an object of quantitative research. The present study fills a gap in our knowledge about statistical features of texts on musicology.

We support corpus-based approach in linguistic research: it has generated an original philosophical trend and developed a novel methodology which facilitates the transition from frequency data and distributional analysis to explanation of discourse phenomena, and builds a bridge between text corpora and cultures [6]. Hereafter we treat corpus as a

The research discussed in the paper is supported by the grant of St.-Petersburg State University № 30.38.305.2014 «Quantitative linguistic parameters for defining stylistic characteristics and subject area of texts».

© Springer International Publishing Switzerland 2015
P. Eismont and N. Konstantinova (Eds.): LMAC 2015, CCIS 561, pp. 69–76, 2015.
DOI: 10.1007/978-3-319-27498-0_6

digital collection of natural language data, large in size, unified, well-structured, linguistically annotated and intended for various experimental procedures [7].

Thus, the aim of our research is to construct the Russian text corpus on musicology and to develop a probabilistic topic model for the given corpus, thus describing distribution of words over topics and topics over texts in our text collection. To meet the need we choose a version of topic models which is based on Latent Dirichlet Allocation and process corpus data with the help of the GenSim statistical toolkit.

The structure of the paper is as follows:

- Section 1 gives an outline of our research,
- Section 2 discusses the notion of a topic model,
- Section 3 is devoted to the software used in the study,
- Section 4 describes the Russian text corpus on musicology,
- Section 5 discusses experimental settings and results achieved in course of experiments,
- Section 6 provides a brief conclusion,
- Section 7 deals with further development of research.

2 Topic Modeling of Text Corpora

Topic modeling is a research procedure which exposes implicit factors constituting the conceptual structure of text corpora. A topic model reflects the transition of a set of texts in a given corpus and a set of words in texts to a set of topics describing the content of a corpus. In fact, the process of topic modeling results in extracting a set of topics from a corpus, i.e. a set of clusters containing words revealing similarity in meaning which is based on distributional similarity within a corpus.

Each word or document within a topic model is related to a number of topics with certain probability. A topic model provides a description of a text corpus in terms of a family of probability distributions over a set of topics. Probabilistic topic model is constituted by

(1) $p(w|d) = \Sigma p(t|d)\, p(w|t)$, where $p(w|d)$ is a certain frequency of occurrence of a word w in a text d,

(2) $p(w|t)$ is an uncertain probability of occurrence of a word w in a topic t,

(3) $p(t|d)$ is an uncertain probability of occurrence of a topic t in a text d.

In order to construct a topic model for a text corpus D it is necessary to find a set of topics T, a distribution $p(w|t)$ for all the topics and a distribution $p(t|d)$ for all the texts. The desired distributions provide a condensed description of text corpora applicable in Natural Language Processing tasks (especially in semantic compression procedures like automatic text indexing and categorization, word and document clustering and classification, extraction of distributionally similar words, etc.).

There are a great variety of topic models, the basic types being algebraic models (Vector Space Model VSM, Latent Semantic Analysis LSA, etc.) and probabilistic models (Probabilistic Latent Semantic Analysis pLSA, Latent Dirichlet Allocation LDA, etc.). LDA model proved to be one of the most productive in processing text collections of both large and moderate size.

Results on topic models for English text corpora are widely discussed in numerous publications, cf. [8–10], etc. In most cases the procedure is performed for scientific and news texts. The paper [11] describes a remarkable study in the field of topic modeling of poetic texts. At the same time, Russian corpora are seldom involved in such research, with few exceptions: positive results have been described in [12–14].

3   Probabilistic Topic Modeling Toolkit

There are computer implementations of various topic models, including LDA, e.g. MALLET [http://mallet.cs.umass.edu/topics.php], Stanford Topic Modeling Tool [http://nlp.stanford.edu/software/tmt/tmt-0.4/], etc. A list of available software is given at [http://www.cs.columbia.edu/~blei/topicmodeling.html].

In our study, the task of topic modeling is fulfilled with the help of a set of Python libraries GenSim [http://radimrehurek.com/gensim/] developed by R. Řehůřek. We have chosen GenSim as it includes a powerful statistical module for developing probabilistic topic models for text corpora. GenSim is also known for its flexibility and operability. We composed a script activating GenSim components and performing automatic text processing based on LDA.

The script provides the following procedures:

(1) extraction of a dictionary from the input corpus (plain text format, UTF8 encoding);
(2) elimination of stop-words and low frequency words;
(3) transformation of a dictionary into a matrix;
(4) construction of LDA model with changeable parameters, the number of iterations, topics, and topic size being assigned by a user;
(5) output of results: topics extracted from a corpus are represented as lists of lemmata with weights and values of perplexity.

4   The Russian Text Corpus on Musicology

The subject area of music seems to be of particular interest in corpus studies, cf. papers on the Corpus of Russian Romances [15, 16]. Our purpose is to construct a resource which gives a general overview of various types of texts dealing with music. In order to perform experiments on probabilistic topic modeling we have developed the Russian text corpus on musicology, covering such areas as theory of music, history of music, performing art, musical instruments, biographies of composers and musicians, etc. Our corpus includes texts of encyclopedias and reference books as well as texts of monographs and collected works on certain subjects.

Pre-processing of texts in our corpus includes the following stages:

(1) elimination of non-text elements (tables, images, diagrams, hyperlinks, etc.);
(2) construction of a stop-list from the Corpus Dictionary of Multi-Word Lexical Units extracted from the Russian National Corpus (RNC) [http://www.ruscorpora. ru/obgrams.html] and frequency lists including lemmata of linkwords, pronouns, numerals, abbreviations from the Frequency Dictionary of Contemporary Russian (RNC) [http://dict.ruslang.ru/freq.php];
(3) Lemmatization and automatic morphological disambiguation with the help of Yandex morphological parser system 3.0 [https://tech.yandex.ru/mystem/];
(4) Splitting texts into documents in accordance with their initial logical structure (chapters, sections, etc.).

Pilot experiments were performed on a subcorpus of over 300 000 tokens in size which included encyclopedic texts [17, 18]. To prove representativeness of the subcorpus we performed its statistical analysis using the functions embedded into AntConc corpus manager [http://laurenceanthony.net/software/antconc/]. We examined the top 100 frequent lemmata, among which we found words *концерт (concerto), музыкант (musician), музыка (music), играть (play* [v]*), игра (play* [n]*), музыкальный (musical), писать (write), скрипач (violinist), оркестр (orchestra), искусство (art), исполнение (performance), пианист (pianist), выступать (perform), скрипка (violin), композитор (composer), произведение (composition), консерватория (concervatoire), джаз (jazz), концертный (concert* [adj]*), выступление (performance), артист (artist), стиль (style), инструмент (instrument), звук (sound),* etc. which also occur in the Russian Associative Dictionary [19]. Lemmata of the upper zone of the frequency list, as will be shown further, constitute the principal part of the topics generated by the LDA model.

5 Design of Experiments and Analysis of Results

Series of tests on probabilistic topic modeling of subcorpus from our collection of Russian texts on musicology were performed with the following parameters:

(1) number of iterations −10;
(2) number of topics – 10, 20, 50, 100;
(3) topic size – 10 lemmata.

Below we list some fragments of output which illustrate our results. Lemmata constituting topics are arranged in accordance with values of the association measure which is automatically calculated but removed from the output.

The model produces topics of general character which partly overlap: such topics include widespread words dealing with music, e.g.:

опера (opera), музыка (music), композитор (composer), произведение (compo-sition), время (time), жизнь (life), музыкальный (musical), новый (new), театр (thearte)...;

музыка (music), композитор (composer), опера (opera), жизнь (life), произве-дение (composition), симфония (symphony), песня (song), время (time), новый (new)...;

концерт (concerto), музыка (music), музыкант (musician), время (time), музы-кальный (musical), игра (play), писать (write), большой (large), искусство (art)....

Alongside general topics, we have managed to form topics of more definite content which refer to particular composers, performers, styles and genres of music, e.g.:

«Шопен (Chopin)»: *Шопен (Chopin), польский (polish), Варшава (Warsaw), Польша (Poland), друг (friend), Жорж (George), Санд (Sand), родина (native land), предчувствие (presentiment), композитор (composer)...*;

«Вена в музыке композиторов (Vienna in the life of composers)»: *Людвиг (Ludwig), Бетховен (Beethoven), Моцарт (Mozart), Гайдн (Haydn), Вена (Vienna), Барток (Bartok), жизнь (life), композитор (composer)...*;

«Скрипачи (violinists)»: *скрипач (violinist), игра (play), музыкант (musician), Крейслер (Kreisler), Байо (Baillot), скрипка (violin), Тартини (Tartini), концерт (concerto), Ромберг (Romberg)...*,

«Джаз (Jazz)»: *группа (group), альбом (album), песня (song), джаз (jazz), Иоахим (Joachim), пластинка (disc), компания (company), записывать (record), Джон (John)...*, etc.

Probably the lemma *Ромберг (Romberg)* within the topic *«Скрипачи (violin-ists)»* implies the family of musicians famous for its cellists, composers, singers, pianists, clarinetists, and violinists. It seems that the topic *«Джаз (Jazz)»* refers to the jazz musician John Coltrane and probably to vinyl discs with jazz records of Joachim Kühn.

We also found several topics of mixed character, e.g.

музыка (music), музыкант (musician), играть (play), гитарист (guitarist), фестиваль (festival), концерт (concert), говорить (talk), Виктор (Viktor), Цой (Tsoi)..., etc.

The given topic combines general terms and the mention of the Russian rock-musician and songwriter Viktor Tsoi.

As regards the inner structure of the topics generated by the LDA model, it is possible to distinguish certain paradigmatic and syntagmatic relations between words within topics. Most of the relations extracted from the topics can be described in terms of lexical functions in «Sense <=> Text» linguistic model (e.g. Syn, Gener, Der, $Oper_{1,2}$, S_i, S_c, Mult, etc.) [20].

A. Paradigmatic relations, e.g.

– synonymy (Syn): *«произведение – сочинение (composition)»*,
– hyponymy (Gener): *«музыкант (musician) – композитор (composer), пианист (pianist), скрипач (violinist), гитарист (guitarist), ...»*, *«произведение (compo-sition) – опера (opera), симфония (symphony), песня (song), ...»*, etc.,

- meronymy (partitive relations): «*произведение (composition) – фраза (phrase), такт (bar)*», etc.
- derivational relations (Der) *музыка (music) – музыкант (musician), музыкальный (musical); Польша (Poland) – польский (polish); опера (opera* [n]*) – оперный (opera* [adj]*), оперетта (operette); скрипка (violin* [n]*) – скрипач (violinist), скрипичный (violin* [adj]*); гитара (guitar) – гитарист (guitarist); выступать (play on the stage) – выступление (performance); играть (play* [v]*) – игра (play* [n]*); джаз (jazz* [n]*) – джазовый (jazz* [adj]*),* etc.,

Further analysis of paradigmatic relations within topics allows us to extract lexical semantic-groups like «*Музыкальные формы и жанры (musical forms and genres)*»: *симфония (symphony), соната (sonata), концерт (concerto), опера (opera), оперетта (operetta), оратория (oratorio), песня (song), пастораль (pastorale)...,* etc.

B. Syntagmatic relations, e.g.

- verb-object relations (Oper$_{1,2}$): *музыка (music) – писать (write); пластинка (disc) – записывать (record);*
- noun-modifier relations (S$_i$, S$_c$): *играть на скрипке (play the violin); играть в оркестре (play in an orchestra);*
- noun-attribute relations: *искусство игры; джазовый музыкант (jazz musician); джазовый оркестр (jazz band);*
- item-set relations (Mult): *музыкант (musician): оркестр (orchestra), консерватория (concervatoire), капелла (choir)...*

Thorough treatment of syntagmatic relations between separate lemmata included in topics provides sets of constructions, e.g.

- full names: e.g. *Людвиг ван Бетховен (Ludwig van Beethoven); Жорж Санд (George Sand);*
- appositive constructions, e.g. *композитор (composer) X (X = Бах (Bach), Бетховен (Beethoven), Гайдн (Haydn), Моцарт (Mozart), Мендельсон (Mendelssohn), Гуно (Gounod), Дворжак (Dvořák), Брамс (Brahms), Шопен (Chopin), Гендель (Handel), Сен-Санс (Saint-Saëns), Глазунов (Glazunov), Рахманинов (Rachmaninov)...); музыкальный критик и композитор Серов (musical critic and composer Serov); пианист Оборин (pianist Oborin); Концерт Виотти (Viotti Concerto); опера Россини (Rossini's opera); опера Вагнера (Vagner's opera); Концерт Венявского для скрипки с оркестром (Wieniawski Concerto for Violin and Orchestra); опера "Царь Давид" (opera "King David"); французский композитор Гуно (the French composer Gounod);* etc.

6 Conclusion

Here we performed linguistic analysis of the data generated by LDA model by:

(1) describing three types of topics as regards their content: general topics, special topics as well as mixed topics, and

(2) analyzing the inner structure of topics in terms of paradigmatic and syntagmatic relations between lexical items.

Evidence obtained in course of our experiments proves consistency of the statistical model and compliance of linguistic results generated by the model with common knowledge on musical terminology.

7 Further Development of Research

We hope to continue our research in the following directions:

(1) enlargement of the Russian text corpus on musicology: addition of texts on musical criticism as well as educational texts (e.g. children's literature on music), development of parallel subcorpus of comparable texts;
(2) refinement of the pre-processing procedure and purification of morphological analysis (lemmatization in particular);
(3) improvement of the topic modeling toolkit, addition of several topic models besides LDA (LSA and pLSA), and investigating optimal parameters for topic modeling;
(4) application of results achieved in course of topic modeling in further studies of musical texts (musical terminology extraction, construction identification, ontology development);
(5) comparison of topical structure of musicology corpus with other specialized corpora.

References

1. Bod, R.: A unified model of structural organization in language and music. J. Artif. Intell. Res. **17**, 289–308 (2002)
2. Scha, R., Bod, R.: Computational aesthetics. J. Informatie en Informatiebeleid **11**(1), 54–63 (1993)
3. Koryhalova, N.P.: Muzykal'no-ispolnitel'skije Terminy (Terminology of Musical Performance) (in Russian). St.-Petersburg (2006)
4. Mitrofanova, O.A.: Regulyarnoje i Irregulyarnoje v Terminologii Muzyki: o Jazykovyh Sposobah Zadanija Risunka Muzykal'nogo Proizvedenija (Regular and irregular items in terminology of music: on linguistic means of defining the contour of the musical composition) (in Russian). In: Materialy XXXI Nauchno-Prakticheskoj Konferencii Filologicheskogo Fakul'teta SPbGU. Vyp. 4. Sekcija Prikladnoj i Matematicheskoj Lingvistiki. (Proceedings of the XXXI Research Conference of the Philological Faculty, St.-Petersburg State University, issue 4. Section of Applied and Mathematical Linguistics), St.-Petersburg (2002)
5. Mitrofanova, O.A.: Jazykovyje Sposoby Zadanija Risunka Muzykal'nogo Proizvedenija: Shtrihi k Lingvisticheskomu Portretu A.N. Skryabina (Language means of defining the contour of the musical composition: the features of A.N. Skryabin's linguistic portrait) (in Russian). In: Avtor. Tekst. Auditorija (Author. Text. Audience). Saratov (2002)
6. Gries, S.T.: What is corpus linguistics. J. Lang. Linguist. Compass **3**, 1–17 (2009)

7. Zakharov, V.P.: Korpusnaja Lingvistika (Corpus Linguistics) (in Russian). St.-Petersburg (2005)
8. Blei, D.M., Ng, A.Y., Jordan, M.I.: Latent dirichlet allocation. J. Mach. Learn. Res. **3**(4–5), 993–1022 (2003)
9. Daud, A., Li, J., Zhou, L., Muhammad, F.: Knowledge discovery through directed probabilistic topic models: a survey. Front. Comput. Sci. China **4**(2), 280–301 (2010)
10. TMB – Topic Modelling Bibliography. http://www.cs.princeton.edu/ ~ mimno/topics.html
11. Rhody, L.M.: Topic modeling and figurative language. J. Digit. Humanit. **2**(1). Winter 2012. http://journalofdigitalhumanities.org/2-1/topic-modeling-and-figurative-language-by-lisa-m-rhody/. (2012)
12. Bodrunova, S., Koltsov, S., Koltsova, O., Nikolenko, S., Shimorina, A.: Interval semi-supervised LDA: classifying needles in a haystack. In: Castro, F., Gelbukh, A., González, M. (eds.) MICAI 2013, Part I. LNCS, vol. 8265, pp. 265–274. Springer, Heidelberg (2013)
13. Vorontsov, K.V., Potapenko, A. Additive regularization of topic models. In: Analysis of Images, Social Networks and Texts. Communications in Computer and Information Science, vol. 436, pp. 29–46 (2014)
14. Mitrofanova, O.A.: Verojatnostnoje Modelirovanije Tematiki Russkojazychnyh Korpusov Tekstov s Ispol'zovanijem Kompjuternogo Instrumenta GenSim (Probabilistic topic modelling of the Russian text corpora by means of GenSim toolkit) (in Russian). In: Trudy Mezhdunarodnoj Konferencii «Korpusnaja Lingvistika – 2015» (Proceedings of the International Conference «Corpus Linguistics – 2015»), St.-Petersburg (2015)
15. Martynenko, G.J.: Semantika Korpusa Russkogo Romansa (Semantics of the Russian romance corpus) (in Russian). In: Trudy Mezhdunarodnoj Konferencii «Korpusnaja Lingvistika – 2006» (Proceedings of the International Conference «Corpus Linguistics – 2006»), St.-Petersburg, pp. 255–262 (2006)
16. Martynenko, G.J.: Korpus Russkogo Romansa kak Osnova Issledovanija Verbal'no-muzykal'nyh Tekstov (The corpus of Russian romances for studying poetry and music) (in Russian). In: Trudy Mezhdunarodnoj Konferencii «Korpusnaja Lingvistika – 2013» (Proceedings of the International Conference «Corpus Linguistics – 2013»), St.-Petersburg (2013)
17. Samin, D.: 100 Velikih Muzykantov (100 Great Musicians) (in Russian). Moscow (2002)
18. Samin, D. 100 velikih kompozitorov (100 Great Composers) (in Russian). Moscow (2006)
19. Karaulov, J.N., et al.: RAS Russkij Assiciativnyj Slovar' (The Russian Associative Dictionary) (in Russian), vol. 1–2. Moscow (2002)
20. Melchuk, I.A.: Opyt Teorii Lingvisticheskih Modelej «Smysl <=> Tekst» (Experience of the Theory of Linguistic Models «Sense <=> Text») (in Russian). Moscow (1999)

Brazilian Portuguese Pronominal Verbs: How to Identify Them?

Aline Camila Lenharo[(⊠)]

College of Letters and Sciences,
Sao Paulo State University (UNESP),
Araraquara, Brazil
alenharo@hotmail.com

Abstract. This paper shows the difficulties in delimiting Brazilian Portuguese Pronominal Verbs (BPPV) and proposes a way based on the theoretical assumptions of functionalism (especially the Dutch current) to formalize them, with a view to treatment of linguistic knowledge into computational-linguistic contexts. In this way, it aims, from a lexical-grammatical characterization of BPPV, to (i) systematize different subtypes of this verb type – such as: verb + $SE_{passive}$, verb + $SE_{inherent}$, and verb + $SE_{reflexive}$, identified from the different types of clitic SE; (ii) establish a comparison between various classifications checked for these verbal subtypes; and finally (iii) to establish a formal proposal to represent these different pronominal verbs subtypes based on Functionalism theoretical assumptions, with the objective of to addressing this linguistic knowledge into linguistic-computational contexts, such as the implementation/refinement of WordNet.Br verbs base. In this way, it is hoped to contribute with two complementary domains of research, the Linguistic Domain and the Linguistic-Computational Domain.

Keywords: Pronominal verbs · Lexicogrammar · Functionalist formal representation · Wordnets

1 Introduction

In Linguistics, the study of certain phenomena can become complex because (i) several authors may assign different meanings to the same term and (ii) several authors may use different terms to describe what is essentially the same phenomenon [1–3]. This is what happens with the terminological and conceptual treatment of Portuguese Pronominal Verbs (BPPV), which can receive different labels – such as "pronominal verbs", "reflexive verbs", "reflexive and reciprocal pronominal verbs", "intrinsically pronominal verbs", "obligatory reflexive verbs", "ex-ergative verbs", between others [4–12]. Many grammarians, lexicographers, linguists and language scholars, trying to explain the use of pronominal clitic next to a verb, often present more or less disparate arguments, generating not only a complex literature, but controversial opinions [13, 14]. In addition, the plurality of functions carried by SE in Portuguese – which serves to, for example,

(i) to transform transitive verbs in verbs with dethematized subject positions (compare (01) and (02));

© Springer International Publishing Switzerland 2015
P. Eismont and N. Konstantinova (Eds.): LMAC 2015, CCIS 561, pp. 77–87, 2015.
DOI: 10.1007/978-3-319-27498-0_7

(ii) to play the role of Agent Passive (03);
(iii) mark the reflexivity of verbal action (04) and (05), etc. – make the task of to define/conceptualize the pronominal verbs further complicated.

1. **"O aluno estuda para o ENEM** como se estivesse estudando para um vestibular".
    'The pupil studies for ENEM as if he were studying for an admission test'
2. **"Estuda-se para a vida**, para o crescimento como ser humano".
    'One studies life, for growth as a human being'
3. **"Vende-se um sítio** com duas casas e água encanada".
    'For sale a farm with two houses and running water'
4. **"Fabinho e Giane se amam"**.
    'Fabinho and Ana love each other'
5. **"Ana se olha no espelho** e se espanta com a transformação em seu visual".
    'Ana looks herself in the mirror and is surprised by the transformation in her look'

In a linguistic-computational interdisciplinary context, as the construction/refining of WordNet.Br – a relational database (structured in terms of synsets, or "synonym sets") that tries to represent one part of language users' lexical knowledge, i.e., the knowledge concerned with relations of similarity (synonymy), opposition (antonym), inclusion (hyponym), decomposition (meronymy) and logic correlation (cause and entailment) senses ([8, 15–17]), in which grammars and dictionaries are adopted as reference works for the development of computational resources. This complexity mentioned about pronominal verbs becomes a problem for the researcher, who is faced with situations such as these illustrated in the two following paragraphs and has doubts on the position he should adopt.

Observing a set of 49 verbs in five lexicographical works – Aurélio [18], Caldas Aulete [19], DUP [5], VOLP [20] and Webster's [21] – it is noted that there is a difference between the number of verbs classified as pronouns: in Aurélio are 28; in Caldas Aulete are 21; in DUP are 24; in Webster's are 15 (classified as "reflexive"); and in VOLP there is no verb. The verb **castrar** *('to castrate')*, for example, is recorded (in at least one sense) with pronominal brand in Caldas Aulete and Aurélio, but is not classified as pronominal (or reflexive) in DUP, VOLP and Webster's.

Comparing 241 verbs recorded with SE in Webster's to 171 verbs registered with pronominal clitic in VOLP, another discrepancy can be observed: 55 verbs are constant concomitantly in the two works. From these 55 verbs, the majority seems to have fallen into disuse in contemporary Brazilian Portuguese, because verbs like **alarpar-se** *('to hide, to cover')*, **endefluxar-se** *('to catch cold')*, **entrefigurar-se** *('to seem to one')*, **fradar-se** *('to become a monk or nun')*, and **hispar-se** *('to bristle')* have few examples located into the research corpus (or none). Among the verbs that obtained several examples located, such as **esbaldar-se** *('to revel')*, there were also located examples without the SE, as illustrated in (06).

6. "A justiça baiana está esbaldando em altos salários".
    'The Bahian justice is reveling in high salaries'

Trying to offer improvements for the interdisciplinary research context cited, this paper proposes that pronominal verbs must be considered as [verb + clitic SE] constructions. In this way, it considers that the term "pronominal verb" includes different verbal subtypes – which must be characterized according to the type of clitic SE that they occur.

In another words, this paper proposes that BPPV can be identified through a lexical-grammatical characterization which includes (i) a systematization of different verb subtypes (such as: verb + $SE_{passive}$, verb + $SE_{inherent}$, and verb + $SE_{reflexive}$), identified from the different types of clitic SE, and (ii) a comparison between various classifications checked for these verbal subtypes (Sect. 2) – which permits heuristic mechanisms of identification.

Besides, due the objective of addressing this linguistic knowledge into linguistic-computational contexts, such as the implementation/refinement of WordNet.Br verbs base, this paper establishes a formal proposal to represent these different pronominal verb sub-types based on Functionalism assumptions (Sect. 3).

To finish, it presents an overview of how the linguistic knowledge about BPPV is related with WordNet.Br (Sect. 4) and traces some final considerations (Sect. 5).

Thus, it is hoped to contribute with two complementary domains of research, the Linguistic Domain and the Linguistic-Computational Domain.

2   The Characterization of BPPV

This paper proposes that BPPV must be considered as [verb + pronominal clitic] constructions, i.e., as lexical items from verb class that occur associated with a clitic SE – which can be conjugate (in number and in person) and can be represented by **me**, **te**, **se** (singular), **nos**, **vos**, and **se** (plural) forms. In this way, it is considered that the term "pronominal verb" includes different verbal subtypes, characterized according to SE clitic type that they occur[1].

Through characteristics from each SE clitic type – such as (a) the ability to modify or not the verb argument structure, (b) receiving specific or arbitrary reference, and (c) the possession or not of se-mantic content (being or not a Theme), among others [2, 8, 10, 11, 22, 24–26] – it is possible to systematize nine different types of SE clitics (Table 1).

So, with this systematization, it is possible to determine nine different subtypes of BPPV: verb + $SE_{reflexive}$, verb + $SE_{anticausative}$, verb + $SE_{ex-ergative}$, verb + $SE_{inherent}$, verb + $SE_{almost-inherent}$, verb + $SE_{stylistic}$, verb + $SE_{passive}$, verb + $SE_{indeterminate}$, and verb + SE_{medial}. Thus it becomes possible to establish a comparison between various verbal classifications available on linguistic works, as illustrated in Table 2 (Cf. [13] for more details).

---

[1] Clitics are a particular type of pronouns matching to unstressed personal pronouns that occur attached to the position of verb complements, but they are not limited "to denote the grammatical person and can display a predicative function, or be overlaid of morphosyntactic features characteristics of some derivational suffixes" [22]. They can be thought as forms that are in the "middle way" between autonomous lexical items and affixes [23].

Table 1. Types of clitic SE.

Types of SE	Mean characteristic	Example
SE_reflexive	To realize the thematic role of internal argument (which may be reciprocal or not).	- Francisco e Bento XVI **se abraçam** em encontro histórico de Papas. *'Francis embraces Benedict XVI in historic meeting of Popes'*
SE_anticausative	Inhibit the realization of Agent or Causer of the situation described by the verb, making it intransitive.	To compare: - Mulher engana bandido que tentava aplicar golpe. (transitive) *'Woman tricks villain who tried to apply blow'* - Casal **se engana** ao reconhecer suspeitos [...] (anti-causative) *'Couple mistaken themselves to recognize suspects'*
SE_ex-ergative	Indicate the agentivization of constructions with SE_anticausative.	- A atriz Sthefany Brito **casa-se** com o jogador Alexandre Pato [...]. *'The actress Sthefany Brito married the player Alexandre Pato'*
SE_inherent	To fuse with the verb, turning into a "fossilized" clitic.	- Em meio aos protestos na Ucrânia, uma jovem manifestante **se apaixonou** por um policial durante os confrontos. *'Amid the protests in Ukraine, a young protester fell in love with a police officer during the clashes'*
SE_almost-inherent	Indicate that Agent and Theme from verbs as **portar-se, comportar-se** e **conduzir-se** (*'behave, conduct oneself'*) merged.	- FHC **comportou-se** como um elegante noivo em sua festa de casamento. *'FHC behaved like an elegant groom on their wedding party'*
SE_stylistic	Highlight traces from Subject's action (especially with motion verbs) or traces of the process or the state change from intransitive verb constructions.	- Enquanto calei, **envelheceram-se** os meus ossos dentro de mim. *'While I kept silence, my bones aged inside me'*
SE_passive	Be the Passive Agent.	- De quatro meses para cá, **vendem-se** ali, por dia, em média, oito camisas 10, contra três com o número 11 de Romário. *'Since four months, sold there, by day, an average of eight shirts 10 against three with Romário's number 11'*
SE_indeterminate	Inhibit the presence of a noun phrase that acts as Subject content described by verb.	- **Ressalta-se** que, no momento da coleta dos dados, a loja [...] autorizou a coleta de preços [...]. *'It is noteworthy that, at the time of data collection, the store authorized the collection of prices'*
SE_medial	To put the process express by verb in perspective through topicalization, passing it to Subject position.	- Agora, essa variação [de vírus da gripe] não está mais nas manchetes internacionais [...] felizmente é predominantemente uma doença aviária e **não se transmite** facilmente entre humanos. *'Now, this variation [of flu virus] is no longer in international headlines [...] fortunately is predominantly a bird disease and not be readily transmitted between humans'*

Table 2. Comparison of different proposals for pronominal verbs classification

type of [verb+SE]	Authors' different denominations of pronominal verb
verb+SE_medial	"Indo-European middle voice" [7]
verb+SE_inherent	"with fossilized unstressed pronouns" [29]; "essentially pronominal" [6]; "intrinsically pronominal" [11]; "with the notion of reflexivity in radical", "ergative without transitive counterparts" and "ex-ergative inherent" [10]; "essential pronoun" [28]; that have a "reflexive oblique form" of personal pronouns as "integral part" [9]; "feelings" [4]; "Subclass 1", "Subclass 2" [27]
verb+SE_reflexive	"accidentally pronominal" [6]; which may have a "pronominal argument" according to the context [11]; "accidental pronominal" [28]; "applied in a reflexive form per se" [4]
verb+SE_anticausative	"com pronome clítico ergativo" [11]
verb+SE_stylistic	"with action attenuated reflexivity and Subject's spontaneity" [28]; "person's movement or attitude in relation to his own body" and "usually not accompanied by an unstressed pronoun to express stylistic aspects" [4]; "Subclass 4" [27]
verb+SE_passive	"Subclass 5" [27]
verb+SE_almost-inherent	"with fused Agente and Theme" [10]; "Subclass 3 (with not pronominal homonym)" [27]
verb+SE_ex-ergative	"with agentive SE_anticausative" [10]

This exercise of comparison permits to establish heuristic mechanisms, based on concatenation of authors' proposals studied – such as [1, 4–6, 9–12, 14, 22, 25–30, between others] – to identify properly the different BPPV (but the establishment of these heuristic mechanisms is subject to another paper). Besides, with this systematization and comparison performed, is possible to affirm that the only two BPPV that are lexical phenomenon, because the clitic SE is not a verb argument (i.e., it cannot change the verb argument structure), are verbs constructed with SE_inherent and SE_stylistic. Others BPPV are considered as syntactic phenomenon be-cause the clitic SE realizes a syntactic function [13].

From these statements, it is possible to propose a formal model of BPPV representation that safeguards the differences between the subtypes identified. Thus, the following section will propose a standard representation for BPPV based on the theoretical assumptions of functionalism (especially the Dutch current), which improves the treatment of linguistic knowledge into computational-linguistic contexts.

3   Proposal for a Formal Representation of Pronominal Verbs Based on Functionalism

The proposal to formalize the BPPV advocated in this article is based on Functionalism – especially the Dutch trend, initiated in 1978 by Cornelis Simon Dik, with his Functional Grammar (FG). The choice of this theoretical model to support the proposal of BPPV formalization is justified by the high degree of formalism and the notational explicitness that the GF provides (due to its aims of integration between functional-communicative considerations and formalization).

In GF, the description of a linguistic expression begins with the construction of a predication, in which properties are determined or relations between different entities, selected during the reference process, are established in a predicate. The predicate is, therefore, the "building block" most basic from morphosemantic level of language organization [31]. Each one is internally organized by means of semantic, syntactic, and pragmatic functions [31, 32].

During verbal interaction, the Speaker selects a predicate frame that expands gradually in broader structures (the predications) to reach the level of linguistic expression, in which the rules of expression are applied. This expansion of predicate in predication occurs with the inclusion of terms – language expressions that refers to entities in a (real or mental) world – into predicate frames, i.e. "blue-prints" representing the argument structures in which the predicate can be constructed [31–33].

In GF, basic predicates and basic terms compose the lexicon of the language and are available to speakers of that language. Through productive rules, they can form derived predicates and derived terms. Thus, in the construction of the underlying clause structure, there is a predicate (designator of properties or relationships) applied to terms (entities designators), producing, through a linguistic encoding, a predication (designating a state of affairs) [31, 32]. In the context (7), for example, there is the predication e_1 (8), where **emprestar** (*'to lend'*) is the predicate which establishes a relationship with three terms: **Bicicloteca, livros** (*'books'*) and **a moradores de rua** (*'to homeless'*). These three terms are the entities of this state of affairs: in a given real world (Sao Paulo city), there is an institution called Bicicloteca – a mixture of **bicicleta** (*'bike'*) with **biblioteca** (*'library'*) – that lends something (from class of books) to humans who do not have a home to live in and, therefore, live on the streets [13]. These three terms, that are obligatory constituents of the clause, are called "arguments" [31, 32].

7. "Bicicloteca empresta livros a moradores de rua".
   'Bicicloteca lends books to homeless'
8. $e_1 = [\text{emprestar}_V [\text{Bicicloteca}]_{Ag} [\text{livros}]_{Go} [\text{a moradores de rua}]_{Rec.}]$

Recapitulating, in second Dutch functionalism, the predicate is a morphosemantic 'building block' in language organization. During the interaction between speakers of a same language community, there is a lexical repertoire, consists of basic predicates and basic terms, that is available to these speakers. This lexical repertoire is used in the communication process for the production of linguistic expressions. As the proposal advocated here is that BPPV of the type [verb + $SE_{inherent}$] are stored in the lexicon, each unit of them is therefore a basic 'building block' available to the speaker in [verb + pronominal clitic] format. In other words, this kind of verb is a predicate that is applied to an appropriate set of terms in the predication. For example, in the context (9), whose nuclear predication e_1 from verb + $SE_{inherent}$ **apaixonar-se** (*'to fall in love'*) is described in (10), the arguments (and also possible operators and satellites) [31, 32] are applied to the basic predicate containing the pronominal clitic.

9. "Amy Winehouse **se apaixonou** por barman no Rio, diz jornal".
   'Amy Winehouse fell in love with a barman in Rio, the newspaper says'
10. e_1 = Past[apaixonar-se$_V$[Amy Winehouse]$_{Exp.}$[por barman]$_{Rec.}$]

As we can see in (10), the clitic $SE_{inherent}$ is part from predication: [apaixonar-se[X]$_{Exp.}$[por Y]$_{Rec.}$]. Thus, it is proposed that [verb + $SE_{inherent}$] BPPV, prototypically, must be formally represented as (11).

11. [verb + se[X]$_{NP}$[Y]$_{PREP+NP}$]

Although the verbs + $SE_{stylistic}$ also can be BPPV formed by a clitic SE that is not an argument (i.e., they are also lexical phenomena), there is a difference between them and the verbs + $SE_{inherent}$: while the $SE_{inherent}$ is a morphological realization of a [verb + clitic], i.e., part of the basic predicate, the $SE_{stylistic}$ is an accessory term used to highlight features of the state of affairs described by the verb, and is therefore unnecessary for the predication (verbs + $SE_{stylistic}$ involve, thus, pragmatic issues that are beyond the scope of this work).

The other BPPV subtypes, in another way, are derived predicates originated from the application of productive rules to basic predicates (i.e., the clitic SE is a term inserted in the basic predicate frame: it fills one argument position of the pronominal verb (or, at least, its presence causes changes in the verbal structure). It is proposed, therefore, that verb + $SE_{anticausative}$, verb + $SE_{ex-ergative}$, verb + $SE_{indeterminate}$, verb + SE_{medial}, verb + $SE_{passive}$, verb + $SE_{almost-inherent}$, and verb + $SE_{reflexive}$ must be formalized as (12).

12. [verb[SE][Y]]

Compare, for example, the contexts of verb **ver** (*'to see'*) (13) and (15), and their respective core predications (14) and (16). The structure of (14) is the same as (16), though (14) is a transitive verb (it is not a pronominal verb) and (16) is an occurrence of a verb + $SE_{reflexive}$.

13. "A kami **viu** o seu reflexo no espelho e ficou fascinada por tamanho brilho e esplendor"
    'The kami saw his reflection in the mirror and was fascinated by glow size and splendor'

14. e_1 = Passado[ver(a kami)(o seu reflexo)(no espelho))]

   'e_1 = *Past[see(the kami)(your reflection)(in the mirror)]*'

15. "Gato **se vê** no espelho e faz poses."

   '*Cat sees itself in the mirror and does poses*'

16. e_1 = [ver(gato)(se)(no espelho)]

   'e_1 = *[see(cat) (itself) (in the mirror)]*'

To materialize one of the most valued assumptions of Dutch functionalism (consider the context of use of linguistic forms and to adopt data actually made (coming from corpora) to illustrate/evaluate the verbal units), it is necessary to highlight that some BPPV show variation of use, where the clitic is erased from the phrase, unlike the prototypical formalization proposed in this paper – as shows the context (17) of verb + $SE_{inherent}$ **suicidar-se** (*'to commit suicide '*)[2].

17. 'Vixii' coitada q[ue] dia ela suicidou?

   '*Poor fellow, when did she committed suicide?*'

So, it is important to represent this possible occurrence on the formal representation proposed here, especially for verbs + $SE_{inherent}$. Thus, it is necessary an alteration from (11) to (18), where the use of parenthesis indicates the possibility of clitic no realization.

18. [verb + (se)[X]$_{NP}$[Y]$_{PREP+NP}$]

With this BPPV representation becomes viable to systematize them in terms of linguistic and computational resources, such as the WordNet.Br.

As the verb + $SE_{inherent}$ are the only lexical phenomenon that realizes morphologically a [verb + pronominal clitic] and WordNet.Br is a database that intends to represent Brazilians' lexical knowledge, it is possible to state that this kind of verb is the only one which must be included in WordNet.Br synsets, such as {acomodar-se, adaptar-se, ajeitar-se, ajustar-se, amoldar-se, conformar-se, engrenar-se, entrosar-se, harmonizar-se, moldar-se}, which has the sense of 'become adapted or harmonized to new/different patterns', as shows (19) – from WordNet.Br database.

19. A Igreja se adaptou aos novos tempos.

   '*The Church adapted itself to new times.*'

4 The BPPV and the WordNet.Br

As stated earlier, the WordNet.Br (WN.Br) is a relational database structured in terms of synsets (sets of words from a same syntactic category that share a concept) [8, 13, 15–17, 40–42]. It is a particular semantic network mirroring Princeton WordNet (WN.Pr) [34–37].

---

[2] It is important to highlight that not all speakers support this type of construction, considering the deletion of the clitic SE a marginal realization of the Portuguese language.

The WN.Br database has been under construction since 2003 [40]. The current WN.Br verbs database has distributed 5,860 verbs in 3713 synsets [13]. Each synset is aligned with WN.Pr through an Inter-Lingual-Index (ILI) ILI [13, 38, 39] and inherits a semantic label and, when it is possible, a gloss from WN.Pr. Each synset also has a key (the lexical unit more representative from the concept) and its constituent units have a sample-sentence.

However, the existing WN.Br verbs base must be refined, augmented and updated, especially in what concerns to BPPV. In this way, the statements of this paper are a contribution to the improvement of this linguistic phenomenon in the database.

The implementation/refinement of BPPV at WN.Br verbs base includes the insertion of a representation of the synset frame.

To conclude this section, Table 3 presents an overview of the information regarding a WN.Br synset (without sample-sentences) and its alignment with a WN.Pr synset. In this example, there is a direct semantic equivalence relation (EQ_SYNONYM) [13, 38, 39] between Brazilian and English synsets.

Table 3. Alignment between WN.Br and WN.Pr through a EQ_SYNONYM relation (Source: adapted from [13], p. 177)

WN	Gloss	Synset
Br	"tornar-se adaptado ou harmonizado a novos ou diferentes padrões"	{acomodar-se, adaptar-se, ajeitar-se, ajustar-se, amoldar-se, conformar-se, engrenar-se, entrosar-se, harmonizar-se, moldar-se}
ILI	00147724 - EQ_SYNONYM	
Pr	"adapt or conform oneself to new or different conditions"	{adjust, conform, adapt}

	Semantic Field	Key	Frame
Br	<verbo de mudança>	ADAPTAR-SE	[[Algo/alguém] [verbo+(SE)] [PP]]
Pr	<verb.change>	ADAPT	Somebody ----s Somebody ----s PP

5   Final Considerations

The lack of consensus (exemplified earlier in this paper) in relation to the classification and/or definition of pronominal verbs pointed to the need to an improved linguistic description for this class of verbs.

This study, from the identification of different types of clitic SE, identified the different subtypes of BPPV, characterized by the properties of the type of clitic SE with which they occur: verb + $SE_{reflexive}$, verb + $SE_{anticausative}$, verb + $SE_{ex\text{-}ergative}$, verb + $SE_{inherent}$, verb + $SE_{almost\text{-}inherent}$, verb + $SE_{stylistic}$, verb + $SE_{passive}$, verb + $SE_{indeterminate}$, and verb + SE_{medial}.

With this identification, it was observed that verb + $SE_{inherent}$ and verb + $SE_{stylistic}$ are lexical phenomena – the former being a morphological realization of a [verb + clitic pronominal] and the latter a pragmatic value realization, i.e., the clitic SE is a "expendable" term for the predication – and the other subtypes of pronominal verbs are dependent on the sentence syntactic structure, i.e., they are derived predicates in which the clitic SE is a term of predication.

In addition, with this identification of BPPV subtypes, it was possible to compare different works, resulting in a terminological correspondence that enables the establishment of criteria to identify each different subtype of BPPV – topic not discussed here, but is essential for the construction/refinement of BPPV synsets.

For now, based on the formalism of Functional Grammar, we proposed frames to BPPV representation, with focus on verb + $SE_{inherent}$ frame: [verb + (se)$[X]_{NP}$ $[Y]_{PREP+NP}$]. This representation allows the development of activities in linguistic-computational context, such as the refinement of BPPV synsets in the WN.Br.

Thus, we consider that this article has achieved its objectives, contributing to two complementary research areas. Although the statements of this paper are a big step for the improvement of the linguistic phenomenon of BPPV in WN.Br, it is important to note that there is still much work to be done.

References

1. Dias-da-Silva, B.C.: A face tecnológica dos estudos da linguagem: o processamento automático das línguas naturais. Tese (Doutorado em Letras). Unesp, Araraquara (1996)
2. Dias-da-Silva, B.C.: O fenômeno da apassivação: em busca da passiva protótipo. Dissertação (Mestrado em Letras). Unesp, Araraquara (1990)
3. Lyons, J.: Semantics 1 & 2. Cambridge University Press, London (1977)
4. Bechara, E.: Moderna gramática portuguesa, 37th edn. Nova Fronteira, Rio de Janeiro (2009)
5. Borba, F.S.: Dicionário de usos do português do Brasil. Ática, São Paulo (2002)
6. D'Albuquerque, A.C.R.C.: A perda dos clíticos num dialeto mineiro. Tempo Brasileiro **78** (79), 97–121 (1984). Rio de Janeiro
7. Dubois, J., Giacomo, M., Guespin, L., Marcellesi, C., Marcellesi, J.B., Mevel, J.P.: Dicionário de linguística. Cultrix, São Paulo (1973)
8. Lenharo, A.C.: Os synsets de verbos do português com o SE inerente e os seus equivalentes do inglês. Dissertação (Mestrado em Linguística e Língua Portuguesa). Unesp, Araraquara (2009)
9. Neves, M.H.: Gramática de usos do português. Unesp, São Paulo (2000)
10. Nunes, J.M.: Ainda o famigerado SE. DELTA **11**(2), 201–240 (1995). São Paulo
11. Peres, J.A., Móia, T.: Áreas críticas da língua portuguesa. Caminho, Lisboa (1995)
12. Perini, M.A.: Gramática do português brasileiro. Parábola, São Paulo (2010)
13. Lenharo, A.C.: Descrição léxico-gramatical e funcional dos verbos pronominais do português brasileiro com vistas à construção da base de verbos da wordnet brasileira e do alinhamento semântico desta à base de verbos da wordnet norte-americana. Tese (Doutorado em Linguística e Língua Portuguesa). Unesp, Araraquara (2014)
14. Seara, I.C.: Estudo de uma hipótese semântico-pragmática para a omissão de clíticos pronominais. Letras de Hoje **14**(119), 165–187 (2000). PUCRS, Porto Alegre
15. Dias-da-Silva, B.C.: Modelagem linguístico-computacional de léxicos. In: Laporte, É., et al. (eds.) Dialogar é preciso: linguística para processamento de línguas, vol. 1, pp. 89–103. PPGEL/UFES, Vitória (2013)

16. Dias-da-Silva, B.C.: A rede wordnet e a compilação de um thesaurus eletrônico. Fórum Linguístico **3**(2), 157–176 (2003). Florianópolis

17. Moraes, H.R.: Aspectos sintaticamente relevantes do significado lexical: estudo dos verbos de movimento. Tese (Doutorado em Linguística e Língua Portuguesa). Unesp, Araraquara (2008)

18. Ferreira, A.B.H.: Dicionário Aurélio eletrônico século XXI, (Versão 3.0). LexiKon Informática Ltda., São Paulo (1999)

19. Geiger, P. (ed.): Dicionário Caldas Aulete da língua portuguesa. LexiKon Digital, Rio de Janeiro (2007)

20. Academia Brasileira de Letras. Vocabulário ortográfico da língua portuguesa, 5th edn. Global, São Paulo (2009)

21. Taylor, J.L.: Webster's: Portuguese-English Dictionary, 16th edn. Record, Rio de Janeiro (2001)

22. Mateus, M.H.M., Brito, A.M., Duarte, I., Faria, I.H., et al.: Gramática da língua portuguesa, p. 827. Lisboa, Caminho (2003)

23. Hopper, P., Traugott, E.C.: Grammaticalization, p. 6. Cambridge University Press, Cambridge (1993)

24. Galves, C., Abaurre, M.B.M.: Os clíticos no português brasileiro: elementos para uma abordagem sintático-fonológica. In: Castilho, A.T., Basílio, M. (Orgs.) Gramática do português falado – volume IV: estudos descritivos, pp. 267–312. Unicamp, Campinas (1996)

25. Pereira, A.L.D.: Os pronomes clíticos do PB contemporâneo na perspectiva teórica da Morfologia Distribuída. Tese (Doutorado em Linguística). UFSC, Florianópolis (2006)

26. Rodrigues, C.A.N.: Aspectos sintáticos e semânticos das estruturas médias no português do Brasil: um estudo comparativo. Dissertação (Mestrado em Linguística). UNB, Brasília (1998)

27. Camacho, R.G.: Em defesa da categoria de voz média no português. DELTA **19**(1), 91–122 (2003). São Paulo

28. Almeida, N.M.: Gramática metódica da língua portuguesa, 44th edn. Saraiva, São Paulo (1999)

29. Rocha Lima, C.H.: Gramática normativa da língua portuguesa, 24th edn. José Olympio, Rio de Janeiro (1984)

30. Mutz, K.: SE-verbs, SE-forms or SE-constructions? SE and its transitional stages between morphology and syntax. In: Gaglia, S., Hinzelin, M.O. (eds.) Inflection and Word Formation in Romance Languages, pp. 319–346. John Benjamins, Amsterdam (2012)

31. Dik, S.C.: The theory of functional grammar. In: Hengeveld, K. (ed.) Part I: The Structure of the Clause, 2nd edn. Mouton de Gruyter, Berlin (1997)

32. Neves, M.H.M.: A gramática funcional. Martins Fontes, São Paulo (1997)

33. Velasco, D.G.: Funcionalismo y lingüística: la Gramática Funcional de S. C. Dik. Servicio de Publicaciones de La Universidad de Oviedo, Oviedo (2003)

34. Saint-Dizier, P.: Predicative Forms in Natural Language and in Lexical Knowledge Bases. Text Speech and Language Technology, vol. 6. Kluwer Academic Publishers, Dordrecht (1999)

35. Fellbaum, C.: A semantic network of English: the mother of all WordNets. Comput. Humanit. **32**, 209–220 (1998)

36. Miller, G.A., Fellbaum, C.: Semantic networks of English. Cognition **41**, 197–229 (1991). Elsevier

37. Miller, G.A., Beckwith, R., Fellbaum, C., Gross, D., Miller, K.: Five papers on WordNet (1990). http://wordnetcode.princeton.edu/5papers.pdf

38. Vossen, P. (ed.): EuroWordNet general document. Version 3. University of Amsterdam (2002). www.vossen.info/docs/2002/EWNGeneral.pdf
39. Vossen, P.: EuroWordNet: a multilingual database with lexical semantic networks. Comput. Humanit. **32**(Special issue), 2–3 (1998)
40. Dias-da-Silva, B.C.: Brazilian Portuguese WordNet: a computational linguistic exercise of encoding bilingual relational lexicons. Int. J. Comput. Linguist. Appl. **1**(1–2), 137–150 (2010). http://www.cicling.org/2010/IJCLA-2010.pdf
41. Dias-da-Silva, B.C.: The WordNet.Br: an exercise of human language technology research. In: Proceedings of International Wordnet Conference – 2006, vol. 3, pp. 301–303. Masaryk University Press, South Jeju Island, Korea (2007). http://gwa.globalwordnet.org/wp-content/uploads/2013/11/gwc2012.pdf
42. Dias-da-Silva, B.C.: Wordnet.Br: An Exercise of Human Language Technology Research, vol. 12, pp. 15–24. Palavra, Rio de Janeiro (2004)

Some Observations on Everyday Singing Behaviour Based on Long-Term Audio Recordings

Tatiana Sherstinova[✉]

St. Petersburg State University,
Universitetskaya Nab. 11, St. Petersburg 199034, Russia
sherstinova@gmail.com

Abstract. This exploratory study deals with the phenomena of singing behaviour in everyday life. A group of 78 people of both sexes between the ages of 16
to 75 and of different occupations were asked to spend a whole day with a
switched on audio recorders to record all their verbal interactions. Participants
were asked to lead a normal life and to do what they usually do in order to capture
real-life communication. The result was 510 h of audio recordings referring to
1950 episodes of everyday life. Singing behaviour of 23 participants (29 %) was
observed in 82 episodes (4.2 %). There are more "everyday singers" among men
(33 %) than among women (25 %). The highest percentage of singing participants is observed for the young people under the age of 25 (41 %) and for
participants older than 55 (40 %). The paper describes the method for gathering
data, outlines the observed types of everyday singing behaviour and gives
examples of how and when individual participants use singing in everyday
contexts.

Keywords: Singing · Everyday life · Songs · Sung utterances · Improvised
singing · Humming · Face-to-face interaction · Real life episodes · Social
groups · Speech corpus

1 Introduction

Music plays an important role in people's everyday activities. Recent studies have
shown that music can have different functions depending on life situations: most often
it acts as a mood-changer or enhancer, it can relax or excite, it gives pleasure and brings
back memories. It helps people – especially the young ones – to provide some kind of
escape from personal problems or gain confidence in themselves (e.g., [1–8]). The
therapeutic function of music is widely used in everyday practice [9], at times of major
life crises [10] and in modern medicine [e.g., 11].

Very often, music is just an accompaniment or background to people's other
everyday activities – doing homework, working, resting, driving, exercising, etc. [5]. In
public settings, people are usually exposed to music despite their individual will (in
cafes, restaurants, fitness clubs, trading centers, etc.), but they can control their use of
music in private environments [6, 12] – by choosing what to listen to or what to sing.

In modern western societies, people usually listen to music more frequently than
sing by themselves on a daily basis. However, the tradition of everyday domestic,

© Springer International Publishing Switzerland 2015
P. Eismont and N. Konstantinova (Eds.): LMAC 2015, CCIS 561, pp. 88–100, 2015.
DOI: 10.1007/978-3-319-27498-0_8

family or solitary singing still exists and many people do sing in everyday life. Thus, according to Mito (2013) 70 % of participants who took part in his experimental study reported a singing episode at least once a week, having an average frequency of 2.5 of such episodes per week [13]. Research and daily observations show that people differ in their singings repertoire as well as in their musical skill levels [14].

As for non-professional "solitary singers", many of them prefer to sing only in cases when nobody can hear them – for example, being alone at home or taking a shower. The latter phenomenon was even called "bathroom singing" or "singing in a shower".

Singing behaviour in everyday life is less studied than music listening, though some papers on the topic do appear [7, 13]. Data for these studies are usually gathered through interviews and diaries (e.g., the volunteer participants are asked to describe in a diary all the occurrences of singing in their everyday life) [13, 15]. These studies are usually aimed at investigating the nature and functions of everyday singing. For example, Faulkner and Davidson (2004) came to a conclusion that men's vocal behaviour is "an important technology of Self" [7]. Recent studies have shown that everyday singing can be used as a mean for performing communicative function, allowing the participants to share their emotional state and to initiate joint activities [16].

Another type of everyday singing behaviour is *singing instead of speaking*, i.e. singing in communication and interaction. This function of everyday singing in modern society is still insufficiently explored. Sung utterances or even short sung monologues sometimes occur in real life conversations when a person speaks to others or just to himself/herself. These fragments of "singing speech" are quite rarely occurring events of short duration. Therefore, it seems difficult to catch and study them via diaries or interviews. This type of singing behaviour has more chances to be found when analyzing audio or video recordings of everyday communication. Thus, Stevanovic and Frick (2014) reports about sung utterances in Finnish conversations from a database of 26 h of video recordings made in three different settings – conversations between family members or friends, instrumental lessons and church workplace meetings [16].

Studying everyday singing behaviour on the material of long-term audio or video recordings – for example, all day long – can bring better understanding of using music in everyday life, as well as of its functions. The aim of this exploratory research, which is based on the large collection of everyday audio recordings, is to describe the most common types of singing behaviour in everyday life, to observe individual variation of everyday singing, and to estimate what social groups are prone to everyday singing activities.

2 Data and Method

2.1 Research Data

The study was performed on material of the ORD corpus – a linguistic resource, which is being created with the primary goal of studying Russian spontaneous speech and oral communication [17]. The participants of both sexes between the ages of 16 to 75 and of different occupations were asked to spend a whole day with a switched on audio recorders to record all their verbal interactions. As the participants made recording during one day, the resource got the Russian title *the One Day of Speech* (*Odin Rechevoy Den'*), which is abbreviated as ORD. The similar method of long-term recordings had been earlier used for gathering data for the British National Corpus [18] and the JST ESP corpus in Japan [19].

When recording, participants were asked to lead a normal life and to do what they usually do. In addition, all of them were requested to complete a diary of their real life everyday situations, to fill out a sociology questionnaire and several psychological tests. In the diary, each participant had to note down general information concerning his major daily episodes including what he/she was doing and where and with whom. We did not ask the participants to make the detailed description of their activities throughout the day, as we considered that the necessity to make notes in the diary frequently would interfere with their natural everyday behavior and impact on the authenticity of the experiment.

The sociological questionnaire contained typical questions about participants' gender, age, place of birth, past and current professions, education, etc. In addition, each respondent was asked to provide the same data concerning his/her principle interlocutors and to supply information concerning their social role in relation to him/her.

A total of 114 participants (54 female and 60 male, representing different social groups) volunteered for the ORD audio recordings by now. Nowadays, the corpus contains more than 1000 h of audio recordings. They were made at home, in offices, in stores, in bars and restaurants, at the university, in transport, outdoors, etc. and contain diverse genres of voice activities – mainly, everyday domestic conversations, professional conversations with colleagues, celebrations, communications with friends, telephone talks, lectures, practical lessons, talking to pets and to themselves, etc. Gathering data for the corpus still continues [20].

All recordings are subjected to expert audition. The phoneticians listen to the recorded data and determine their quality for further analysis. As these recordings are made in real life circumstances – not in laboratory soundproof chambers – their quality may diverse a lot, despite using professional voice recorders. If the majority of participant's daily episodes are recorded with a moderate or low noise level the recordings are enrolled in the corpus for further acoustic and linguistic analysis.

2.2   Episodes of Everyday Life

Further, the ORD recordings are segmented into large episodes called *macro episodes*, united by (1) a setting or scene of communication, (2) social roles of participants, and (3) their general activity. These macro episodes are, in some way, similar to stages within acts in theatrical plot structure [21]. If a real life episode lasts longer than half of an hour, it is divided into smaller parts for practical reason, because annotating and processing of long audio files are not always convenient. For example, if an evening party lasts during 1, 5 h – even if it is of homogenous nature – we divide this fragment into at least 3 parts (episodes). Audio files corresponding to these episodes became the main units of the corpus. The long fragments of recordings not containing speech or other voice activity of participants (for example, the periods of silence, the sound from the radio or TV alone) are not included in the corpus, though they may be available in the archive of original recordings.

All episodes get a verbal description in three aspects: (1) *Where does the situation take place?* (2) *What are participants doing?* (3) *Who is (are) the main interlocutor(s)?* [22]. Then, these descriptions are normalized to standard codes, which help to provide data search and selection, and are supplied by additional markers (e.g., humor, positive emotions, negative emotions, "drinking" conversation, phone conversation, etc.) [22]. One of such markers was introduced to distinguish episodes containing fragments of *singing* behaviour [17], because it turned out that the gathered audio data contain not only the recordings of participants' conversations with other people, but in many cases the participant's singing as well. The episodes of everyday singing in the ORD recordings occur quite regularly. It was this fact that motivated us to carry out this study.

2.3   Participants

The material for this exploratory research is the part of the ORD corpus which has been already annotated on the level of episodes. It includes 1950 episodes of everyday life, or 510 h of audio data, and refers to daily communication of 78 people (42 men and 36 women) between the ages of 16 and 75 and of different occupations. One of the participants was a professional musician (female, 70) – a pianist and a vocal coach; another participant (male, 53) is a teacher in his own private school and conducts choral classes to his schoolchildren along with the other disciplines. Professional occupations of 76 other participants do not relate to music in any way.

2.4   Definitions

In this study, we use the following definitions:

Singing participants are those, whose recordings contain at least one fragment of their singing behaviour.

Event of singing behaviour is one the following: (1) singings of some known song or melody (with or without words, with original lyrics or with quite new, improvised words), or any part of it; (2) humming a tune (either existing or *improvised*); (3) joining in singing to radio, TV, computer or CD player, etc.; (4) vocalizing spoken utterances in a singing-a-song way with a "musical" timing structure and melodic features (not just "sing-song prosody" alone) [cf, 16], (5) imitation of somebody else's singing, and (6) improvising ("composing" ad-hoc) and performing "couplets" for pragmatic purposes.

An episode was marked as *"containing singing"* if it contained at least one fragment of any type of singing behaviour. In most of the cases it refers to the participant's own singing, but may define as well singing of his/her family members, friends or colleagues, who participated in the recorded episode. Absolute or relative duration of singing fragments as opposed to non-singing ones was neither measured nor estimated. For this research we took into consideration only the number of different fragments of singing behaviour for each episode.

2.5   Limitations of Data and Method

At the stage of gathering audio data for the ORD corpus, we didn't expect to get any relevant material for musical studies. Because of that we didn't include in the questionnaire special questions concerning participants' musical education, their engagement in non-professional musical activities, musical preferences, and other information which might be helpful in current research.

Despite our intention to gather all-day-long recordings, we have got inevitable pauses in audio registration in the following cases: (1) either participant themself or one of his/her interlocutors was against of recording of some particular conversation or episode for ethical or other reasons; (2) if a participant decided to make a pause in recording just because he/she did not expect any communication for some while (e.g., if they were alone at home – a situation, which is known to be the best condition for solitary singing); (3) a participant forgot to change batteries of the voice recorder in time. In the result, from different participants we gather recordings of different duration.

There were difficulties in analyzing recordings made in noisy environment (e.g., aloud TV in the background), in such situations singing in a low voice and especially humming may be aurally imperceptible.

Some songs – especially those which are sung without words and little-known foreign songs – were not possible to identify.

3   Results

3.1   Singing Activity of Participants

Live singing was found in 82 episodes (4.2 %) related to daily life of 23 participants (14 men and 9 women). According to our data, 29 % of the participants sing in everyday life – 33 % men and 25 % women. Thus, we may claim that singing behaviour is a regular phenomenon of daily life.

Figure 1 shows distribution of real-life episodes (macro episodes of the ORD corpus) containing singing in the recordings made by each participant. In this graph, the participants were arranged according to the number of such episodes. This chart shows how singing activities are scattered during a day (however, it does not reflect how many events of singing behaviour took place in each episode). The maximum singing activity measured in episodes was found in recordings of participant S125 (11 episodes). Singing behaviour of 39 % "singing participants" was concentrated within one single episode.

For participants on the left side of the graph, singing behaviour reveals itself in more than one setting (at home, at work, visiting friends, etc.) and at different time of the day (in the morning, in the afternoon or in the evening). This group of participants

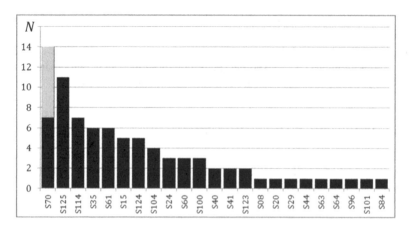

Fig. 1. Distribution of episodes containing singing events for individual participants (the grey zone for S70 denotes singing activities of other family members)

may be called "regular singers", because they practice different types of singing behaviour on a regular basis.

The engagement of participants in everyday singing may be also evaluated by numbers of singing events during a day. In this aspect, analysis revealed three main types of singing participants: (1) active singers, (2) moderate singers, and (3) occasional singers.

The border lines between these groups are quite vague. Basing on actual data, we have decided to draw the borders between groups at the points of 5 and 15 singing events per day. Thus, we consider participants to be occasional singers if they were engaged in less than 5 singing events per day, moderate singers were observed in 5–14 singing events, and we consider a participant to be an active singer if he/she is engaged in 15 or more singing events during a day and demonstrates singing behaviour in a variety of ways.

With this approach to classification we have obtained the following results:

(1) There are four **active singers** in our sample: S15 (m, 20, cadet), S24 (f, 63, professor), S35 (m, 70, technical inspector), S125 (m, 52, security guard). Three quarters of this group are male, and three quarters are older than 50 years old (though all three seniors are working).

(2) The group of **moderate singers** consists of 7 participants: S60 (f, 20, student), S61 (f, 25, managing director), S104 (m, 27, locksmith), S124 (m, 47, plumber), S123 (m, 53, teacher), S70 (f, 63, retiree), and S114 (f, 70, vocal teacher).

(3) The group of **occasional singers** is the most numerous (12 people). Here you can find a schoolgirl (f, 16), a hockey player (m, 21), a network analyst (f, 23), an economist (m, 24), archaeologist (m, 27), pediatrician (m, 41), an accountant (f, 44), an economist (m, 51), a retired engineer (m, 66), and several other participants.

Preliminary study did not reveal correlation between professional occupation of participants and their singing behavior.

We have already noted that the percentage of singing men (33 %) is a bit higher than of singing women (25 %). Another factor having influence on participants' singing activity seems to be their age. Let us consider this factor in some detail.

3.2   Age Distribution of Singing Participants

Figure 2 shows the age distribution of singing participants as opposed to those who were not engaged in singing activities during the day of recordings. The time axis is divided into 12 five-years periods.

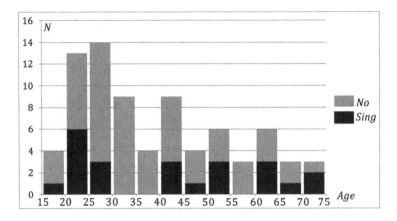

Fig. 2. Age distribution of the groups of participants: singing (*Sing*) vs. non-singing (*No*)

The largest absolute value of singing participants (6 persons) is observed for people between the ages of 20 to 25. Taking account of involvement of the youth in various musical activities, this fact is not surprising. We may also see "everyday singers" among the other age categories – both middle-aged and elderly. It is however interesting to note that we did not find any examples of singing behaviour of participants between the ages of 30 to 40 years, i.e. in a period, which is usually characterized as a time of active family and career development.

As the number of participants who took part in the recordings differs for different ages, it is expedient to use some normalizing method. For example, we may analyze the proportion of singing participants to non-singing ones (S/N index) in its dynamics.

The corresponding graph is presented on the Fig. 3. Actual values of S/N index are given in grey (each dot refers for a 5 year period, e. g. the initial value of 0.33 characterizes the period between 15 and 20 years old). The general trend of the index is obtained by means of the distance-weighted least squares smoothing.

This chart reveals an interesting tendency. There is a local maximum of S/N index at the age between 20 to 25, but after that singing activity abruptly disappears,

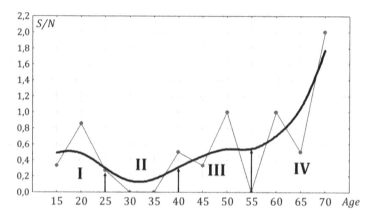

Fig. 3. Time series of *S/N* index (*ratio of singing participants to non-singing ones*, grey dots and polyline), its general trend (black curve) and four age groups of participants

practically fading away for participants at the ages between 30 and 40. Later on, we observe its gradual revival, so that for participants at the ages between 50 and 55, as well as between 60 and 65, the share of singing people is higher than that for twenty-years-old participants. The highest value of *S/N* index has been achieved for elderly people of 70 years and above.

The fitting curve has three inflection points, marked on the graph by arrows. These points located at the ages of 25, 40 and 55 years divide lifetime into four age groups with the two mid periods of 15 years.

Calculating the percentage of singing people for each age group, we obtain the following statistics:

I group (under 25 years old) – 41 %,
II group (25–39) -- 11 %,
III group (40–54) – 37 %,
IV group (55 years and above) – 40 %.

Thus, elderly people in our sample turned out to be engaged in singing activities practically at the same degree as the young people. This conclusion is consistent with that of other researchers asserting that music plays an important role in the lives of older adults (e.g., [24]).

3.3 Participants' Singing Behaviour

As we have seen before, the most typical regular singers in our sample are participants S35 and S125. The first – S35 (m, 70, engineer working as a technical inspector) – engages himself in a solitary singing activity both being at home and at work – being alone or in the presence of others. However, singing was never in focus of his daily activities: he is singing while doing housework, going somewhere, working, and going to bed. Sometimes, he forgets the words of the song but continues humming the melody. During the day, he sang – wholly or partly – 13 different songs. His repertoire consists mainly of the songs from popular movies, traditional Russian songs (romances), and other popular music.

Another regular singer is a participant S125 (m, 52, historian currently working as a security guard). He made the recording in his day off, so we cannot judge his singing activities at work. He lives alone and sings at home being alone, in communication with his 70-years-old mother and while visiting his teenage children, who live separately from him. Unlike many other participants, he is actively engaged in music activities: in his leisure time, he regularly plays guitar, sings to a guitar, and teaches his children how to play songs on the guitar. His repertoire is mainly "bard" songs with simple guitar accompaniment. He sings while cooking and doing housework, too. Besides singing songs, this participant regularly sings common utterances – as if they were lines of some song – addressing the other people or just for himself. Once, he even improvised a whole sung monologue – an answer to his daughter – performed in a couplets form.

According to Fig. 1, the leader in this distribution is a participant S70 (f, 63, retired journalist), who made recordings at home being with her family. However, if we analyze the content of her recordings, it is seen that it is not the participant herself who is the main singer in the family. The majority of registered singing events refer to her 11-years-old grandson who is singing at home all day long. Participant S70 demonstrates her own singing behaviour in just 7 episodes. She can join her grandson's modern repertoire singing, though for her solitary chant she prefers songs that were popular in the days of her youth.

The other regular singing participant is S114 (f, 70, pianist), who is working as an accompanist, piano and vocal teacher. The registered episodes of her singing behaviour refer to her professional activities – vocal lessons with amateur singers and piano lessons with a child. This is not surprising as it is known that singing is an essential part of the process of teaching and learning music [16] and may occur in other professional musical activities (for example, during orchestra rehearsals [23]). Unfortunately, we do not have information, whether this participant sings at home just for herself or not, as she – currently living alone – refused to record her home episodes, justifying her decision by the fact that "there is nothing interesting for recording" during her domestic activities.

Participant S61 (f, 25, specialist in political sciences working as a managing director) made recordings during vacations. Spending time with her girlfriends, she is actively engaged in listening to popular music in background, and she starts singing along with the radio when she likes the song. She is also singing or humming popular tunes by herself when walking on the street or being at home. The other event of her singing behaviour was imitating the singing of an unknown street musician, whose performance she did not like.

We should also mention two other participants, whose singing activity is less scattered during the day (i.e., concentrated within few macro episodes), however is presented by numerous different singing events.

One of them is the youngest participant in our "top list" – S15 (m, 20, cadet) – who spent the whole day of recordings in caserne. Together with his classmates, he is actively engaged in singing in his free time. Young men sing to a guitar, accordion, and play mouth organ. These recordings contain a polyphony of various music being heard at the same time here and there, and most of this music is live. Therefore, we may suppose that cadets prefer to sing songs along or play instruments rather than listening to recordings. Participant S15 itself can play accordion and harmonica, he is singing or humming being in casern or when he is going somewhere. He and his classmates sing primarily military songs, "street songs", rock and pop music.

Finally, participant S24 (f, 63, university professor) is another active singer in our research. Her singing activities are limited to a single setting – when she is at home alone. She demonstrates singing behaviour in a variety of ways while she is working on computer and then preparing to go to work. She sings several songs and produces – like the described above participant S125 – song-like utterances along with the "normal" speech. Her repertoire consists of songs which were popular at the time of her youth, some of which are almost forgotten today, and children's songs. Later, she is singing while walking alone along the street. She was not observed to be singing in the presence of other people, even with her husband.

Thus, singing behavior of participants is characterized by an evident diversity. However, everyday singing events seem impossible to occur in a formal setting. People are usually engaged in singing behaviour when they are alone (e.g., being at home or walking somewhere) or in some friendly informal setting.

Singing repertoire differs greatly between participants, but most people sang popular music, songs from the movies, bard and chansons songs, traditional music and children's songs. The older people tended to sing songs of their youth.

3.4   Types of Everyday Singing Activities

In this section we shall briefly list general types of everyday singing behaviour observed in our material during this exploratory study. All singing events in analyzed recordings are split into three groups:

(1) Singing of some known song or melody is the most common and frequent type. Its following subtypes have been already observed on the material of the ORD corpus:

- choral singing (at school),
- group singing in the family or with friends/comrades,
- crowd-singing together (e.g., after the victory of the city's favorite football team),
- ritual singing during a marriage,
- singing at vocal, instrumental and solfeggio lessons,
- solitary singing accompanying himself/herself on a musical instrument (e.g., a guitar),
- joining in singing to a song on the radio/TV/CD-player/computer,
- individual singing along without accompaniment (a cappella),
- humming a tune,
- imitation of somebody else's singing.

All 23 singing participants in our sample were engaged in this traditional singing. If this type of singing activity is a simple reproducing of the song – which is similar in a way to reciting poems, in the next two types of activities the participants function like the composers themselves.

(2) Sung utterances appear when participant cardinally changes his speaking style vocalizing utterances in a singing-a-song way. In some cases, vocalized utterances have even got "musical" timing structure and melodic features, so that they begin to resemble the lines from some unknown song rather than fragments of ordinary speech. They are rather rare phenomena which may occur in oral communication both addressed to other people or when talking to himself/herself. Besides, semi-vocalized utterances that are somewhat in the middle between singing and speaking styles rarely occur as well.

Two of our participants – S24 and S125 – repeatedly use sung utterances in their everyday life, the others rarely use speech vocalizing style if ever. We did not find examples of sung utterances in recordings of participants who do not sing songs in everyday life.

(3) Improvised composing is improvising a "song" ad-hoc. We have observed three song-like improvised monologues in recordings of two participants. Participant S124 (m, 47, plumper) applies to such improvising twice a day – in both cases as a musical greeting to colleagues. Described above participant S125 used improvised couplets answering to his daughter when she asked him for money, which he did not have. Using the form of an improvised song, the father softens and extenuates his failure to fulfill the request of his daughter.

The other singing-related improvised phenomena are modifying melodies of the known songs or singing new words to the old songs.

4 Conclusions

Long-term audio recordings of everyday life turned out to be a valuable resource for studying singing behaviour in everyday contexts. As opposed to the diary method, it allows capturing "minor" singing events such as sung utterances or humming and draw researchers' attention to a very broad palette of individual singing behaviour. Moreover, audio or video recordings are ideal material for further phonetic and pragmatic analysis of how singing is used in face-to-face interaction and what functions does it have. For example, we have observed that sung utterances may appear instead of common greetings in informal settings. Singing elements bring additional – unusual – expressiveness in spoken interaction. Singing helps to vividly express people's feelings, views and attitudes, as well as to enhance the mood of interlocutors or mitigate a complicated situation.

The research has shown that singing in everyday life is a regular phenomenon. Singing behavior events have been observed in daily life of 29 % participants. There are more singing men (33 %) than singing women (25 %) in our sample. We did not find any evident links between singing behaviour of participants and their professions or current occupations. However, the age of participants seems to be a factor that has an influence on their singing activity. The highest percentage of singing participants is observed for the young people under the age of 25 (41 %) and for participants older than 55 (40 %). Thus, elderly people in our sample turned out to be engaged in singing activities practically at the same degree as the young people. It is also interesting to note that we did not find any examples of singing behaviour of participants between the ages of 30 to 40 years, i.e. in a period, which is usually considered to be the peak of a person's social maturity, normally characterized by active work and career development.

Regarding the conditions of everyday singing, our observations are consistent with the results, presented in earlier papers on everyday use of music (e. g., [5, 6]): people are engaged in singing behaviour usually when being alone (e.g., being at home or walking somewhere) or in some friendly informal setting.

Though singing repertoire differs greatly between participants, most often people sing popular music, songs from the movies, bard and chansons songs, traditional music and children's songs. The older people are prone to sing songs of their youth.

In this brief overview, it is hard to describe all the peculiarities of singing behaviour in everyday life, which were observed here – they are worth of further, detailed investigation. Therefore, this study is planned to continue, involving both qualitative and quantitative methods of analysis.

Acknowledgements. The research is supported by the Russian Scientific Foundation, project # 14-18-02070 "Everyday Russian Language in Different Social Groups".

References

1. Larson, R.: Secrets in the bedroom: adolescents' private use of media. J. Youth Adolesc. **24**, 535–550 (1995)
2. Frith, S.: Music and identity. In: Hall, S., Du Gay, P. (eds.) Questions of Cultural Identity, pp. 108–128. Sage, Thousand Oaks (1996)
3. Behne, K.E.: The development of "Musikerleben" in adolescence: how and why young people listen to music. In: Deliege, I., Sloboda, J.A. (eds.) Perception and Cognition of Music, pp. 143–160. Psychology Press, Hove (1997)
4. DeNora, T.: Music in Everyday Life. Cambridge University Press, Cambridge (2000)
5. Sloboda, J.A., O'Neill, S.A., Ivaldi, A.: Functions of music in everyday life: an exploratory study using the experience sampling method. Musicae Sci. **5**, 9–32 (2001)
6. North, A.C., Hargreaves, D.J., Hargreaves, J.J.: Uses of music in everyday life. Music Percept. **22**(10), 41–77 (2004)
7. Faulkner, R., Davidson, J.: Men's vocal behaviour and the construction of self. Musicae Sci. **8**(2), 231–255 (2004)
8. Davidson, J.W.: Singing for self-healing, health and wellbeing. Music Forum **14**(2), 29–32 (2007)
9. Stevens, C.: Music Medicine: the Science and Spirit of Healing Yourself with Sound. Sound True Inc., Boulder (2012)
10. Faulkner, R.: Men's Ways of Singing. Phenom. Singing **4**, 67–75 (2003)

11. Hegi-Portmann, F., Lutz Hochreutener, S., Rüdisüli-Voerkel, M.: Musiktherapie als Wissenschaft: Grundlagen, Praxis, Forschung und Ausbildung. Eigenverlag, Zürich, Switzerland (2006)
12. Greasley, A., Lamont, A.: Exploring engagement with music in everyday life using experience sampling methodology. In: Louhivuori, J., Eerola, T., Saarikallio, S., Himberg, T., Eerola, P.-S. (eds.) Proceedings of the 7th Triennial Conference of European Society for the Cognitive Sciences of Music (ESCOM 2009), pp. 165–174. Jyväskylä, Finland (2009)
13. Mito, H., Boal-Palheiros, G.: Why do young people sing in everyday life and at school? In: Proceedings of the 24th International Seminar on Research in Music Education, vol. 9, pp. 172–178. Thessaloniki, Greece (2013)
14. Müllensiefen, D., Gingras, B., Musil, J., Stewart, L.: The musicality of non-musicians: an index for assessing musical sophistication in the general population. PLoS ONE **9**(2), e89642 (2014)
15. Bolger, N., Davis, A., Rafaeli, E.: Diary methods: capturing life as it is lived. Annu. Rev. Psychol. **54**, 579–616 (2003)
16. Stevanovic, M., Frick, M.: Singing in Interaction. Soc. Semiot. **24**(4), 495–513 (2014)
17. Asinovsky, A., Bogdanova, N., Rusakova, M., Ryko, A., Stepanova, S., Sherstinova, T., Sherstinova, T.: The structure of the ORD speech corpus of Russian everyday communication. In: Matoušek, V., Mautner, P. (eds.) TSD 2009. LNCS, vol. 5729, pp. 250–257. Springer, Heidelberg (2009)
18. Reference Guide for the British National Corpus. http://www.natcorp.ox.ac.uk/docs/URG.xml
19. Campbell, N.: Speech & expression; the value of a longitudinal corpus. In: LREC 2004, pp. 183–186 (2004)
20. Bogdanova-Beglarian, N., Martynenko, G., Sherstinova, T.: The "One Day of Speech" corpus: phonetic and syntactic studies of everyday spoken Russian. In: Ronzhin, A., Potapova, R., Fakotakis, N. (eds.) SPECOM 2015. LNCS, vol. 9319, pp. 429–437. Springer, Heidelberg (2015)
21. Sherstinova, T.: Macro episodes of Russian everyday oral communication: towards pragmatic annotation of the ORD speech corpus. In: Ronzhin, A., Potapova, R., Fakotakis, N. (eds.) SPECOM 2015. LNCS, vol. 9319, pp. 268–276. Springer, Heidelberg (2015)
22. Sherstinova, T.: The structure of the ORD speech corpus of Russian everyday communication. In: Matoušek, V., Mautner, P. (eds.) TSD 2009. LNCS, vol. 5729, pp. 258–265. Springer, Heidelberg (2009)
23. Weeks, P.: A rehearsal of a Beethoven passage: an analysis of correction talk. Res. Lang. Soc. Interact. **29**(3), 247–290 (1996)
24. Creech, A., Hallam, S., McQueen, H., Varvarigou, M.: The power of music in the lives of older adults. Res. Stud. Music Educ. **35**(1), 87–102 (2013)

Problems of Notation

Shaping Tunes: Sharing Musical Information Across Cultural Boundaries

Indranil Roy[(⊠)]

Independent Scholar, Kolkata, India
indronil@yahoo.com

Abstract. Indian music and its notation system has always been a complicated subject for Western musicologists due to differences in their fundamental structure and contradictory axioms. Distinct (and often subjective) note intervals and scale structures, prevalence of microtones, grace notes, intrinsic ornamentals, rhythmic control and absence of harmony in Indian music contrast it against Western music, which largely builds on equal temperament scales, mean tones and ubiquitous primacy of harmony. These differences make rendering Indian music notation into Western Staff notation extremely difficult. Another contention is that printed music is inherently limited in usefulness and it is worth considering an audio-visual digital notation format to supersede sheet music. This paper explains the structural differences between Indian and Western musical systems and proposes a new digital audio visual notation system for Indian music to reconcile them while addressing the limitations of printed sheet music through computer software solutions.

Keywords: Indian music · Notation · Staff · Tuning · Scales · Raga · Shruti

1 Introduction

The story of music is pitted with discords, especially so when one looks at the perception of Indian music by Western musicologists. Eminent experts among the Western musical fraternity often neglected nuances of Indian music to make it easily transferable, thereby rendering it off-colour. The reason behind this is partly historical and partly vocational. Early Western musicologists viewed Indian culture in an Orientalist framework which often has been condescending or patronizing: It is something from a lost past, folk, rustic, sweet but archaic. Even a scholar like A. H. Fox Strangways, in his classic 'The Music of Hindostan' writes [1]:

> *The study of Indian music is of interest to all who care for song, and of special interest to those who have studied the early stages of song in medieval Europe or ancient Greece. For here is the living language of which in those we have only dead examples. It is hardly possible in the case of modern European Folksong to study melody pure and simple, for we have no large body of such song of which we can certainly say that it was not influenced at all by the current conception of harmony.'

Yet it was Strangways himself who meticulously collected Indian songs, analyzed the modes and wrote about them, showing that culture can surely be overcome. E. Clements summed up this view succinctly in his 'Introduction to the study of Indian Music.' In his words [2]:

© Springer International Publishing Switzerland 2015
P. Eismont and N. Konstantinova (Eds.): LMAC 2015, CCIS 561, pp. 103–114, 2015.
DOI: 10.1007/978-3-319-27498-0_9

'Europeans, on their part, are too ready to assume that the Indian scales are artificial and capricious, and too prone to ascribe to "quarter tones" distinctions between intervals with which they are not familiar, such as the difference between the major tone and the minor tone. Intervals less than a semitone are frequently employed in grace or embellishment, but very seldom in scales. When they form part of a scale, it is possible in many cases to regard them as constituents of natural chords of the seventh, the tempered equivalents of which are well known to the Western musician as discords. It is also a prevalent idea that, in the study of Indian music, intonation may be neglected as being of minor importance. This view is, however, demonstrably wrong; the student who masters the subject of intonation will find no difficulty in solving the remaining problems of Indian musical theory'.

It is through rigorous comparative analysis that the differences between these two systems could have been understood; not to define superiority of one or primitiveness of the other, but to create a framework that can help to share musical expertise. Instead, Western scales and techniques were freely inducted into Indian music, culling its complexities and making it easier for performers, but destroying the subtleties.

To the uninitiated Western ear, Indian classical music might appear to be monotonous, simplistic, lacking in harmony, even discordant. One of the primary causes for this comes from how the listener, trained in one form of music, anticipates and expects a musical progression to develop. However, the difference between Western and Indian classical music is not only a matter of subjective cultural mode that can be reconciled with due exposure; their fundamental structures, scales, tuning are different too. This dissonance needs to be understood and accounted for to make Indian musical modes sharable with Western listeners. H.A. Popley, in his 'The Music of India' quoted the observation of a correspondent in the Madras Mail, over a century ago [3]:

'I owe that Indian music, though it interests me, does not appeal to me the least. I have tried again and again to catch some comprehensive idea and grasp a beginning or an ending, to discover whether the music is pathetic or sublime, erotic or religious, and I have never yet succeeded...The conclusion to be drawn is not that the art is inferior or that it does not exist. It is the ears of our musical understanding which are deaf to those sounds, which have so powerful an effect upon our neighbours.'

2   Two Cultures

Indian classical music can be broadly classified into two geographically separate streams – northern and southern. The North Indian stream is known as *Hindustani* and the South Indian as *Carnatic*. Having evolved from the same stock they are similar in many ways, the major differences being in scale creations, ornamentation and articulation. In the present context these differences can be ignored and both collectively referred to as Indian music.

Western classical music is based on harmony, a major/minor tonal system and uses tonic progression and counterpoint abundantly. Indian music is built on melody; harmony, counterpoint and tonic progression are not used. Most performances of Indian music feature a primary voice or instrument creating melody with tonal support from drones and rhythm from percussions.

Western music uses major and minor scales and equal temperament notes. Indian music uses a much more complex system of scales, with parent scales and descendant families that sound quite different from each other. While there are only two sets of pitch ratios between the notes in Western system, one for all major scales and another for all minor scales, Indian music uses different pitch ratio for the notes in different scales.

Classical Indian texts such as *Natyashastra* (*Bharata*) and *Sangeet Ratnakara* (*Sharangdev*) mentions three fundamental scales – *shadaja gram*, *madhyam gram* and *gandhar gram* – the last one rarely used. Within a scale, transposing the tonic to another note gives rise to new sub-scales or modes, some of them very similar in structure to Greek modes. These modes are known as *That* in *Hindustani* and *Mela* in *Carnatic* system. Ten common *Thats* are used in *Hindustani* system and seventy two *Melas* in *Carnatic* system. The actual scales used in performance are further derived from these modes.

Like twelve tone chromatic octave of Western music, Indian music also uses an octave of twelve notes but these notes are selected from a gamut of 22 microtones or *shrutis*, with seven natural notes (*shuddha swar*) and five sharp/flat notes (*vikrit swar*). Each *vikrit swar* is again selected from a set of 2–3 *shrutis* assigned to each *shuddha swar*, selection depending on the scale being considered. The tonic, or first note of a scale, and the fifth note are considered pure and immovable (*achala swar*). These two notes are used in the accompanying drone as a constant reference upon which all other notes are built.

The pitch ratios between the microtones are not defined as frequencies; instead there is a qualitative and subjective aspect to them. Each *shruti* is assigned a name, a quality and a family. The ratio and frequency of *shrutis* can be calculated using elaborate and complex theories. Notes at a distance of 9 or 13 *shrutis* from each other are considered mutually consonant (*samvadi*), notes at a distance of two or twenty *shrutis* are mutually dissonant (*vivadi*) and the rest assonant (*anuvadi*). A close inspection of the *shruti* system shows that some notes in Indian music do not correspond exactly to the notes in Western music, causing the sound produced to be, at times, fundamentally different.

The classical music frameworks, *Ragas*, form the basis of compositions. A *Raga* uses minimum five and maximum nine (in some schools, ten) notes from an octave. In some *ragas* the same note can be different in ascending and descending tune. A *raga* scale can begin on any pitch, the tonic roughly corresponding to 'C' in Western scales, but unlike Western 'C' it need not have a specific frequency and all other notes are generated in reference to the constant tonic. But a *raga* is not just a scale and ascendant/descendant rules; there are other aspects that defines it such as the sonant, consonant and dissonant notes, the typical musical phrases that signify a *raga*, the primacy of upper or lower tetrachords and allowed/forbidden sequences of notes.

Barring certain free form improvised performances; melody in Indian music is structured around definite rhythm patterns. These rhythms or *taal* range from simple 6 beat to complex 28 beat forms and can be symmetric (like 3/3 or 4/4/4/4) or asymmetric (like 4/3 or 3/2/2). Tempo (*laya*) is specified only as a general guideline, like fast (*drut laya*), moderate (*madhya laya*), or slow (*vilambit laya*). Rhythm plays an important role and often complicated musical structures are built spanning multiple units of the base rhythm. Percussion instruments play important role in supporting melody and at times they complement melody too.

Though Indian music is melodic and performed in a note-after-note form, the progression is rarely staccato. Movement from one note to next is legato, through glissando or portamento. Ornamentation and grace notes are used frequently to embellish continuity. There are specific ornamentations pertinent to Indian music with no direct Western equivalent.

It is very difficult to express Indian music in Western staff notation. Existing symbols are insufficient to transcribe the gamut of 22 notes or typical ornamentations used in Indian music. Either way it is a tenuous and non intuitive process. It also implies that fixed note equal temperament instruments like piano are unsuitable for Indian music.

In Ananda Coomaraswamy's words [4]:

'The theory of scale is everywhere a generalisation from the facts of song. The European art scale has been reduced to twelve fixed notes by merging nearly identical intervals such as D sharp and E flat, and it is also tempered to facilitate modulation and free change of key. In other words, the piano is out of tune by hypothesis. Only this compromise, necessitated in the development of harmony, has made possible the triumphs of modern orchestration. A purely melodic art, however, may be no less intensely cultivated, and remains the advantage of pure intonation and modal colouring.

Apart from the keyed instruments of modern Europe there scarcely exists an absolutely fixed scale: at any rate, in India the thing fixed is a group of intervals, and the precise vibration value of a note depends on its position in a progression, not on its relation to a tonic...the strange tonality of the Indian song is due to the use of unfamiliar intervals, and not to the use of many successive notes with small divisions.'

The argument on dissonance between Indian and Western music can thus be summarized in two points: Limitation of equal temperament scales and instruments in the context of Indian music and a lack of compatible notation systems. While Western Staff notation doesn't have symbols for notes and ornamentations specific to Indian music, Indian notation system too is inherently tentative, limited and underutilized.

3   Writing Music Down

Historically India had a strong oral tradition with little systematically written documentation. Indian musical notation was also mostly oral causing significant distortions over time and rise of parochial versions of same compositions. Many compositions vanished due to lack of performance. Difference in rendition of same composition and modes by different schools made it difficult to assimilate a definitive canon.

Oral transfer of musical knowledge lacks standardization and promotes local interpretations of ornamentation and graces. Each performance is unique to the performer and no reliable record of the same remains except in the listener's memory. A systematic notation system can help in documentation and preserving musical knowledge and assist learning and performance by new aspirants.

It has been observed that no significant body of Indian musical notation exists that's more than a century or so old. From the mid- to late nineteenth century, interests in development of a notation system for Indian music began to take shape. Among the primary exponents, Jyotirindra Nath Tagore developed danda matrik swaralipi – the notation format created by Kshetra Mohan Goswami, and created aakarmatrik swar-alipi, the de-facto standard for Bengali musical notations now. Vishnu Narayan Bhatkhande wrote the seminal treatise on Hindustani classical music and devised Bhatkhande notation system that is still in use. However, these notation systems did not account for the Western audience and their particular requirements.

Since late eighteenth century there have been attempts, mostly by western musicologists interested in Indian music, to transcribe Indian music in staff notation. However the rendered samples were few compared to the vast body of compositions available and the transcriptions were mostly of compositions by a selected few. Lack of formal correspondence between Indian and Western music made the work difficult and the results were mostly untenable for practitioners. It was not surprising that most of the early staff notation transcriptions of Indian music were rarely popular and fell into obscurity soon. If we look at some samples of Indian music rendered into staff notation by different persons, the complications will be obvious (Figs. 1 and 2).

Fig. 1. One of the oldest samples of Indian music in Staff Notation by Sir William Jones (On the Musical Modes of the Hindoos, Sir William Jones, Asiatic Researches Vol 3, The Asiatic Society of India, 1799.)

Fig. 2. Notation by A.H. Fox Strangways [1]

This is one of the first few notations of a modern Indian composition systematically transcribed by a Western musicologist. Though groundbreaking work, it still suffers from the mostly unavoidable issues plaguing such work: matching syllables with notes, handling Indian legato form and grace notes.

He prepared notation of many other Indian compositions and though being a highly useful and important documentation work, they too are of limited use to musicians for practical purpose.

John Alden Carpenter set music to the translated compositions from *Gitanjali* by Tagore and modified Tagore's tunes too. His compositions from Tagore are some of the hardest to read and perform from the same corpus (Fig. 3).

Indira Devi Chaudharani, Tagore's niece, transcribed 100 compositions from Tagore keeping them as close to the original as possible. However the issues with Strangways surface here too (Fig. 4).

It has been observed that these notations, when rendered by musicians absolutely unfamiliar with the original, sound absolutely different and complicated. It is not the fault of the composers or performers; instead it shows the inherent limitations in conventional translation of Indian music into Western Staff notation system and also of printed sheet music on the whole.

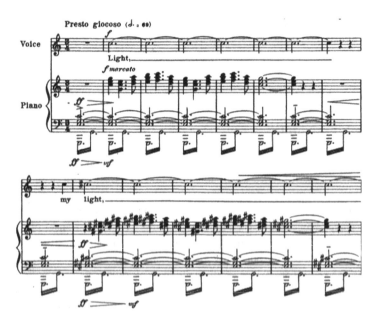

Fig. 3. Notation by John Alden Carpenter (John Alden Carpenter, Gitanjali (Song Offerings) Poems by Rabindranath Tagore Music by John Alden Carpenter, G Schirmer, 1918.)

Fig. 4. Notation by Indira Devi Chaudharani (Indira Devi Chaudhurani, Rabindranath Tagore One Hundred Songs in Staff Notation, Sangeet Natak Academy, 1961.)

When performing Indian music in true form, it seems imperative that the nuances and subtleties of the system must be mastered first. Often this becomes harder for someone proficient in the Western musical system than for an untrained person. This is because a lot of temporary unlearning is needed from the former in the areas where the two systems contradict each other. A new framework for translation of Indian music notation to Western staff notation, keeping intricacies intact, could be of great help in this case. Also the use of digital audio visual technologies could give us a radically different approach towards notations and sheet music that would be much simpler and functional for students and practitioners.

4   Rethinking Notations

It is a common belief among Indian musicians that notation is an inadequate and incomplete instrument for representing music. While it is true that for primarily melodic compositions a mechanical rendition of notation produces a colorless performance, one must not forget that the reason is not notation per se, but the inherent limitation of printed material to 'carry' a tune. Paper is an imperfect medium for music transcription; they are to be heard, not read. An expert musician would be able to sight read the music from printed notation effortlessly, but many special components of music can't be written down unless one creates an ever expanding and overtly complicated symbolic referential framework that would involve an unnecessary and ever continuing learning process, not to mention lack of standardization. This also excludes a major part of the audience since the sight reading music needs thorough training and practice. Further, rhythm and tempo can't be represented that well in printed notation except as guidance.

Calling up a simple analogy, one can say that printed notation is like a color-by-numbers painting. The young artist colors in to create the picture, but availability and perception of various shades and hues might make one completed painting differ from another. It also takes much more effort to visualize the colors just by looking at the outline and instructions, just like sight reading a music notation. In fact the case for music becomes far more critical when we remember that color shades can be documented and universalized (like notes in Western music), but notes are not mathematically precise for Indian music.

For music compositions, especially Indian melody, a better alternative to traditional printed notation is a digital audio-visual one. However this idea is absolutely new to Indian music scenario. There has been only one demonstrable such system designed and tested with a substantial corpus of Indian notations and the traditionalists are yet to be fully aware and proficient with the new approach.

Traditions aside, digital technology provides us a much better and far reaching way of storing music notations. The archival, longevity, search and retrieval benefits notwithstanding, digital audio-visual notations can provide a dynamic representation of music, with structure, nuances and ornaments shown as is in real time. A digital notation would not be an audio-visual recording but a dynamically generated audio-visual representation of notation, with option to change every parameter allowable, like scale, tempo, playing instrument or even language/notation format.

It is essential and useful to separate form and content within a digital notation. The backend would store all musical and structural information as well as sampled instruments to play the notation and the interface would be a mechanism to generate dynamic audio visual rendering on demand. In this way the same content can be used to generate notations in different systems, play them as per user-selected parameters so that the listeners can hear and see the notation perform itself in their own scale, tempo, notation system and instrument of choice.

4.1   *Swarasruti*: An Audio-Visual Notation System for Indian Music

The digital notation system described has been prototyped and demonstrated as *Swarasruti*, an Audio-Visual Notation Project. The system handles notations in three formats, two of them Indian (Bengali *aakarmatrik* and Hindustani Bhatkhande) and one Western (staff notation) It can dynamically change the displayed notation between any of these formats, play the music with syllable highlighting in real time, set and use tempo, scale and instruments as per listener's choice. It can also search and retrieve notation from its database, both exact match and similar sounding phrases. It can loop sections, handle ornaments, play grace notes gracefully and dynamically change rhythm and recreate the displayed notation as per tonic change as required by Indian music. It can also prepare multi-format sheet music output ready to be printed when needed. Over 2000 Indian compositions have been digitized to create the initial corpus for testing.

The internal part of the system is based on MIDI format with extensions necessary to represent Indian musical notes. The most important of them is the ability to handle 22 and 24 microtones. The other important features are ability to link syllables to sustained notes, handling grace notes and various ornaments from Indian music. The interface handles display and playback of notations, highlights syllables as the corresponding notes are played and changes rhythm and tempo automatically as needed. The issue of changing notation when the scale or tonic changes, a peculiarity of the Indian

Fig. 5. Bengali and Devanagari script with *Aakarmatrik* and *Bhatkhande* notation formats

musical system, has been specifically addressed to enable listening in one's natural scale, instead of a predetermined one.

Here are a couple of sample multilingual notations as generated by *Swarasruti*. They have been generated from the compositions of Rabindranath Tagore (Figs. 5 and 6).

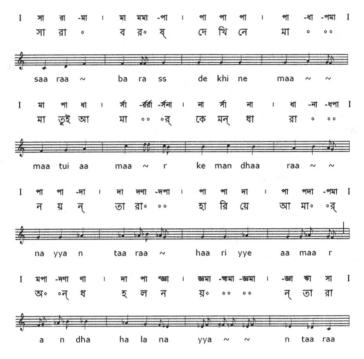

Fig. 6. Bengali and Roman script with *Aakarmatrik* and Staff notation formats

5   Conclusions

While the difference in musical framework is a subjective cultural separation, the mathematical difference in tuning and scale is a more stringent and barring phenomenon. Modal differences can be bridged with exposure but the notes and scales in Indian classical music tend to create a potentially stronger barrier for the Western audience. This is even more pertinent because while the position and ratio of notes in Western music are mathematically fixed, Indian classical music permits (even at times requires) individual notes frequencies to change according to scales or raga, even during ascending and descending phrases within a single composition.

Representing Indian classical music with staff notation is extremely difficult, if not impossible. At best such representation approximates the notes thereby rendering any performance flat and unnatural. The prototype audio-visual notation system for Indian music demonstrates a new paradigm in representation of Indian music notation. It has been tested and appreciated by experts and students both. However the efficacy and acceptance of any such new system needs time and understanding by community, a slow process in Indian musical scenario. There is also a lot of promising development, both in terms of enriching the corpus database and adding new features. For the Western audience, it is expected that in due time this new format will prove to be immensely useful and preferred over traditional sheet music for Indian compositions and provide them an easier way to learn and perform Indian music.

Indian and Western music both are rich and wonderful traditions. Sharing musical experience between them without compromising or culling the uniqueness of any one is a daunting task, needing efforts from both ends. As Popley quotes Lord Ronaldshay [3]:

> 'The future of the land we live in may be likened to a splendid edifice built up on a firm foundation of pillared arches. The pillars are two great races...The keystones of the arches are the will on the part of both races to understand and co-operate with one another in this task.'

The words may be dated but they're still true. Establishing a middle ground, without cutting down or dressing up the nuances of any culture, is perhaps the only way to making a shared effort worthwhile. Unshackling music and freeing notation from mute sheets for it to fly straight to the ear could be a definitive step in that direction.

Acknowledgments. Swarasruti has been a private initiative, without any institutional funding. I would like to acknowledge the efforts put up by my father, M.N. Roy, who after his retirement single handedly transcribed and digitized over 2000 notations in this new prototype and created the corpus that formed the base of Swarasruti project.

References

1. Fox Strangways, A.H.: The Music of Hindostan. Clarendon Press, Oxford (1914)
2. Clements, E.: Introduction to the Study of Indian Music. Longmans Green & Co., London (1913)
3. Popley, H.A.: The Music of India. LPP, New Delhi (1996)
4. Coomaraswamy, A.: The Dance with Siva. The Sunwise Turn Inc, New York (1918)

Further Reading

5. Arnold, J., Bel, B.: A scientific study of north Indian music. National Centre Perform. Arts Q. J. **XII**(2-3), Mumbai (1983)
6. Bharat, N.: Manisha Granthalaya, Kolkata (1967)
7. Bhatkhande, V.N.: Hindustani Sangeet Paddhati. Sangeet Karyalaya, Hathras (1979)
8. Danielou, A.: Introduction to the Study of Musical Scales. The India Society, London (1943)
9. Danielou, A.: The Ragas of Northern Indian Music. Munshiram Manoharlal, New Delhi (1980)
10. Framjee, F.: Text Book of Indian Music. Sakhi Prakashan, Hathras (1990)
11. Gangoly, O.C.: Ragas and Raginis. Munshiram Manoharlal Publishers, New Delhi (1947)

12. Kaufmann, W.: Musical Notations of the Orient; Notational Systems of Continental, East, South and Central Asia. Indiana University Press, Bloomington (1967)
13. Brhaddeshi, M.: Motilal Banarsidas, Kolkata (1992)
14. Prajnanananda, S.: A History of Indian Music. Ramakrishna Vedanta Math, Kolkata (1963)
15. Prajnanananda, S.: Music of the Nations; a Comparative Study. Munshiram Manoharlal Publishers, New Delhi (1973)
16. Ratanjankar, S.: Shruti as a unit of measurement of musical intervals. In: Commemorative Volume for S. N. Ratanjankar. K. G. Ginde, Mumbai (1961)
17. Sharangdev: Sangit Ratnakar. Mumnshiram Manoharlal Publishers, New Delhi (1996)
18. Tagore, S.M.: Six Principal Rags. Neeraj Publishing House, New Delhi (1982)

A Proposal for a New System of Reading and Writing Music for the Blind

María-Teresa Campos-Arcaraz[(✉)]

Faculty of Music, UNAM, Mexico City, Mexico
tkmpos@gmail.com

Abstract. Braille musicography is a notation for music based on Braille code. It is a very useful tool for blind musicians, but it is more difficult to read and write than conventional music notation [1, p. 41]. This is because the Braille system is linear while music notation is a bidimensional system. Also, Braille allows 64 combinations of raised dots while there are at least 292 music signs [2, p. 60], thus signs repeat and change their meaning according to the context. As a consequence, music transcription to Braille musicography cannot be fully automatic [3, p. 61, 85] and cannot be obtained easily by blind musicians. I propose a basic set of new signs based on combinations of 9 raised dots. These should be coherent to blind musicians. Tests of the new proposed code are being held with blind students of the Faculty of Music in UNAM, Mexico.

Keywords: Braille musicography · Braille music transcription

1 Introduction

This article describes part of the project developed to get a Master in Music Technology in the Faculty of Music of UNAM, Mexico. It is limited to the notation of common music practice, also called conventional music notation[1]. Among academic practices in this context, to be able to read and write music is very important: most characteristics of music are learned and analyzed from notation. It is an efficient way of communication between composers and interpreters, and it allows new proposals for interpretation. In music studies it becomes an essential tool, for example in group classes like harmony or counterpoint.

As it is a visual tool, it should be translated to a tactile code in order to make the information available to blind people. Because of the characteristics of Braille code and conventional music notation, some significant changes are made in the transcription, but a score for the blind should cover the same information as a conventional one.

---

[1] According to Donald Byrd [4, p. 13] "CMN (Conventional Music Notation) includes any arrangement of the symbols in general use by composers in the European art music tradition from about 1700–1935, used with meanings that were standard: if the notation was made between 1700 and 1935, at the time it was made; (2) if the notation was made before 1700, with the meanings of 1700; or (3) if the notation was made after 1935, with the meanings of 1935." Tablatures and special signs for contemporary music are excluded from this definition.

© Springer International Publishing Switzerland 2015
P. Eismont and N. Konstantinova (Eds.): LMAC 2015, CCIS 561, pp. 115–124, 2015.
DOI: 10.1007/978-3-319-27498-0_10

1.1   Conventional Music Notation

Conventional Music Notation is a written system of signs organized in graphic space [5, p. 42]. The signs are at least 292 [2, p. 60] and the set includes numbers, letters, syllables, words, phrases, and specific music signs [6, p. 83]. Position is part of the meaning - the symbol which represents the duration of a note gets a specific sound when put in a certain position. A staff and clefs as references establish the exact height of each note. The vertical axis represents the heights and the horizontal axis the time in which the sounds are played.

There are signs that put together with another change their meaning, like alterations or flags in the stems of the notes which shorten the duration.

As it is a bidimensional system, simultaneity can be easily represented. Every sign over the same horizontal point represents something happening at that same time. Then, several notes, articulation, expressions, etc. can be represented to happen at the same time. As the sense of sight allows us to catch a lot of information in one glimpse, this is an efficient way of representation.

1.2   The Braille System[2]

The way in which most blind people read and write is through the Braille Code. It is based on combinations of 6 raised dots in a cell (also: box) organized in two columns with 3 dots each. The dots are numbered 1, 2 and 3 in the left column, and 4, 5 and 6 on the right one. There are 64 possible combinations, including the empty cell where no dots are raised.

In literary Braille, each combination represents a letter or a punctuation mark. The 10 combinations representing letters a to j are the same as the ones representing letters k to t, but adding dot 3. The next set of letters[3] are repetitions of the last ones but adding dot 6. In this way, there are not many different signs to learn, but some letters can be deduced.

The same signs that represent the first 10 letters are used for numbers 0 to 9 by adding the prefix for numbers (dots 3, 4, 5 and 6), which indicates a change of context. Braille can be used in many contexts with the adequate prefix (for example math, chemistry, programming and music).

This code was published in 1825 by the Frenchman Louis Braille while he was a student in the Royal Institute for the Blind in Paris, and it has since proved to be the most efficient system for reading and writing for the blind.

Other systems like raised letters, coiled letters or other raised symbols have been proposed [8], but raised dots are the easiest and clearest to read currently[4].

---

[2] The information from this section is taken from the Braille Manual [7].

[3] Except for letter w which is considered a special character.

[4] Actually, many cases of blindness are due to diabetes or aging, and both of them cause a loss of sensibility in fingers so reading Braille becomes almost impossible. Another alternative in these cases is Moon System [9].

There have been other proposals of 8 points for music [10], and today some computer programmers who need 256 signs (combinations for 8 raised dot) use them; but in a large scale these systems have not worked. There is a physiological reason for this: our fingers can distinguish precisely the position and quantity of Braille raised dots only within a small area in the fingertip [11, pp. 434–435]. This is because of the type and number of specific skin receptors we have for these tasks. Outside this area, the mental image is blurred. In order to read a cell of 2 × 4 raised dots, the finger has to move up and down through each sign, and then continue the horizontal movement to read the others. This makes reading slow and impractical.

1.3 Braille Musicography[5]

Every music symbol has a representation in Braille Musicography. As it has been pointed out before, 6 dots have only 64 different combinations, but there are at least 292 music signs. These means it is necessary to use combinations of 2 or more boxes to represent some music symbols. Also, as Braille is a linear system, there is no possibility of using position as part of the meaning, so all that information must be written with extra signs.

As shown in the Braille Music Manual, the name of the note and its duration are included in the same box. The notes Do, Re, Mi, Fa, Sol, La, and Si are represented by letters d–j with the higher dots 1, 2, 4 and 5, and durations represented by lower dots 3 and 6. As there are more than 4 durations (the number of combinations allowed by 2 dots), one sign represents more than one duration. In case the correct durations of the notes in a measure is not clear, extra signs for 'greater' or 'lesser' value are used. In case of an anacrusis, the use of these is obligatory. Measures are always separated by empty boxes. Although rests have the same durations as notes, they are written differently. Points 3 and 6 do not represent duration, but still one sign represents two different values.

To specify the pitch of a note, it is necessary to write the octave to which the note belongs and the alteration (if there is one). The order to write these signs is: alteration, octave and note+duration. The octave is not written before every note, but before the first note of the score, before notes that make a greater interval than a sixth with the respective previous note, or before a note a fifth apart from the previous note (if there is a change of octave).

There is a sign for each of the clefs. Even if in Braille Musicography they have no real meaning, their use facilitates the communication between a blind musician and a sighted one. There are also signs to indicate if the stems of the notes point up or down, if the notes are grouped in a certain way, if there are passages that repeat identically or if there is a pattern that can be abbreviated. This system intends to use the less space possible and it should help the memory and the understanding of the structure of the musical work.

---

[5] All the information of Braille Music is taken from the manual [12].

Difficulties. Though Braille Musicography is the most-used system at present, it has characteristics which make it much more complicated than conventional notation. Only a few are mentioned in this section.

To write key signatures, the alteration signs are used following this rule: if a key has up to 3 alterations, the corresponding flat or sharp is written these number of times; if there are more than 3, then the prefix for numbers and the number of alterations is written down, followed by the type. One of the problems with this way of writing comes when a student is learning music: he must know the theory first and then must interpret the notation [13, p. 85].

Another complicated characteristic of Braille Musicography is the use of ties and slurs. In conventional notation both are represented by the same sign; context makes the reader decide if it is a duration, phrasing or an expression sign. In Braille, slurs and ties are written differently, and each kind of slur is distinguished. As Braille is a linear system, the note on which slurs begin and end should be indicated with extra signs, including information if the slur ends in a different voice or staff.

But the greatest difficulties are related to the transcription of simultaneous voices. There are 3 possible ways to write simultaneous notes:

(1) If notes start and end at the same time, these are chords and are written as intervals from a certain note. If the voice is written in a higher clef (like G) then the higher note is written and the intervals are descendant. If the voice is written in a bass voice (for example in an F clef), the lowest note is written and the intervals are ascendant. The duration of the notes are specified only for the first note.

(2) If there are two or more independent voices in a measure or a phrase, one of the voices is written, then an in-accord sign that indicates a simultaneous voice in the same measure, and next to it the second voice. These can be repeated for several voices in the same staff and measure. If the independent voices coexist only in one segment of the measure, the partial in-accord sign is used.

(3) When the voices are totally independent it is convenient to write them separately, and there are 2 accepted formats: bar over bar or phrase over phrase. For each measure or phrase, each of the voices is written in separate lines of the page. In scores like the ones for the piano, the signs for left hand and right hand are used.

All rests must be written, even if in the original score rests are not visible for clarity.

Repetitions and abbreviations are also used in polyphony whenever possible, but sometimes there are different ways to write the same passage. Depending on the characteristics of the music that need to be remarked, one way or another is chosen.

Score Transcription. Because of the difficulties of Braille Musicography (some of them mentioned earlier), transcription of a conventional score cannot be fully automatic. Sometimes many decisions have to be made during the transcription [3, p. 86]. Many efforts in the world to make a software able to transcribe any score are being made. There are different computer programs that contain plug-ins that allow to change a score to Braille notation, but to avoid non-clear passages the scores have to be revised by an expert.

Unfortunately, there are not enough transcriptors [14, p. 123] and transcriptions take a lot of time and are generally expensive. As an example, according to one of the blind students of the Faculty of Music, at least 3 weeks and up to a month and a half is the average time to receive a transcription of a piece of the Book of Anna Magdalena Bach when ordered.

2 Objectives and Justification

Braille Musicography is a tool that allows blind people to read and analyze music, but it is not as efficient as conventional notation. Transcribing a score requires a lot of effort and time, and it cannot be made automatically. This is why there is a need to look for other systems or codes to write music for the blind in a more efficient way and with the possibility of an efficient automatic transcription.

Within this research a new system is developed, a set of basic music signs that is expandable. If a box of 3 × 3 raised dots is used, 512 possible combinations are allowed and the problem of repeating combinations with different meanings could be solved, making musicography more efficient and clear.

3 Proposal

3.1 Description of the System

This system proposes a sign generator of 9 dots, in a matrix of 3 rows and 3 columns numbered as shown in Fig. 1. The size of the dots and the distance between them respect the ones established for standard Braille. It can be read fluently because it doesn't exceed the area of the fingertip with which we can read and understand each sign. There is no need of going vertically on each to identify it. It allows 512 different combinations, so no sign will be repeated or change its meaning depending on the context.

The set of basic music signs proposed is formed by the names of the notes, durations, octaves, alterations, ties, dot and staccato. In Fig. 2 some of these are shown. It is a system for melodies of only one voice. A solution for simplifying the writing of several simultaneous voices is still to be found.

As this image shows, the name of the note and its duration are written in the same box. All of the notes have dots 4 and 7 raised. Any other sign not containing dots 4 and 7 raised is not a note.

The names of the notes are represented by dots 1, 2 and 3, and silence is represented by none of these dots raised. Combinations of the dots of the other two columns are the durations, having 16 options. When choosing the meaning of the signs a pattern was followed, so that some meanings could be deduced.

Fig. 1. 3 × 3 matrix sign generator

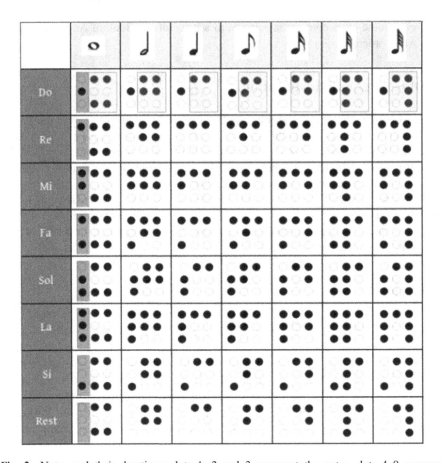

Fig. 2. Notes and their durations: dots 1, 2 and 3 represent the notes, dots 4–9 represent durations

Fig. 3. (a) Octaves (b) alterations

Figure 3a shows the signs for octaves. These are the same as in Braille Musicography, but in a 9 × 9 box. Alterations are shown in Fig. 3b; they use only the last column of the matrix.

When indicating the key, a combination of the signs of the notes in the first column and the alterations on the second column can be used, as shown in Fig. 4.

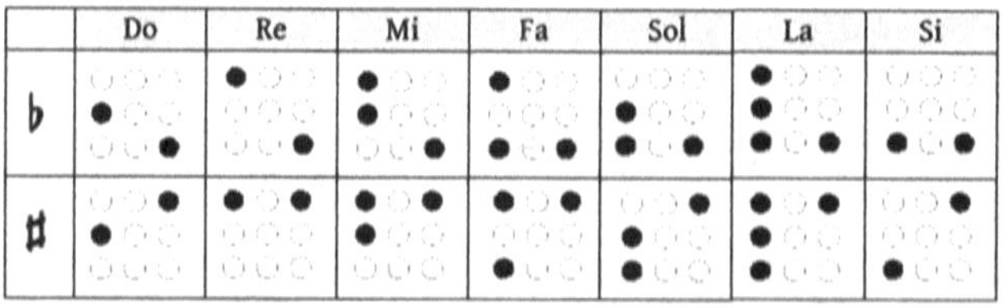

Fig. 4. Key signatures: the first column will show the name of the note and the last one the corresponding alteration

The proposed signs for the G and F clefs are shown in Fig. 5. They should be written at the beginning of the score in a line including only the clef, the time signature (the same as in Braille) and the key signature, in the order mentioned.

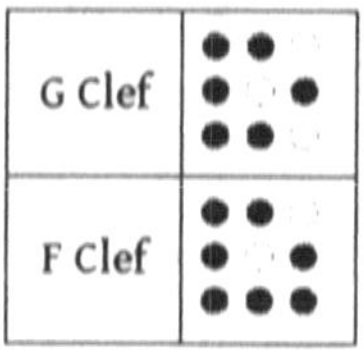

G Clef	(braille pattern)
F Clef	(braille pattern)

Fig. 5. G and F clefs

Signs for the duration dot and staccato are shown in Fig. 6a and b. The order in which the signs should be written is "octave - alteration - note+duration - dot - articulation" (in this basic set staccato is the only sign proposed).

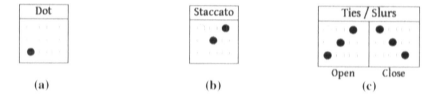

Fig. 6. (a) Dot, (b) *Staccato*, (c) Tie/Slur

The sign for slurs (Fig. 6c) is changed from Braille Musicography. Dots 3, 5 and 7 before the note form an opening slur or tie. After the last note affected by the slur a closing sign with dots 1, 5 and 9 is used. All the notes in the middle will be affected. As in conventional notation, if the notes are the same then it will be a tie, if the notes are different then it will represent a slur. An example of a transcription of a segment of a traditional Mexican song is shown on Fig. 7b.

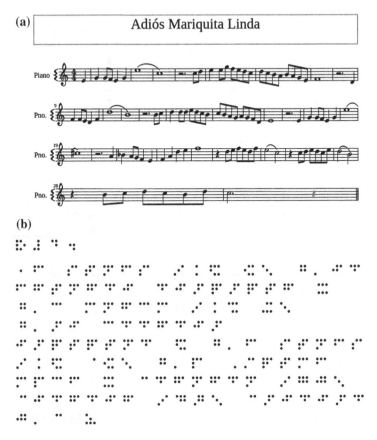

Fig. 7. (a) Segment of traditional mexican song "Adiós Mariquita Linda" (b) transcription to the new proposed musicography

This set of signs is intended to be expandible. Some signs should be 'deducible', and the system should be as clear and simple as possible.

3.2 Tests

Some tests were made with blind students of the faculty of music: 3 children of 11–13 years in courses of piano, a pianist about to obtain his degree and a second-year Vocal Performance student. First, an interview was conducted asking them if they used Braille Musicography, if it was useful for them, if they liked it, and what they thought should change. Two of the children had no interest in learning musicography because it was complicated and, in their words, 'you have to put like a thousand signs to write one little thing'. The older students said they understood the need to use it, and thought it was good except for writing polyphony, where it was very inefficient. Most of the students, once learning a piece, do not review the notation again.

After this, a 3 × 3 matrix of 9 raised dots was proposed, and it was tested by the same students. The 9-dot system was explained and the dots numbered, and a paper with several combinations of the 9 dots was given to them. All of the students recognized and numbered the raised dots correctly at their first attempt every time.

After this test, the conclusion is that a 9-dot matrix is feasible to use as a generator of signs.

These were only preliminary tests, so more studies should be done. A greater quantity of students is needed to prove the efficiency of this new proposal.

4   Conclusion

There is a need of a new way of writing music for the blind. The difficulty of reading and transcribing Braille Music compared to conventional notation is significantly greater. Furthermore, the lack of clarity when analyzing a piece emphasizes this need. Although there is a necessity to make a worldwide standard notation, it is not convenient when the system is not optimal.

With the proposal presented in this work, I intend to show that there could be more efficient ways to write music for the blind. It has to be studied in more depth and tested by a greater number of people. A lot of work is yet to be done, and the participation of blind musicians and experts in music and music cognition is fundamental. Also, new slates and printers for a 9-dot code have to be produced.

Many comments on the difficulty of learning a new notation while already knowing another have arisen, but blind musicians find the actual system still not satisfying. If a new adequate system, where transcription can be fully automatic (and distribution much easier as a consequence) is found, then there will be less struggle with the change.

This system is still at a primary stage. Many signs must be added, and the way of writing polyphony is still a matter of investigation.

Besides this search of the code, it is necessary to find the means to make it available for everyone who needs it. A software has been developed to transcribe an .XML file with a melody of one voice, using only the basic set of signs explained in this article. It is written in JavaScript language and soon it will be accessible on the Internet for free. Manuals and a forum to get the comments and suggestions of teachers and musicians are important, and they are part of the work intended for the future.

Acknowledgements. I would like to thank UNAM and the Music Graduate Studies department for the opportunity and the help offered in the project, and the economic aid to attend the International Workshop on Language, Music and Computing held in Saint Petersburg.

This work would be useless without the help of the blind students of the Faculty and their piano teacher Ms. Adriana Sepulveda

References

1. Herrera, R.: Las representaciones internas de la altura y la escritura musical. In: Schifres, F., Herrera, R. (eds.) Seminario sobre Adquisicion y Desarrollo del Lenguaje Musical en la Enseñanza Formal de la música. Aspectos educacionales, psicologicos, y musicologicos, pp. 37–42. Universidad de La Plata, Argentina (2010)
2. Díaz, I.: La educacion musical de personas con deficiencia visual y la Musicografía Braille: De la musicalizacion a la lectura y escritura de la partitura en Braille. In: Fillottrani, L., Mansilla, A. (eds.) Tradicion y Diversidad en los aspectos psicologicos, socioculturales y musicologicos de la formacion musical. Actas de la IX reunion de SACCoM, pp. 58–64 (2010)
3. Accessible Music: The state of the art. In: Mus4VIP Project: Music for Visually Impaired People. LLP - KA3 ICT: Multilateral Projects. Consortium of the MUS4VIP project coordinated by Conservatorio di Musica Pollini di Padova, p. 61 (2013). http://www.music4vip.org
4. Byrd, D.A.: Music notation by computer. Ph.D. thesis. Ann Arbor: Indiana University (1984)
5. Wadle, D.C.: Meaningful scribbles: an approach to textual analysis of unconventional musical notations. JMM J. Music Meaning **9**, 38–68 (2010)
6. Notation. In: Stanley, S. (ed.) The New Grove's Dictionary of Music and Musicians, vol. 13. MacMillan Publishers Limited, London (1980)
7. Risjord, C.: Instruction Manual for Braille Transcribing, 6th edn. American Printing House for the Blind, Louisville (2013)
8. Gascon Ricao, A.: La ensenanza de los ciegos en Espana. Universidad Complutense de Madrid, Madrid (2004)
9. Moon Literacy. http://www.moonliteracy.org.uk/
10. Burgos, E.: The first Spanish music codes for the blind and their comparison with the American ones. Fontes Artis Musicae **57**(2), 167–185 (2010)
11. Gardner, E., Martin, J., Jessell, T.: The bodily senses. In: Kandel, E.R., Schwartz, J.H., Jessell, T.M. (eds.) Principles of Neural Science, 4th edn. University and The Howard Hughes Medical Institute, McGraw-Hill, New York (2000)
12. Braille Authority of North America. In: Music Braille Code. American Printing House for the Blind, Louisville (1997)
13. Herrera, R.: La musicografía Braille en el aprendizaje de la musica. In: Fillottrani, L., Mansilla, A. (eds.) Tradicion y Diversidad en los aspectos psicologicos, socioculturales y musicologicos de la formacion musical. Actas de la IX reunion de SACCoM, pp. 80–89 (2010)
14. Encelle, B., Jessel, N., Mothe, J., Ralalason, B., Asensio, J.: BMML: braille music MarkUp language. Open Inf. Syst. **3**, 123–135 (2009)

Linguistic Studies of Music

Structural Interaction of Poetry and Music Components in Songs by Sergei Rachmaninoff

Gregory Martynenko[✉]

St. Petersburg State University, St. Petersburg, Russia
g.martynenko@gmail.com

Abstract. The songs by Rachmaninoff represent the superlative manifestation of Russian vocal lyrics, making these songs a perfect material to research interrelations between music and poetry. Structural interaction between poetry and musical components in Rachmaninoff's songs is studied by time series analysis. Time dynamics of two indices are compared. Stress index is used for describing poetry component of the song and pitch/duration index is used for describing its musical part. The methodology of comparative study is demonstrated on three songs: *All was Taken from Me*, *The Fountain* and *What Happiness*. Time dynamics of the pitch/duration index has turned out to be a complex phenomenon. It combines a general trend with cyclical fluctuations, for description of which the notion of *a poetry-musical period* (*strophe*) was introduced. As a rule, a whole period corresponds to four lines. The intonational contrasts are more explicitly expressed in musical components of the songs than in poetry ones.

Keywords: Songs · Russian romance · Rachmaninoff · Poetry · Music · Statistical analysis · Time series · Stress index · Pitch/duration index · Trend · Cyclical fluctuations

1 Introduction

In Ancient Greece, the word music (Gr. *mousike*, "art of the Muses") referred to any "temporal" art – poetry, dance and the music itself [1]. Being an integral part of the Ancient Greek life, music was inseparable from song and dance since all three components came together in civic occasions and religious ceremonies [2]. At present time, music and poetry are separated arts, though some musical forms are syncretic, combining poetry with instrumental and vocal music.

Poetry and music are usually studied separately. However, there are papers dedicated to comparative studies of poetry and music. For example, Kon made a comparative rhythmic research of poetry by Velimir Khlebnikov and musical compositions by Stravinsky [3]. Shubnikov and Koptsik analyze both musical and poetry texts from the standpoint of the theory of symmetry [4]. Martinovich uses musical terms for description of rhythm and meter in Russian poetry [5]. A general overview of the interdisciplinary character of current musicology and its approaches is given in [6].

In recent years, there were attempts to parallel the study of musical and poetry components in vocal compositions (e.g., [7]). Patel in [8] considers the grounds for this approach: "For languages with clearly defined stress, such as English, each sentence

© Springer International Publishing Switzerland 2015
P. Eismont and N. Konstantinova (Eds.): LMAC 2015, CCIS 561, pp. 127–139, 2015.
DOI: 10.1007/978-3-319-27498-0_11

comes with a distinct pattern of stronger and weaker syllables. When words in these languages are set to metrical music, a relationship is established between the syllabic accent patterns and musical metrical accent patterns".

Searching out the common formation principles in literary and music compositions is a rather complicated task. It is thoroughly discussed in works by Makhov [9], who proposes tendency to affinity between literary and musical forms. For example, a large-scale musical structure known as sonata form consists of three parts. Many literary genres are also based on triform structures: e.g., the canonical form of the sonnet (*thesis – antithesis – synthesis*), oratorical speeches (*exordium – medium – finis*) or literary compositions (*exposition – climax – dénuement*) [10, 11]. It seems that a "triad structure" goes beyond the scope of art and can be associated with any human activity, which implies *beginning – development – end*.

The objective of this investigation is to study structural interaction between poetry and musical components in songs by Sergei Rachmaninoff, in which poetry and music are made indivisible. The research is made on the complete collection of 83 Rachmaninoff's songs [12].

2 Rachmaninoff's Songs (Romances)

In terms of Russian musicology, Rachmaninoff's songs belong to the genre of Russian classical *romance*, which is a chamber poetry-and-musical composition for voice with instrumental accompaniment. In Russia, romance is the most popular genre of vocal chamber music, which has many varieties, from folk songs to classical art songs written by the prominent Russian composers – Mikhail Glinka, Pyotr Ilyich Tchaikovsky, Nikolai Rimsky-Korsakov, Sergei Rachmaninoff and others [13]. In German an art song is called *Lieder*, in French it is *mélodie* [14].

In contrast to more "serious" vocal genres (e.g., opera), Russian classical romance is based on short poetic forms – lyric, elegy, ballad, poetry miniature, etc. Poetic words provide the songs with some certainty, individuality, and picturesque visibility, whereas the music enhances their expressiveness, enriches their emotional component, and uncovers the hidden or implicit meanings of unspoken lyrics. The musical component of Russian romances is presented by the unity of vocal and instrumental (mainly, piano or guitar) parts.

When writing a romance, Russian composers usually choose a lyric poem and set it to music by creating vocal and instrumental (mostly piano) part. Most of Rachmaninoff's songs are based on poetic texts. However, Rachmaninoff has a unique experience in writing songs with non-poetic words. For example, his song *We shall rest* (1906) is based on a fragment from the play *Uncle Vanya*, by the Russian playwright Anton Chekhov. Another example is Rachmaninoff's own letter to the well-known Russian actor and theatre director Konstantin Stanislavski that was set to music in a romance *Letter to Stanislavsky* (1908).

The songs by Rachmaninoff represent the superlative manifestation of Russian vocal lyrics. Most of these songs are monologues. Some of them resemble confessions, revealing the inner world of the lyrical hero. In general, they are characterized by the high grade of passion and powerful dynamics in expression, which is usually increasing (from the beginning of the song to its end), though in some cases, on the contrary, decreasing.

Poetic texts, by getting into the creative laboratory of the composer, acquire additional qualities – the convexity, brightness and sharp distinction of the hero's emotional state.

Lyric poems that Rachmaninoff chose for his songs belong to different eras and styles, their authors are the writers of different background and literary schools. Most often Rachmaninoff chose the poetry by Alexander Pushkin, Afanasy Fet, Fyodor Tyutchev and other great authors. One of Rachmaninoff's songs – *Vocalise* – has no poetry component. For the song *From the Gospel of John* the composer set to music the canonical biblical text. Rarely when composing a song Rachmaninoff picked out the lyric by less-known or even unknown poets. Unlike other contemporary composers, he often set to music the verses by Russian modernist poets – Dmitry Merezhkovsky, Konstantin Balmont, Valery Bryusov, Igor Severyanin and others.

Table 1 presents the distribution of poets ranked according to the number of their verses in Rachmaninoff's songs. There are a lot of names on the list but the poets who are on top are especially known for their lyricism and musicality.

Table 1. Distribution of poets in Rachmaninoff's songs

Rank	Poet	Number of songs	Rank	Poet	Number of songs
1	Tolstoy Aleksey K	6	21	Maykov Apollon	1
2	Tyutchev Fyodor	5	22	Bunin Ivan	1
3	Fet Afanasy	5	23	Chekhov Anton	1
4	Rathaus Dmitry	5	24	Yanov Mikhail	1
5	Pushkin Alexander	4	25	Grekov Nikolay	1
6	Apukhtin Aleksey	3	26	Beketova Catherine	1
7	Koltsov Aleksey	3	27	Kruglov Aleksey	1
8	Golenischev-Kutusov Pavel	3	28	Korinfsky Apollon	1
9	Merezhkovsky Dmitry	3	29	Davidova Margarita	1
10	Nadson Semyon	3	30	Goethe Johann Wolfgang von	1
11	Galina Glafira	3	31	Shelley Percy Bysshe	1
12	Polonsky Yakov	3	32	Guyau Jean-Marie	1
13	Heine Heinrich	3	33	Hugo Victor	1
14	Shevchenko Taras	3	34	Isaakyan Avetik	1
15	Minsky Nikolai	2	35	Bely Andrei	1
16	Khomyakov Aleksey	2	36	Severyanin Igor	1
17	Balmont Konstantin	2	37	Sologub Fyodor	1
18	Lermontov Mikhail	1	38	Bryusov Valery	1
19	Vyazemsky Pyotr	1	39	Rachmaninoff Sergey	1
20	Zhukovsky Vasily	1	**In total**		80

3 Studies in Temporal Dynamics of Literary and Musical Texts

In recent years, significant results have been obtained in mathematical description of literary texts in terms of the change in time of their outer structure [15–19]. These are two examples.

Figure 1 shows a chart depicting dependence of average stress index (i.e., the ratio of the number of stressed syllables to all syllables) on the line number in Russian classical sonnets [17]. Figure 2 presents the dependence of average sentence length (the number of words in the sentence) on the sentence position in different structural parts of short stories by Anton Chekhov [18].

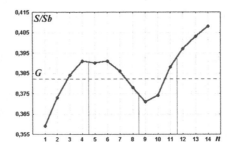

Fig. 1. The dependence of average stress index on the line number in Russian sonnets

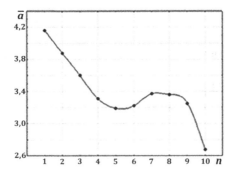

Fig. 2. The dependence of average sentence length from its position in Chekhov's short stories

These both charts have a notable S-shaped form, which reflects the compositional structure of the given text types – Russian sonnets and Chekhov's short stories [18].

This shape of the graphs cannot be just an accident. We assume that it relates to some fundamental features of any creative activity.

Let us consider the examples of creativity in fine arts.

The English painter and critic William Hogarth (1697–1764) claimed that he discovered the secret by which the ancient Greeks managed to surpass other nations in the arts [20]. Hogarth believed that this secret was a waving or serpentine line, which he

Fig. 3. Hogarth's line of beauty

called "*the line of beauty*", or "*line of grace*" (see Fig. 3) [21]. Two contrasted curves of this line give an impression of the letters "*S*". In a manner, it resembles an incomplete *clothoid* (*Cornu spiral*).

Hogarth's ideas were later continued in aesthetics studies. For example, the concept of a serpentine line – *Figura serpantinata* – was used in description of sculpture or painting compositions. The spiral pose of figures and the waving character of configuration were used to achieve additional lightness, dynamics, and grace. The classic examples of the line of beauty and serpentine lines may be found in works by Leonardo da Vinci, Rafael, Michelangelo and others.

The studies of temporal dynamics in musical texts are described in works by Rozenov [22] and Sabaneev [23]. Both musicologists analyzed structures of musical pieces, associating the culmination of the whole composition with the golden section on the axis of time.

4 Research Methodology

The method of time series analysis, which is widely used in statistics, forms the basis of our method. This statistic method allows studying sequential data and analyzing their dynamic structure. In time series charts, there are usually time intervals or other time-related measurements on x-axis, and correspondent parameter values are given as a sequence of data points on y-axis.

For the given research, we confined ourselves to two parameters: (1) stress index (*SI*) – a ratio of stressed syllables to all syllables – is used for describing poetry component of the song, and (2) pitch/duration index (*PDI*) – calculated as multiplication of duration and pitch for each note – is used for describing its musical component.

Our choice of these parameters is justified by our hypothesis that there exists a correlation between them, since word stress in Russian implies increasing both duration and intensity of stressed syllables. When studying poetry texts, specialists in poetics usually analyze interrelations between rhythm and meter as well as different types of feet (iamb, trochee, dactyl, etc.) and deviations from them. In the context of the proposed approach, studying poetry lines in songs, we neglect particular feet, emphasizing attention to proportion between stressed and non-stressed syllables in poetry segments of different length.

Duration and pitch of sounds, which are necessary for calculation of *PD* index, are explicitly defined by the composer's musical notation. Here, we have not taken into account musical dynamics – the volume of particular sounds – as well as the other nuances of song performance. These musical components should be better studied on recorded performances [24, 25].

When studying poetry and musical time series, we took into account three components: (1) a general trend, (2) cyclical fluctuations, and (3) random variations. The prevailing tendency and cyclical fluctuations were calculated by means of the moving averages method based on the moving intervals of different durations.

Taking into consideration the complexity of dynamic interaction between poetry and musical components of songs, we tried to grasp some elements which could help us to make a formal and comparable description of both song's components.

For the pilot investigation presented here we confined ourselves to analysis of the song's vocal line and the correspondent poetry component. The piano part of Rachmaninoff's songs was temporary left aside. It might be considered an oversimplification of the musical component – especially for vocal compositions by Rachmaninoff, known for the importance of their instrumental (piano) part. However, this is a stepping stone for further more complex investigations.

Since the structure of any time series depends on the total length of investigated object or phenomenon, first we should evaluate its variability (i.e., to analyze the length of Rachmaninoff's songs).

5   Rachmaninoff's Song Length

Initially, we calculated the length of all Rachmaninoff's songs in measures. Figure 4 shows this distribution.

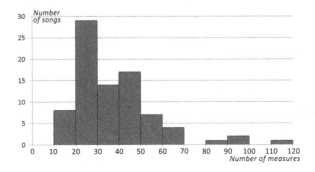

Fig. 4. Rachmaninoff's song length

Statistics of this distribution are as follows. The average Rachmaninoff's song length is 38.49 measures, standard deviation (SD) is 17.43, and coefficient of variation (CV) is 45.3 %. CV is considerably above its critical level of 33 %, which is typical for the normal distribution [26]. Therefore, we can doubt that this distribution is homogeneous. Indeed, the distribution curve has three modes and may be divided into three parts. The first part refers to the short songs whose length is less than approximately 35 measures. The second group consists of the average-length songs, and the third group refers to the longest romances. However, it would be difficult to determine exact borders for these groups. The shortest Rachmaninoff song is *From the Gospel of*

St. John (1915), which consists of 14 measures, and his longest song – *Fate* (1900) – consists of 114 measures.

The heterogeneity of Rachmaninoff's song length distribution reveals itself in song's chronological dynamics shown in Fig. 5. In this graph, the average number of measures is calculated for each 5-year period during which Rachmaninoff wrote his vocal compositions. The number of songs composed during each period is given above the *x*-axis. The chronological data for this chart are taken from [12, 27]. We can see that the first songs by Rachmaninoff in the early 1890s were rather long compared to others. For the composer, it was the most fruitful period, during which he wrote 22 songs. During the next period (1895–1899), on the opposite, it looks like that Rachmaninoff a little "lost interest" to song-writing, as he composed only 11 songs and they are the shortest among his other vocal compositions. In 1910–1915, Rachmaninoff came back to longer songs, as the average number of measures has its peak for this period. Finally, the composer's last romances written just before the Russian revolution in 1917 are few in number and short again.

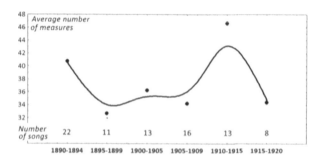

Fig. 5. Chronological dynamics of Rachmaninoff's song length

6 Analysis of Pitch/Duration Dynamics in Rachmaninoff's Songs

The pitch/duration index (*PDI*) is calculated as multiplication of duration and pitch for each note of the vocal line and the resulting values are summed up for each measure. Previously, the corresponding pitch range for each song was determined depending on the type of singing voice (high, medium or low). For example, for a soprano, the range of notes is usually between middle C (C_4) and "soprano C" (C_6). Then each note is assigned a corresponding number starting from 1 and up to 15: $C_4 = 1$, $Cis_4(Des_4) = 1.5$, $D_4 = 2$, etc.

The methodology of pitch/duration series study we shall demonstrate on three Rachmaninoff songs: *All was Taken from Me, The Fountain* (both published in 1906, lyric by Fyodor Tyutchev), and *What Happiness* (1912, lyric by Afanasy Fet). In Fig. 6 you may see three dynamic profiles of pitch/duration index calculated for these songs. The grey dotted lines indicate the trends for each chart based on musical data polynomial fitting.

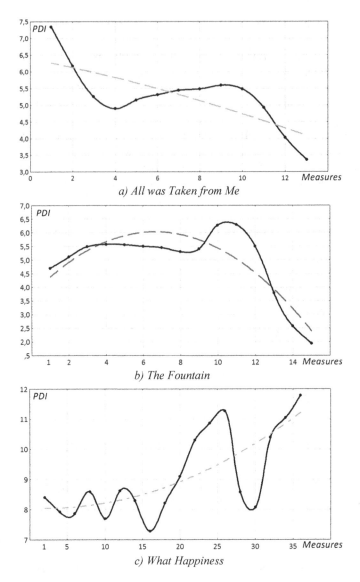

Fig. 6. Dynamic profiles for pitch/duration index (*PDI*) in Rachmaninoff's songs and its general trend.

The *PDI*-dynamics curves for the given songs (as, indeed, for other Rachmaninoff's romances) are rather complex. They combine a general trend (upward, downward or composite) with cyclical fluctuations. Several local extremums and inflection points are observed on these charts. The segments of the graphs look like a sequence of *S*-shaped curves resembling the above-mentioned Hogarth's line and forming a serpentine line.

This fact induces us to make an intriguing assumption: Could such a musical segment with an *S*-shape on the graphic be a minimal prosody unit of poetry line that is woven into the musical texture? We would call such unit *a poetry-musical period* (*strophe*). The number of these periods naturally depend on the song's length: the longer the song the more periods it has.

We have studied these poetry-musical periods in 26 of Rachmaninoff's songs. The average length for a period is 7.52 measures, SD = 2.01. The coefficient of variation equals to 18.9 %, indicating a high concentration of empirical values around the mean. This stability in data analysis in humanities is an extremely rare phenomenon. The statistical error of 0.788 calculated at 95 % confidence level also proves such stability: even for the small sample size, the average number of measures in each period lies in the range of 7.52 ± 0,788 (i. e., between 6.73–8.31). At a 99 % confidence level, the length of periods lies between 5.94–9.10. This last interval resembles the "magic" Miller's number 7 ± 2 [28]. Thus, we can claim that the period's length in measures is rather stable.

As a rule, a quarter of the musical period corresponds to one poetry line, a half of the period refers to a distich, and the whole period corresponds to a quatrain.

Musical notation facilitates comprehension of musical structure. Besides pitch and duration of sounds described in this paper, it contains information about pauses between periods and lines, as well as various kinds of articulation marks, dynamic symbols, slurs, notation symbols for rhythm and tempo, etc. These composer's notations remain outside this research. We should mention that Rachmaninoff's songs, especially the later ones, are fully notated, but their statistic analysis is hardly feasible.

7 Dynamic Interaction of Poetry and Musical Components

Parallel time series of a poetry stress index (*SI*) and musical pitch/duration index (*PDI*) calculated for each poetry line in the same three Rachmaninoff songs are given in Fig. 7. As these two indices have different dimensions and different scales, their values have been normalized by division by the mean. Thus, we achieved comparability between two indices and drew the graphs conveying structural interaction between poetry and musical components of Rachmaninoff's songs.

The first song to be analyzed here is *All was Taken from Me*. The lyric of this romance is a tragic quatrain by Fyodor Tyutchev, which the poet dedicated to his wife shortly before his death. Reflecting on his fate on the threshold of eternity and waiting for Divine Providence, he turns to his wife, saying:

Vsjo otnjal u menja kaznjaschij bog:	*The Lord took everything away from me:*
Zdorovje, silu voli, vozdukh, son,	*My will, my health, my rest, my breath of air,*
Ondu tebja pri mne ostavil on,	*You only has He left to care for me*
Chtob ja jemu escho molit'sja mog.	*That I could pray to Him in my despair.*
	(Translated by Eugene M. Kayden)

The pitch/duration index chart is a *S*-shaped downward curve. It is extremely "depressed", sharply falling down. As for the stress index, it is the same in each line, creating the monotony that escalates the sense of desperation and hopelessness of the lyric hero.

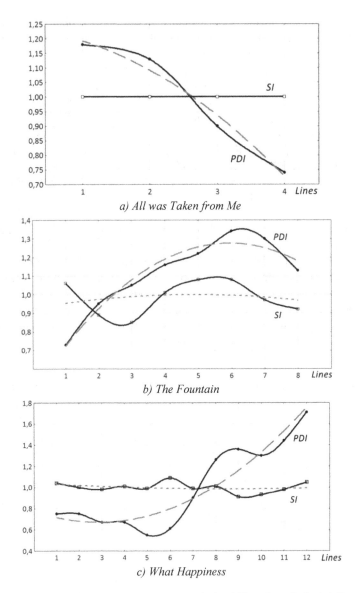

Fig. 7. Dynamic interaction between poetry stress index (*SI*) and musical pitch/duration index (*PDI*) in three Rachmaninoff's songs with their trends

The second song, *The Fountain*, is also based on lyrics by Fyodor Tyutchev. Tyutchev's original verse consists of 16 lines divided into two parts. The first part introduces the author's idea in general. The fountain here is a symbol of everything that strives upward but is inevitably doomed to fall. The meaning of the second part concretizes the initial one. It introduces an idea of the seething thought, which soars higher and higher, but is destined to fade away.

Rachmaninoff set to music only the first part of this Tyutchev's lyric. In this way he achieved a generalizing picture. Rachmaninoff's *The Fountain* is not about just flourishing and fading thoughts, not about acute and dying feelings, and not about some rough activity and the fatigue which inevitably follows. This song is about everything that is ever born, reaches its climax, but is doomed to disappear. This idea is reflected as well in the movement of the *PD* index, which first increases to the maximum and then – like a fountain – falls down.

As for the poetry stress index, in the beginning of the song, it moves in antiphase with the *PD* index. Later, its dynamics corresponds with PDI, maintaining and enhancing the musical component. However, the upward tendency is expressed by *S*-index modestly enough: we observe here minor cyclical fluctuations around a weakly expressed trend.

Finally, for the song *What Happiness* Rachmaninoff set to music an extremely emotional poem by Afanasy Fet. In this Rachmaninoff's composition the emotionality is delivered rather implicitly at first, but then it fully reveals itself and reaches its extreme intensity on the verge of collapse. This can be observed by the profile of *PD* index, too. This index sharply rises over the *x*-axis and approaches "infinity". At the same time, the stress index shows here no distinct features and creates a monotonous background in contrast to the musical culmination.

8 Conclusions

1. The dynamic curves of poetry and musical components in Rachmaninoff's songs consist of the *S*-shaped segments. The full "zigzag" of the curve we call a poetry-musical period, and most often it corresponds to four lines (a quatrain).
2. Cooperative dynamics of analyzed poetry and musical components is of ambiguous nature. The intonation contrasts are more explicitly expressed in musical components of the songs than in poetry ones.
3. Any poetic text set to music undergoes substantial transformation. In musical compositions, it is subject to restructuring. As a result, the vocal line becomes more expressive and explicit that the original verse.
4. For this pilot analysis, we deliberately left aside the piano part of songs despite its undisputable importance for musical architecture of Rachmaninoff's romances.
5. Individual performing style has a significant impact on dynamical expression of songs. The new acoustic properties that cannot be simply described in the music notation appear during a live performance. This is another potential direction of further research.
6. Dynamic interaction of poetry and musical components may be studied as well on the material of songs by different composers that set to music the same poetry text. For example the following verses were set to music by more than 20 composers: *Sing not, O Lovely One* by Alexander Pushkin, *Say Why Thou Came* by Sergei Golitsyn, *Cradle Song* and *No, It Is Not Thou I Love So Fervently* by Mikhail Lermontov, *Tears* and *Spring Waters* by Fyodor Tyutchev and others [29]. Thus, we can enter an exciting not yet well explored area of poetic and musical hermeneutics.

References

1. Latham, A.: The Oxford Companion to Music. Oxford University Press, Oxford (2011)
2. Howatson, M.C.: The Oxford Companion to Classical Literature. Oxford University Press, Oxford (2011)
3. Kon, Y.G.: O nekotorykh stilisticheskikh paralleljakh v russkoj kul'ture nachala XX veka: Stravinskij i Khlebnikov (On Some Stylistic Parallels in the Russian Culture of the Early Twentieth Century: Stravinsky and Khlebnikov) (in Russian) In: Aktual'nye voprosy iskusstvoznanija: Sovremennoe Kompozitorskoe Tvorchestvo. Fol'klor Karelii. Khudozhestvennoe nasledie, Petrozavodsk (1986)
4. Shubnikov, A.V., Kopcik, V.A.: Simmetrija v nauke i iskusstve (Symmetry in Science and Art) (in Russian). Nauka, Moscow (1972)
5. Martinovich, G.A.: O metre i ritme russkogo stikha (On the meter and rhythm of Russian verse) (in Russian). J. Mir russkogo slova 3, 66–74 (2001)
6. Greer, D. (ed.): Musicology and sister disciplines: past, present, future. In: Proceedings of the 16th International Congress of the International Musicology Society. Oxford University Press, Oxford (1997)
7. Palmer, C., Kelly, M.: Linguistic Prosody and Musical Meter in Song. J. Mem. Lang. 31, 525–542 (1992)
8. Patel, A.H.: Music, Language, and the Brain. Oxford University Press, Oxford (2008)
9. Makhov, A.E.: Musica literaria. Ideja slovesnoj musyki v evropejskoj poetike (The Idea of Verbal Music in the European Poetics) (in Russian). Intrada, Moscow (2005)
10. Freytag, G.: Die Technik des Dramas. Verlag von Pirzel, Leipzig (1863)
11. Martynenko, G.Y., Sherstinova, T.Y.: Chislovoj profil' sjuzheta (Quantitative Profile of Literary Plots) (in Russian). In: Proceedings of the International Congress "Russian Language: its Historical Destiny and Present State". Moscow State University, Moscow, pp. 524–525 (2010)
12. Rachmaninoff, S.: Romancy (Songs) (in Russian). Vol. I–II. Music, Moscow (1989–1990)
13. Kratkaja Literaturnaja Entsiklopedija (The Brief Literary Encyclopedia) (in Russian). Soviet Encyclopedia, Moscow (1962–1978)
14. Olin, E.: Singing in Russian: A Guide to Language and Performance. Rowman & Littlefield, New York (2012)
15. Cheremisina-Enikolopova, N.V. Zakony i pravila russkoj intonatsii (The Laws and Regulations of Russian Intonation) (in Russian). Flinta, Moscow (1999)
16. Grinbaum, O.N.: Garmonija stroficheskogo ritma v estetiko-formal'nom izmerenii (The Harmony of Strophic Rhythm in Esthetic and Formal Measurement) (in Russian). St. Petersburg State University, St. Petersburg (2000)
17. Martynenko, G.Y.: Ritmiko-smyslovaja dinamika russkogo klassicheskogo soneta (Rhythmic and Meaning Dynamics of Russian Classical Sonnet) (in Russian). St. Petersburg State University, St. Petersburg (2004)
18. Martynenko, G.Y.: Chislovaja garmonija teksta (Numeral Harmony of Text) (in Russian). St. Petersburg State University, St. Petersburg (2009)
19. Grinbaum, O.N.: Roman A.S.Pushkina Evgenij Onegin: ritmiko-smyslovoj kommentarij. Gravy pervaja, vtoraja, tret'ja, chetvjortaja (Novel Eugene Onegin by Alexander Pushkin: Rhythmic and Semantic Comment. Chapters I–IV) (in Russian). St. Petersburg State University, St. Petersburg (2012)
20. Gilbert, K.E., Kuhn, H.: History of Aesthetics. Indiana University Press, Bloomington (1939)

21. Hogarth, W.: The Analysis of Beauty: Written with a View of Fixing the Fluctuating Ideas of Taste. Reeves, London (1753)
22. Rozenov, E.K.: Zakon zolotogo sechenija v poezii i musyke (The Law of the Golden Section in Poetry and Music). In: Rozenov, E.K. Statji o muzyke. Moscow, Music (1982)
23. Sabaneev, L.L.: Et'udy Shopena v osveschenii zolotogo sechenija. Opyt pozitivnogo obosnovanija (Chopin's Etudes and the Golden Section. An Experience of Positive Justification) (in Russian). J. Iskusstvo. Iss. 2 (1925)
24. Repp, B.: A microcosm of musical expression: II. Quantitative analysis of pianists' dynamics in the initial measures of Chopin's Etude in E major. J. Acoust. Soc. Am. **104**(2), 1085–1100 (1998)
25. Todd, N.: The dynamics of dynamics: a model of musical expression. J. Acoust. Soc. Am. **91**, 3540–3550 (1992)
26. Sis'kov, V.I.: Korreljacionnyj analiz v ekonomicheskikh issledovanijakh (Correlation analysis in Economy Studies) (in Russian). Statistics, Moscow (1975)
27. Sylverster, R.D.: Rachmaninoff's Complete Songs: A Companion with Texts and Translations. Indiana University Press, Bloomington (2014)
28. Miller, G.A.: The magical number seven, plus or minus two: some limits on our capacity for processing information. J. Psychol. Rev. **63**(2), 81–97 (1956)
29. Pesni i romancy russkikh poetov. Serija "Biblioteka poeta" (Songs and Romances by Russian Poets. The Poet's Library Series) (in Russian). Sovetskij pisatel', Moscow-Leningrad (1965)

A Linguistic Approach to the Syntax of Early Music: Representation of the Hexachord System by X-Bar Method as an Excavation Tool

Oğuzhan Tuğral[✉]

ITU/MIAM (Dr. Erol Ucer Centre for Advanced Studies in Music),
ITU Macka Kampusu, Yabanci Diller Binasi Macka, Istanbul 34367, Turkey
oguzhantugral@gmail.com

Abstract. In their pioneering Generative Theory of Tonal Music (1983, 'GTTM'), Lerdahl and Jackendoff attempted to apply Chomsky's Transformational Generative Theory method to music, with the aim of explaining the musical structures as a language. Their insight has been further developed by Katz and Pesetsky's "Identity Thesis" within the framework of the Minimalist Program of linguistics. While those studies are concerned with the "common practice" period in music, the aim of the present study is to point out that while GTTM and Identity Thesis are genuine approaches to music in tonal tradition, they do not address the issue of early periods (pre-tonal period). To answer this question, this study uses Generative Theory's X-Bar approach to analyze "early music" repertoires and associate it with Foucault's archaeological approach to the historical documents. It proposes hierarchical relationships within the intervals of hexachord system as an approach to the theory of early music and applies its output to the "Annus Novus versus" of Aquitanian Polyphony.

Keywords: Archaeology of knowledge · Linguistics · Generative theory · X-Bar · Early music · Hexachord system · Gamut · Deep structure · Surface structure

1   The Problems, Background and Method

Was there any period in history when music had been treated as a language? Could there be any continuity in music as a natural substitution of language as interdependent relationships with their features and constituents? This study investigates to find evidence in the light of the studies of musicology and to answer these questions in Modal Period of Early Music by representing them within the Generative approach in linguistics. Finally, it calls this synthesis an excavation tool to collaborate with Foucault's approach in the "Archaeology of Knowledge".

In order to find out a consistent evaluation scheme for the early music, there have been numerous endeavors for decades. In this respect, the studies which came down to us by Treitler and Fuller have been lightening the trajectories of the duration of the medieval music, while they were contemplating about the term to transform the

© Springer International Publishing Switzerland 2015
P. Eismont and N. Konstantinova (Eds.): LMAC 2015, CCIS 561, pp. 140–165, 2015.
DOI: 10.1007/978-3-319-27498-0_12

paradigm to a progressive level. Accordingly, Margaret Bent criticizes the anachronistic approaches of "presentist" scholars and encourages those people who may make studies which may be able to analyze the individual pieces of the term in an analytical manner in line with Lerdahl and Jackendoff's GTTM [1: 23].

So GTTM still expects the value it deserves, one case of which is the recent study of Pesetsky and Katz, which, as in the verbal realm, seems to bring about sufficient answers to these needs which have kept the hopes of the researchers alive [2]. However, Cohen draws the boundaries of this realm; "… the systematic borrowing of grammatical terms in the Middle Ages, beginning with the Carolingians, was of crucial importance for the history of western music theory. Grammatical discussions of such matters as the nature of the voice, the elements of language, the articulation of a text by means of punctuation and pauses, the correct rendering of verbal accents and syllabic quantities, and the correct writing of the graphic symbols for accents provided the Carolingian cantors with a variety of terms and verbal strategies for the description of melodic events" [3: 314].

Finally, while Harold Powers revealed that "Given my present belief in the much greater range of variability as to both order and kind of complexity in the world's musics versus the world's languages, I can hardly imagine how a model developed really satisfactorily for the detailed structural explanation of one musical language is so easily to be modified to another, and all the more so if the original model be evolved from linguistics rather than from the musical disciplines" [4: 48][1]. Blair Sullivan claims that early grammar studies in the Carolingian Era projected their own characteristics into musical structures and he states his aims in his work; "The investigation is conducted in two fundamental intellectual terrains: grammatical theory and harmonic theory, …. A large collection of treatises has been read with a single purpose: the location of materials pertaining to the written representation of sound and the exploration and comparison of the underlying assumptions that produced Greek pitch notation and neumatic systems" [5: viii].

1.1   Traces of Word Segmentation and Phonologic Analogy

7By the time of the first political unity of Europe under Charlemagne (who paid special attention to cultural and educational organizations in his famous palace school Aix-La-Chapel), the most important art in the traditional seven arts of the medieval period was grammar. These studies, organized under Alcuin, an influential scholar of the period, offered his successors what could be considered the musical counterparts of the essentials of language to music. For highlighting these endeavors, Sullivan's dissertation is especially important. In his dissertation, Sullivan refers these studies as "A tightly woven net of circumstances-music historical, socio linguistic, and socio-political direct the focus of the investigation toward the Carolingian culture and writers such as Hrabanus Maurus, Alcuin, Johannes Scottus, Aurelian of Reome, Hildemar of Corbie,

---

[1] Same quotation takes place in [1]. The citation is taken from the original source.

Hucbald of St.-Amand, Regino of Prum, Remigius of Auxerre, and the theorists of Musica enchiriadis, Scolica enchiriadis, and Commemoratio brevis" [5: ix].

In this study, we will refer to two principles which show the strong linguistic characteristics of medieval music. The first one of the principles is the Frankish treatise of early medieval music presented by Sullivan that refers to Peter Wagner's "Un piccolo trattato sul canto ecclesiastico in un manuscritto del secolo X XI" and indicates the phonologic background:

Principal 1 (Phonologic Analogy). "What is chant (song)? It is skill in the musical art, inflection of the voice, and melody.... Its source and composition are revealed by the accentuations of tone and the metric patterns of syllables. Indeed, it is described by acute, grave, and circumflex accentuations of tone.... The musical note known as neuma originated from the accentual patterns of the tones" [5: 103].

The second principle indicates the syntactical analogy which Sullivan refers to as Aurelian's Musica Disciplina.

Principal 2 (Word Segmentation). "The tone is the basic element of music, in addition to being a rule, just as the basic element of grammar is the letter and the basic arithmetical element the unit. In the same way that speech arises from and is guided by letters, and that large numbers arise from and are guided by units, so every melody is governed by the limits of its sounds and its tones" [5: 34].

These are the essential principles of our study. After describing the X-Bar method and Excavation approach, by using the X-Bar method of Generative theory, we will demonstrate that we can use an analytical tool which we develop through this study to parse and analyze to the individual scores of the manuscripts in the medieval era. We consider this technique as an excavation into Foucault's approach.

1.2   X-Bar Method[2]

In 1970, Chomsky introduced to first appearances of the X-Bar method to the linguistics discipline with his "Remarks on Nominalization" [6]. The system he developed was to become the main analytical representation tool of the Generative theory in the following years. In this study, Chomsky discusses how a nominalization process works in our minds with respect to two categorizations: Gerundive nominals and derived nominals. In the study he gives forty examples to analyze their transformations. He also specifies the representational levels of his approach: "Deep Structure" and "Surface Structure". "The context-free grammar generates phrase-markers, with a dummy symbol as one of the terminal elements. A general principle of lexical insertion permits lexical entries to replace the dummy symbol in ways determined by their feature content. The formal object constructed in this way is a deep structure. The grammar contains a system of transformations, each of which maps phrase-markers. Application of a sequence of transformations to a deep structure, in accordance with certain universal conditions and certain particular constraints of the grammar in question,

---

[2] Many special thanks to A. Sumru Özsoy who has helped me to understand the compelling topics in Generative Theory.

determines ultimately a phrase-marker which we call surface structure" [6: 12]. On the other hand, we can present the introductory description of the X-Bar Method as "In generative syntax ..., X-bar theory is the module of the grammar that regulates constituent structure. It aims at characterizing a possible syntactic configuration. In interaction with the other principles of the grammar, X-bar theory determines structural representations" [7].

The present study uses the X-Bar method of the Generative Theory and applies it to Foucault's Archaeological approach as an excavation tool. At this point, one of the main differences needs to be emphasized; when Chomsky says that "I will assume that a grammar contains a base consisting of a categorical component (which I will assume to be a context free grammar) and a lexicon. The lexicon consists of lexical entries, each of which is a system of specified features" [6: 12], he points out two properties of the language competence: categorical components and lexicon. However, Katz and Pesetsky emphasize the differences and also similarities of music and language, "... language, unlike music, makes use of a lexicon. So many other details of music and linguistic structure will turn out to be identical that the two domains might quite reasonably be viewed as products of a single cognitive system" [2: 2]. Accordingly, in the light of this evidence, the properties of music and language are identical, although the lexical properties of the language are locked out in music. In this paper, we propose a new phrase-markers tool which consists of intervals of the music as the deep structures which generate the individual surface structures of the musical phrases. The main justification of the intervallic deep structures takes its essentials from Patel's observation. In his relatively recent study, Patel has given musicology new insights about the cognitive properties of music. Patel divides the pitch intervals to four categories [8], and especially with respect to the categorical perception he points out their identification and distinction. "CP (categorical perception) refers to two related phenomena. First, sounds that lie along a physical continuum are perceived as belonging to distinct categories, rather than gradually changing from one category to another. Second, sounds of a given degree of physical difference are much easier to discriminate if they straddle a category boundary than if they fall within the same category. CP is thus studied using both identification and discrimination tasks" [8: 24]. In the same section, Patel alerts the interested scholars, to how music may be related to the realm of neuroscience; "The question of interest is if the size of the MMN [9] simply grows linearly with frequency difference, or if there is a jump in MMN size as the interval crosses into a new category. If so, this would be neural evidence that pitch intervals were acting as sound categories in perception" [8: 28].

When we exclude the lexical properties of language from the representation process of Generative theory, those representational tools of categorical components of language as Noun Phrase (NP), Verb Phrase (VP), Adjective Phrase (AdjP) etc. could be replaced with the new categories in our study: Diapason Phrase (DpasP), Diatesseron Phrase (DtesP), Diapente Phrase (DpenP) etc. Finally, we represent our categories with the five essential structural relations of Generative theory: Daughter, Sister, Adjunct, Complement and Specifier relationships.

Daughter. If one node is immediately dominated by another node, it is the daughter of that dominating node. Determiner Phrase (DP) and Determiner (D') that are the first binary branches of maximal projection DP are also its daughters in Fig. 1).

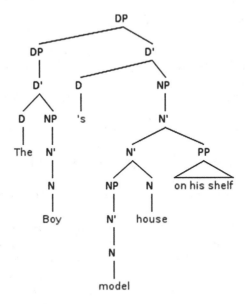

Fig. 1. Daughter relation

Sister. If two components are adjacent to each other, it is a sister relationship. The nodes which are denoted in the rectangle are sister relationships in Fig. 2.

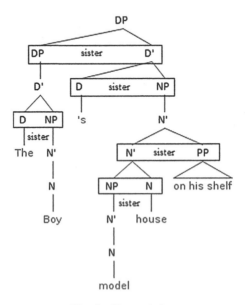

Fig. 2. Sister relation

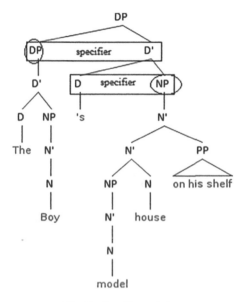

Fig. 3. Specifier relation

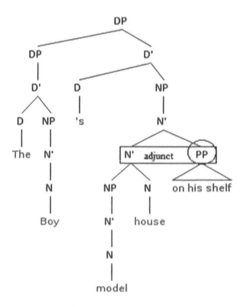

Fig. 4. Adjunct relation

Specifier. It is a "Sister to X', daughter of XP" [10: 186]. In this sense, DP is a specifier (Spec) position of first DP and NP is the second specifier of maximal projection, DP in Fig. 3.

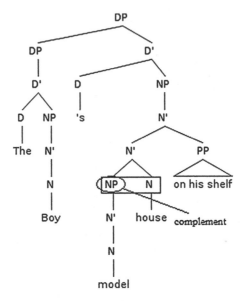

Fig. 5. Complement relation

Adjunct. If one XP is adjacent to a bar node (at the right or left of the bar) and is the daughter of another bar node, it is an adjunct relationship. In verbal, when we consider "on his shelf" part, it is an adjunct of the NP.

Complement. If one XP is adjacent to a head level, it has a complement relationship. Verbally, when we consider "model house", first noun "model" is a complement of the head of NP.

In the description process of five functions, we used the linguistic representation. At the end of this study, we will examine these functions with the musical segmentations.

1.3   Archealogic Approach

In his Archaeology of Knowledge, Foucault describes his approach to the episteme; "By episteme, mean, in fact, the total set of relations that unite, at a given period, the discursive practices that give rise to epistemological figures, sciences, and possibly formalized systems; the way in which, in each of these discursive formations, the transitions to epistemologization, scientificity, and formalization are situated and operate; the distribution of these thresholds, which may coincide, be subordinated to one another, or be separated by shifts in time; the lateral relations that may exist between epistemological figures or sciences in so far as they belong to neighboring, but distinct, discursive practices" [11: 191].

The present study extends the boundaries of the archeological approach to the individual music pieces and collaborates its analysis to the various recursive musical figures. In this sense, through the analysis of this study's approach, we will present the epistemological figures–such as melismas, differentiae, tonaries, psalm tones, modes etc. - which have discursive characteristics but are also recursive. And at a given period - 12th century, 13th century etc. - we will try to understand what are the total set of relations – common properties of the corpus or collections - that unite those characteristics, for example consonance-dissonance treatment, sequences of the intervals, rhythmic properties, transformations of note against note treatment, etc. By this analysis, we see the transformations of a simple structure to conceptualization of that structure (e.g. which period call the some recursive structures from piece to piece) as 1st species that once upon a time were called simply organum style, when a simple recursive feature began to be called "directed progression", "cadence", or "occursus" and what were their origins unintentionally or without any conceptualizations took place in the pieces etc. We hope this analytical system will bring the formal units of music a new perspective as referred to in Foucault's "Recurrent redistribution", "Recurrent redistributions reveal several pasts, several forms of connection, several hierarchies of importance, several networks of determination, several teleologies, for one and the same science, as its present undergoes change: thus historical descriptions are necessarily ordered by the present state of knowledge, they increase with every transformation and never cease, in turn, to break with themselves..." [11: 5].

After all, this system that develops a mathematical model locks out all the speculative tradition for the term for a while, but then after some analytical organization to the early music pieces, it will apply syntactic organization as the provider of their grammaticality at a given period and it will detect transformations of their grammaticality between three discontinuities and two continuities placed between them. We apply the terms Discontinuity and Continuity concepts of Foucault to the external phrases in our approach. In Foucault's words, "… the notion of discontinuity assumes a major role in the historical disciplines. For history in its classical form, the discontinuous was both the given and the unthinkable: the raw material of history, which presented itself in the form of dispersed events - decisions, accidents, initiatives, discoveries; the material, which, through analysis, had to be rearranged, reduced, effaced in order to reveal the continuity of events" [11: 8]. Consequently, we hope to hear a voice crying in the wilderness in the ruins of the ancients by these methods of present study.

2 Practical Aspects

In this part, we will demonstrate the two principles of phonological and syntactical analogies which refer to sentences represented in Sullivan's dissertation. However, before further investigation, we will clarify three concepts: Phrase, Bar and Head, used in X-Bar method. In order to understand their differences in musical meanings, we will clarify some complexities about the conceptualizations which coincide with the concepts of music discipline with the linguistics.

Phrase (Music). "A term adopted from linguistic syntax and used for short musical units of various lengths; a phrase is generally regarded as longer than a Motif but shorter than a Period. It carries a melodic connotation, insofar as the term 'phrasing' is usually applied to the subdivision of a melodic line. As a formal unit, however, it must be considered in its polyphonic entirety, like 'period', 'sentence' and even 'theme'" [12].

Phrase (Linguistics). "The term Phrase is used to mean simply a set of elements which form the constituent, with no restriction on the number of elements that the set may or must contain" [13: 85].

Bar (Music). "A line drawn vertically through a staff or staves of musical notation, normally indicating division into metrical units (of two, three, four beats, etc.); now also the name for the metrical unit itself, the line being commonly called a 'bar-line'. American usage, however, normally reserves the term 'bar' for the line itself, describing the metrical unit as a 'measure'" [14].

Bar (Linguistics). "A Bar in linguistics is an intermediate projection between phrase and head nodes" [10: 186].

Head (Music). The head concept for the music was used first time in the GTTM. While its description gives cue to the problems what about the phrase-markers which generate those heads, it is important it stimulates such questions. Although, there is no literal description of the head in GTTM, we understand from a lots of example of which it proceeds, it is the "... a single event is chosen as the most important event..." [15: 120].

In our study, the head is a music unit indicated by interval phrases, and described as word initials and word endings by the way of the segmentation principles which we describe them in the present study.

Head (Linguistics). "The word that gives its category to the phrase" [10: 186]. Now, we will see the main categories of the practical aspects. They include four parts: External Phrases, Hexachordal Features as the Phonological Analogy, Internal Phrases and Textural Segmentations.

2.1 External Phrases (Maximals)

An external phrase is not placed in the realization of musical pieces, however as the main projections, they direct the cognitive properties of the performers as the deep structures. They are;

Time Phrase (TP). As a maximal projection, TP dominates all the branches as the feeling of the beats in a bar. The bar concept is used in the sense of X-Bar method rather than notation of music. Feeling can change from one point to the other, and these cognitive transformations in the feelings of the performers indicate the place of the piece in time. Accordingly, in a study which published in 2009 could be strong supporter of this approach "We show that newborn infants develop expectation for the onset of the rhythmic cycles (the downbeat), even when it is not marked by stress or other distinguishing spectral features. Omitting the downbeat elicits brain activity associated with violating sensory expectation. Thus, our results strongly support the view that beat perception is innate" [16].

Discontinuity Phrase (DiscP). Discontinuity is a major event in the piece (e.g. beginning of the sentences, transformation of the modes). It takes its source from Foucault's Archaeological approach. DiscP is usually placed in specifier position (Spec) of the TP. It means the beginning of the piece by a DiscP gives first impressions of the beats which direct the perceptual trajectories of following constituents. Because of this fact, it has a special importance. On the other hand, as an external phrase DiscP is not placed on the realization of the music; however it is specified by first Dpas1s and Dpas1s subordinated constituents under its head. This fact gives a cue that the "Spec CP" position in Generative Linguistic can functionally be applied to the present music representation and analysis system. In the future studies, we assume that the Byzantine Octoechos and Intonational formulas, psalm tones of the medieval music could be able to have strong relationships to perceive music of the medieval peoples which specify the direction of the music perception. We expect to associate them to Spec MCP (Specifier Music Clause Position).

Continuity Phrase (ConP). The time span which extends from first DiscP to the last one in the ConP Region. It takes as its source Foucault's Archaeological approach. ConP is the complement of TP. It means the rhythmic determination specified by DiscP in the TP is tried to be constant through the ConP. However, unless a metronome indicates what a certain tempo is, it is almost impossible staying consistently in the certain tempo marker. Accordingly, the Dpas1s specify these slight tempo transformations through the ConP region. Therefore, the first Dpas1 is Spec position in the region[3] except for last Dpas1 which is the starting dyad of the ConP and it is functioned as the complement of the ConP. And the Dpas1s which places between Spec MCP and complement of the ConP are adjunct to ConP. Finally, in the representation process, *Hierarchically Dpas5, Dpas4, Dpen1, Dpen5, Dpen4 and Dtes1, Dtes5 and Dtes4 are adjunct to Dpas1. All other intervals are complement of aforementioned intervals and complements with each other.* The last underlined sentence will be called as the hierarchical formula through the study.

DiscP Region. It is the boundaries of the Specifier Music Clause Phrases (Spec MCP) position from first Dpas1 to second Dpas1 (from left to right in DiscP Region). Its features are head initial. The hierarchical formula is also valid for this maximal.

ConP Region. It is the boundaries of the Spec MCP position from first Dpas1 to last Dpas1 in ConP (from right to left in ConP Region). Its features are head final. The hierarchical formula is also valid for this maximal.

2.2   Hexachordal Features as the Phonologic Analogy[4]

The features which are explained in this part stem from the order of the Hexachord system. They are;

Realm. Indicates where the individual notes take place as Grave, Acutae and Super Acutae in the hexachord system.

Loca. Denotes the particular point of an individual realm in the Loca. For example G is the 8th point of the Grave realm.

---

[3] In future studies, we will assume that "differentia" parts of the medieval music could be associated by this conceptualization.

[4] [17] is a well-organized website to basic knowledge for hexachord system.

Syllables. Indicates the Ut, Re, Mi, Fa, Sol and La notes. Their successive intervallic characteristics collaborate with Loca points and transform them.

Deductio. The cluster of the syllables as Hard, Natural and Soft.

Phonologic Relationship. In phonology, we see two main categories: Consonant and Vowels. Consonants are represented by three features - manner, place and voice, and vowels are represented by two features - monophthongs and diphthongs. Consonants' three features have some sub features as the following; Manner sub features are stop, fricative, affricate, nasal, liquid, glide; Place sub features are bilabial, labiodentals, lingua-dental, lingua-alveolar, lingua-palatal, lingua-velar, glottal and Voice sub features are voiced and voiceless. When we observe the vowel subcategories, a monophthong has three sub features as front, central and back and diphthongs has only one feature. Table 1 represents these characteristics.

Table 1. Phonologic features

Consonances			Vowels	
Manner	Place	Voice	Monophthongs	Diphthongs
stop	bilabial	Voiced	Front	Diphthongs has only one feature
fricative	labiodentals	Voiceless	Central	
affricate	lingua-dental		Back	
nasal	lingua-alveolar			
liquid	lingua-palatal			
glide	lingua-velar			
	glottal			

Since we do not need to further investigate why the features of the hexachordal system are completely different, we will not give examples of the representation of these phonological features. What we try to denote is to show the analogies of parsed hexachord system to these distinctive features of the phonetic properties that humans can produce. For further investigation, [18] is a well-organized website to study these features.

Referring to Katamba's explanation regarding the generative approach's interpretation of distinctive features, he states that "Chomsky and Halle (1968) in their book The Sound Pattern of English (henceforth SPE) proposed a major revision of the theory of distinctive features. They replaced acoustically-defined phonological features with a set of features that have, in most cases, articulatory correlates. Furthermore, the number of features was also substantially increased. ... SPE features remain binary. They have only two coefficients or values, plus (+) indicating the presence of a feature and minus (—) its absence, so that, for example, among other things, a sound like [p] is said to be [—voice] and [— nasal] while [m] is [+voice] and [+nasal]" [19: 42]. In the following section, representation of the present study's hexachord system collaborates its own features (represented in the preceding part) as an analogy to that of the generative approach.

Hexachord System and Features of Deductios. By synthesizing the Musica Enchiriadis, Musica Scholarum, and Alia Musica compilations, Benedictine monk Guido Arezzo devised a new analytical system for music in the beginning of the 11th century.

In Guido D'Arezzo's approach, three components have the main functional categories in the system: Syllables, Loca and Deductios.

In the Table 2, it presents the all the individual notes unique features. The brackets are organized in the following order;

Table 2. Hexachordal features

GENERATIONS OF THE DEDUCTIOS (FEATURES)				
LOCA	Feature1	Feature2	Feature3	Notes
e'	[+Sac, +e', +la, +Hard]	[+Sac, +e', +mi, +Nat]		E5
d'	[+Sac, +d', +sol, +Hard]	[+Sac, +d', +re, +Nat]	[+Sac, +d', +la, +Soft]	D5
c'	[+Sac, +c', +fa, +Hard]	[+Sac, +c', +do, +Nat]	[+Sac, +c', +sol, +Soft]	C5
b'	[+Sac, +b', +mi, +Hard]	[+Sac, +b', +fa, +Soft]		B4
a'	[+Sac, +a', +re, +Hard]	[+Sac, +a', +la, +Nat]	[+Sac, +a', +mi, +Soft]	A4
g	[+Ac, +g, +do, +Hard]	[+Ac, +g, +sol, +Nat]	[+Ac, +g, +re, +Soft]	G4
f	[+Ac, +f, +fa, +Nat]	[+Ac, +f, +do, +Soft]		F4
e	[+Ac, +e, +la, +Hard]	[+Ac, +e, +mi, +Nat]		E4
d	[+Ac, +d, +sol, +Hard]	[+Ac, +d, +re, +Nat]	[+Ac, +d, +la, +Soft]	D4
c	[+Ac, +c, +fa, +Hard]	[+Ac, +c, +do, +Nat]	[+Ac, +c, +sol, +Soft]	C4
b	[+Ac, +b, +mi, +Hard]	[+Ac, +b, +fa, +Soft]		B3
a	[+Ac, +a, +re, +Hard]	[+Ac, +a, +la, +Nat]	[+Ac, +a, +mi, +Soft]	A3
G	[+Gr, +g, +do, +Hard]	[+Gr, +G, +sol, +Nat]	[+Gr, +G, +re, +Soft]	G3
F	[+Gr, +F, +fa, +Nat]	[+Gr, +F, +do, +Soft]		F3
E	[+Gr, +E, +la, +Hard]	[+Gr, +E, +mi, +Nat]		E3
D	[+Gr, +D, +sol, +Hard]	[+Gr, +D, +re, +Nat]		D3
C	[+Gr, +C, +fa, +Hard]	[+Gr, +C, +do, +Nat]		C3
B	[+Gr, +B, +mi, +Hard]			B2
A	[+Gr, +A, +re, +Hard]			A2
I	[+Gr, +G, +do, +Hard]			G2

[Realm, Loca, Syllables, Deductio]. On the left side the locas denote the places of the syllables. Some locas take one, two or three syllables depending on which deduction they belong to. Dark grey highlights show the hard deductios, grey natural and light grey soft deductios. For example, the "d" loca refers to three distinct syllables which belong to hard, natural and soft deductios. At the most right it denotes the places of modern notational system.

2.3   Internal Phrases (Step and Interval Hierarchy)

These are the intervallic features which are also deep structures. They are associated with divine origins, according to the Pythagorean Tradition of The Harmony of the Spheres and are doctrinized by those conceptualizations of Musica Mundane, Musica

Humana and Musica Instrumentalis as Macrocosms and Microcosms by, 6th century scholar Boethius. Now, we will see their hierarchies:

Step Hierarchy. The Direction Phrase (DirP) which shows the linear and vertical ways of the lines is the maximal projection. Step Hierarchies are dominated by linear ways which we call Melody Phrase (MelP)[5] and it c-commands the Vertical Phrase (VerP) of the Intervals. The"-"means step.

1-P. Indicates the 1st step of the modes and depending on the modes its first step takes those notes respectively: D, A, E, B, F, C, G, D. The first step of the modes therefore specifies the other steps' numerical characters which is the most important step.

5-P. The second most important step which has transformative character depending on the first note.

4-P. In the third order of the hierarchy tree and it has a transformative character depends on the first note of the mode.

DPP. (Directed Progression Phrase) takes its essential from Fuller's [20]. It consists of 3-P and 6-P. These steps are evaluated under this phrase in order to provide consistency to the binary system of the X-Bar Method. DPP is a non-head phrase as an exocentric construction (Fig. 6).

3-P. Immediately dominated by 4-P and also occurs preceding step phrase. It has transformative character depends on the first note of the mode.

6-P. The sister of the 3-P and shares the same features as 3-P.

DisP. DisP takes its essence from the steps in question are evaluated as the main dissonance steps in music theory. It is evaluated under this phrase since it provides consistency to binary system of the X-Bar Method. DisP is non-head phrase as an exocentric construction.

2-P. Dominated by 3-P and it c-commands the 7-P. It has a transformative character dependent on the first step of the mode.

7-P. Dominated by 6-P and it c-commands the 2-P, It also has a transformative character dependent on the first step of the mode it belongs to.

Interval Hierarchy. Interval Hierarchies belong to VerP and are dominated by LinP and c-commanded by every individual step, but do not c-command the LinP and its sub-branches;

Dpas (P1st and P8th). The most important interval by the words of Marsilio Ficino "The Ratio 2 to 1... fills the ears with wonderful pleasure by means of octave" [21: 165]. It dominates all the intervals.

Dpen (P5th). Dpen is the second important interval in the medieval period together with Dtes. They are dominated by Dpas and dominate the rest of the intervals.

---

[5] Many thanks to Professor A. Sumru Özsoy who suggested this for representation.

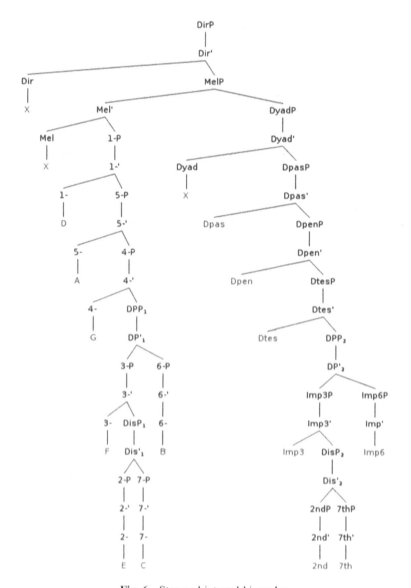

Fig. 6. Step and interval hierarchy

Dtes (P4th). Dominated by DpenP, DpasP and DpenP immediately dominates the DtesP and respectively dominate the rest of the intervals.

DPP. (Directed Progression Phrase), As in DPP in the section of the step hierarchy, this takes its essential from Fuller's [30]. It consists of 3-P and 6-P. These intervals are evaluated under this phrase in order to provide consistency to binary system of the X-Bar Method. DPP is a non-head phrase as an exocentric construction.

Imp3 (m3 and M3). Intervals of the Imp3 are sisters of the intervals of the Imp6P. They are immediately dominated by DtesP. Imp3P and Imp6P mutually c-command to each other's domains.

Imp6 (m6 and M6). Intervals of the Imp6 are sister of the intervals of the Imp3P. They are immediately dominated by DtesP. Imp6P and Imp3P are mutually c-commands to each other.

DisP. As in DisP in step hierarchy section, takes its essential from the steps in question which are evaluated as the main dissonance steps. They are evaluated under this phrase in order to conform to the binary system of the X-Bar Method. DisP is non-head phrase as an exocentric construction.

Second (m2 and M2). Regarded as dissonances. They are immediately dominated by Imperfect sonorities and respectively c-command each other's domains.

Seventh (m7 and M7). Regarded as dissonances and they are immediately dominated by Imperfect sonorities and respectively c-commanded by DpasP, DpenP and DtesP.

Second (m2 and M2). Regarded as dissonances. They are immediately dominated by Imperfect sonorities.

Seventh (m7 and M7). Regarded as dissonances and they are immediately dominated by Imperfect sonorities.

Diabolus in Musica (DMP). The interval not used in chant repertoires, therefore not represented in the tree, and even if rarely used, includes the detailed treatment in the counterpoint of the discantus. It is placed in the lowest part of the hierarchy.

2.4   Textural Structures and Segmentation Principles

There are three species of textural segmentation processes: Monorhythmic (MRS), Homorhythmic (HRS) and Florid (FS). And there are two levels of each of the segmentations: Phonologic Level (PL) and Syntactical Level (SL).

Monorhythmic Segmentation (MRS). MRS is analyzed in the two levels PL and SL.

PL. PL level of MRS is determined by word boundaries of the relevant text and all articles, prepositions, and conjunctions are evaluated in the following words they belong to. The intervallic characters of every step (this is the only differences between MRS and HRS analysis) indicate the prosodic accentuations.

SL. SLS level of the MRS is determined by the steps which specify the beginning and ending of the words. Depending on the step hierarchy, the dominant step gives its own name to the segmentation. At this point, we need to say that since close interdependency exists between intervals and steps, the hierarchical formula which takes its essential from intervals is considered in line with steps in MRS. Accordingly, the hierarchical formula (Henceforth, "I-Formula" Interval Formula) *Hierarchically*

Dpas5, Dpas4, Dpen1, Dpen5, Dpen4 and Dtes1, Dtes5 and Dtes4 are adjunct to Dpas1. All other intervals are complement of aforementioned intervals and complements with each other is changed by that principle as we call "S-Formula" (Step Formula). *Hierarchically 5th, 4th, adjunct to 1st, All other steps (2nd, 3rd, #4th, 6th and 7th) are complement of aforementioned intervals and complements with each other* (Score 1).

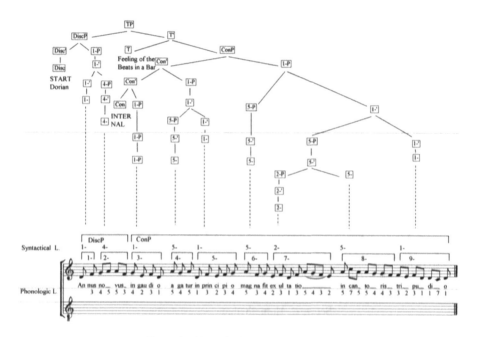

Score 1. Monorhythmic segmentation

Homorhythmic Segmentation (HRS).

HRS is analyzed in the two levels PL and SL.

PL. PL level of the HRS is determined by simply word boundaries of the relevant text and all the articles, prepositions, and conjunctions are evaluated in the following words they belong to. The intervallic characters of the every dyad indicate the prosodic accentuations.

SL. SL level of the HRS is determined by the intervals which specify the beginning and ending of the words. And depends on the intervallic hierarchy, the dominant interval gives its own name to the segmentation (Score 2).

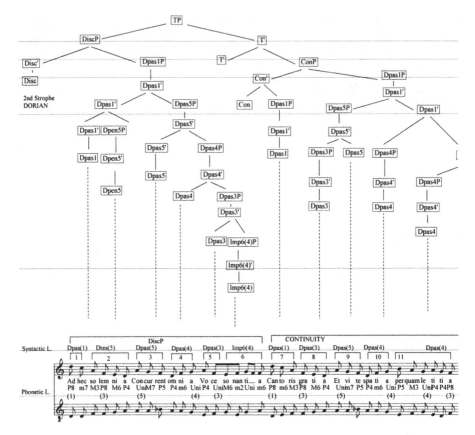

Score 2. Homorhythmic segmentation

Florid Segmentation (FS)[6]. FS is analyzed in two levels PL and SL.

PL. PL level of FS is determined by the long notes which were called tenore in early music generally in the tenor part and occasionally in the other parts of the pieces. In the florid texture, the analysis process breaks down the restriction of verbal and dives into the purely musical representation of its individual language.

SL. SL level of FS is determined by the intervals which specify the beginning and ending of the words. Depending on the intervallic hierarchy, the dominant interval gives its own name to the segmentation (Score 3).

---

[6] Many thanks to Professor Paul Whitehead acquiring this concept to our study by making me aware of various historical facts as to the period we study.

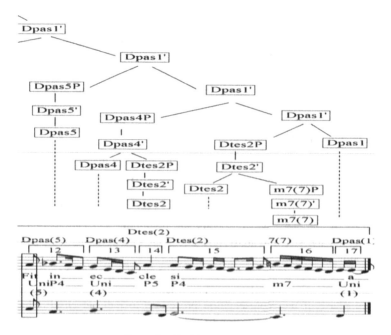

Score 3. Florid Segmentation

3 Application of the Analytical Principles

Since the middle of the last century, a lot of work as to demystify the Middle Ages music have been practiced and these studies enliven the ways of the new and early researchers who want to develop these accelerations one step more. In this respect, it would be important to refer to the scholars who studied Aquitanian Polyphony: Treitler and Fuller, particularly Fuller's 1969 dissertation [22] and contemplation about early music syntax and Treitler's syntactical explanations as to the essentials of early music have illuminated the way of this study.

Firstly, the exercises we practice are "Annus Novus" piece of Aquitanian Polyphony. "Annus Novus" is the first piece transcribed in Fuller's dissertation, for this term was pointed out by the same quotation in Fuller's dissertation. Treitler's identifications of the maximal segmentation of the piece gives the essential determination of the analysis system: "Groups of phrases usually form balanced units of musical structure that span an entire strophe or outline a rhyme grouping within a strophe. An unflagging sense of melodic direction and balance and symmetry in the large phrase groupings are the prevailing artistic principles of this chant—principles which have direct analogues in the poetic structure" [23]. In this respect, the analysis of Annus Novus is in line with the essentials of Treitler's indication.

3.1   Evaluation of the First Strophe

The first strophe of Annus Novus versus is the monophonic textural structure, so we will examine it in the principles of the relevant texture. When we observe the Score 4, under the lyrics we see that the step numbers of the individual mode is Dorian. These step numbers originate the PL, although in this phase the boundaries of the word segmentation are not indicated. This is the first phase of the representation which will be modified by the next phases. For the representation process, we will indicate the description in the following bullets;

- Above the notes, there are two levels of brackets, one of them denoting the SL and specifying the word boundaries, and therefore modifying the PL. The subject of this phase is SL.
- The second phase of the representation process indicates the SLS level of the MRS determined by the steps which specify the beginning and ending of the words. Depending on the step hierarchy, the dominant step gives its own name to the segmentation.
- The second level brackets above the PL brackets, specify the Maximals that are DiscP and ConP. The subject of this phase is the DiscP.
- The third phase of the representation process is to indicate DiscP which is the boundary of the Spec MCP position from first 1- to second 1-[7]. Its features are head initial in the DiscP. Hierarchically S-formula is valid for MRS representation.
- Now, we will examine the DiscP's internals as Deep Structures. DiscP is a major event in the piece. Accordingly, the head of the DiscP is the Dorian and beginning of the piece. These features are not placed in the realization of the structure, however as a proposal, they are rather intention of the performers or experienced listeners in a performing or listening process. The intention is specified by the 1-P (Segment1) as a Spec position which consists of a adjunct that is 4-P (Segment2). This adjunction is determined by S-Formula[8].

We see another bracket adjacent to DiscP. It is the ConP. In this phase we will examine this maximal by the following levels.

- The fourth phase of the representation process is to denote the ConP, until the end of the musical sentence. It is determined by the strophe while respectively first 1- are specifier of ConP, following 1-s - except the last one which is complement of the ConP - are adjunct of the ConP and S- Formula gives the essential representation.
- As a last section of evaluation of the first strophe of the Annus Novus, we will examine the ConP's internals. ConP is the internal structure of the sentence.
- In the ConP, we see one Spec MCP consisting of two adjuncts and one default complement structure of the ConP.

---

[7] Numbering is from left to right in DiscP.

[8] In the representation, we see under a single bar level, a sister relationship as 1-'and 4-P. To show the adjunct function of the 4-P to 1-P, we have to draw the tree in this way. On the other hand, the validation of this representation in language could be arguable in Verbal/ Linguistics discipline.

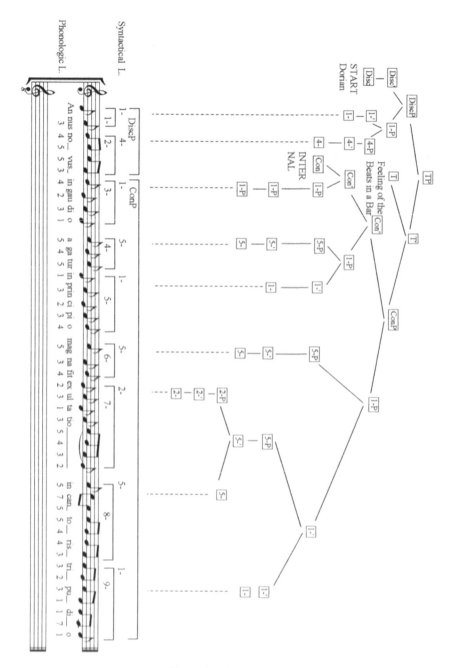

Score 4. First strophe

- The Spec MCP of the ConP is First 1-P[9]. Its head is at the end of the sentence and is the last segment consisting of two adjuncts. From right to left, first adjunct of 1-P is 5-P which has one complement as 2-P and second adjunct of the 1-P is the 5-P.
- The adjunct of the ConP is second 1-P in the middle of the piece which has its own adjunct that is 5-P.
- Finally, the complement of the ConP is another 1-P which is third from right the left.
- In the ConP, the most dominant head which places at the most left because the feature of the ConP is head final.

Detection of the "Mutatios" by Features. In the "Hexachord System and Features of Deductios", the features of the deductios of the hexachord system are denoted. In this part, by showing the unique features of the each voice on the score we will indicate the mutatios[10] -if any- from one hexachord or deductio to another.

In the Score 4, 9 segments are seen; two of them in the DiscP and rest are in the ConP. Now, we will list the segments and their features.

Segments of the DiscP.
    [+Ac, +d, +re, +Nat]
    [+Ac, +g, +sol, +Nat]
Segments of the ConP.
    [+Ac, +g, +sol, +Nat]
    [+Sac, +a', +la, +Nat]
    [+Ac, +d, +re, +Nat]
    [+Sac, +a', +la, +Nat]
    [+Ac, +e, +mi, +Nat]
    [+Ac, +a', +la, +Nat]
    [+Ac, +d, +re, +Nat]

There is no mutation in the features of the segments in the first strophe of versus, and all the segments have the features of the natural deduction.

3.2   Evaluation of the Second Strophe

The second strophe of Annus Novus versus includes HRS from first to 12th segments and FS textures from 12th to 17th. The four phases that were explained in the preceding section are valid for second strophe. In this evaluation of the 2nd strophe, there will be some modifications depending on the textural transformations. In the preceding section, the steps indicated the deep structures, however in this part the intervals will specify the

---

[9] Numbering starts to begin from right in the ConP Region.

[10] To the transformations between natural, hard and soft hexachords, the most fundamental characteristic of the hard hexachord is the natural b and of soft is bb and of the natural is that it does not include b note.

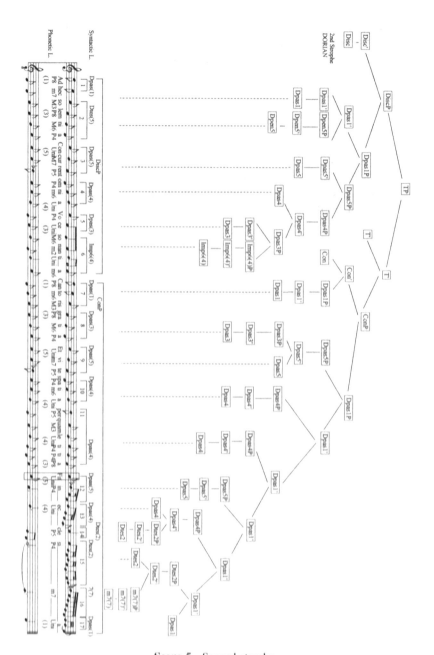

Score 5. Second strophe

deep structures of the strophe because HRS and FS levels the main characteristics of the organization come from the intervals.

The strophe is the homophonic and florid textural character, so we will examine it in the principles of the relevant texture. When we see Score 5, under the lyrics the interval number of the individual mode Dorian will be seen. As for the representation process, we will indicate the description in the following bullets:

- The first phase of the representation process is to indicate the PL level.
- Above the notes, there are two levels of brackets, one of them denoting the SLs and specify the word boundaries and therefore modifies the PL. The subject of this phase SL.
- The second phase of the representation process is to indicate the SLS level of the HRS and FS determined by the steps which specify the beginning and ending of the musical segments. Depending on interval hierarchy, the dominant interval gives their own name to the segmentation.

Above SL, we see two brackets as DiscP and ConP. In this phase we will examine the DiscP.

- The third phase of the representation process is to indicate DiscP, the boundaries of maximal from 1st segment to 6th segment. Hierarchically, first Dpas1 Spec MCP of DiscP dominates the other constituent of the DiscP and it has two adjuncts, Dpas5P and Dpen5P.
- Then, Dpas5P consists of one adjunct which is Dpas4. Dpas4 has a complement which is Dpas3P and finally Dpas3P has a complement Imp6 (4).
- Another adjunct of the DiscP is Dpen5P.

We have seen another bracket adjacent to DiscP, the ConP. In this phase we will examine this maximal region.

- The fourth phase of the representation process is to denote the ConP from 7th to 17th segment. ConP is until the end of the musical sentence that is specified by the strophe and I-Formula is valid for this representation.
- As a last section of evaluating of second strophe of the Annus Novus, we will examine the ConP's internals.
- In the ConP, it is seen 1 Spec MCP and 1 complement structure. The Spec MCP of the ConP places at the end of the sentence which is Dpas1. The Dpas1 has 5 adjunct and one complement respectively from the last segments to the preceding ones;
- Dpas1's complement is Dtes2 which has one complement: m7(P).
- The first adjunct of the Dpas1 is Dpas4P which has one complement: Dtes2P.
- The second adjunct of the Dpas1 is Dpas5P.
- The third and fourth adjunct of the Dpas1 is Dpas4Ps.
- The fifth adjunct of the Dpas1 is Dpas5P which has one complement that is Dpas3P.
- Finally, the complement of the ConP is Dpas1 which does not consist of any constituent in its bar.

Detection of the "Mutatios" by Features. In the Score 4, it is seen 19 segments; six of them in the DiscP and rest of the segments are in the ConP. Now, we will list the segments and their features.

Segments of the DiscP.

1. [+Gr, +d, +re, +Nat]
2. [+Gr, +f, +fa, +Nat]
3. [+Ac, +a, +mi, +soft]
4. [+Ac, +a, +mi, +soft]
5. [+Gr, +e, +mi, +Nat]
6. [+Ac, +g, +sol, +Nat]

Segments of the ConP.

 7. [+Gr, +d, +re, +Nat]
 8. [+Gr, +f', +fa, +Nat]
 9. [+Ac, +a, +mi, +Soft]
10. [+Ac, +a', +la, +Nat]
11. [+Gr, +f, +fa, +Nat]
12. [+Ac, +a, +mi, +Soft]
13. [+Ac, +g', +sol, +Nat]
14. [+Gr, +e, +mi, +Nat]
15. [+Gr, +e, +mi, +Nat]
16. [+Gr, +c, +fa, +Hard]
17. [+Gr, +d, +re, +Hard]

In the first 6 segments of the DiscP, we see one mutation to the soft hexachord through the middle of the region and it turn back into the natural hexachord.

ConP begins on the natural hexachord and by the third segment starts to waver between natural and soft hexachord, and shows a consistency on the natural hexachord through the middle of the ConP and, finally it ends on the hard hexachord.

4   Conclusion

As a first step to a novel analytical tool for early music which also shows the first implications of a cognitive approach to it, the present study synthesizes musicology and linguistic aspects as applied to the repertory of Aquitanian Polyphony. In conclusion, its main contributions to the relevant studies are the following;

- The study extends the boundaries of the GTTM (Generative Theory of Tonal Music) to music of the 12th century. In this sense, we call it GTMM (Generative Theory of Modal Music).
- X-Bar method of Generative theory is applied to the repertories of the Aquitanian Polyphony of Twelfth Century,
- As the main distinction of present study to Pesetsky and Katz's "Identity Thesis", the conceptualizations of musical structures which take their essential historical

terms of the intervals are described as the "deep structures," and these structures denoted the evidences of the implications of intervallic impacts which are revealed by Patel in his "Music, Language and Brain".

- While musical spaces are described as taking place in two maximals every individual notes are described in a conceptualized domain.

This paper presents a novel approach to early music. This need arose from the fact that though in the evaluation process to the pre-tonal period there have been a lots of subjective interpretation form to discursive pieces, there has not been a tool to provide a consistent understanding for the individual corpus i.e. Aquitanian Polyphony, Montpellier Codex. To provide a contribution to bring a solution about these problems, present study's implications are following:

- All the essentials which are presented through the study are the components of a syntactical tool applied to early music.
- This new syntactical tool may show the cognitive tendencies of the composers of the term, because it takes its essentials from Linguistics, a cognitive discipline.
- Historically, early grammar studies in the Carolingian era and its permeating characteristics into the music structures in the epistemological sense may redefine the compositional process of Western Classical Music by inheriting the mindset of their creators and its evolutionary trajectories.
- A retrospective excavation of the minds of the composers via analyzing the signs that they left could show some new paths to the music analysis generally, and not solely early music repertoire.
- This syntactical analysis tool may be able to be a preset analysis tool for early music repertoires.

Acknowledgment. To my dear mother and sister, thanks to you for always standing behind on my decisions and I am grateful to my dear professors Paul Whitehead in Historical Musicology and A. Sumru Özsoy in Linguistics. If there had not been their guidance and intellects, this study would not exceed a threshold of a positivity but marks time in its myths.

References

1. Bent, M.: The grammar of early music: preconditions for analysis. In: Judd, C. (ed.) Tonal Structures in Early Music. Garland Pub, New York (1998)
2. Katz, J., Pesetsky, D.: The Identity Thesis for Language and Music, version 2.1 (January 2011). http://ling.auf.net/lingbuzz/000959
3. Cohen, D.E.: Notes, scales, and modes in the earlier middle ages. In: Christensen, T. (ed.) The Cambridge History of Western Music Theory. Cambridge University Press, Cambridge (2002)
4. Powers, H.: Language models and musical analysis. J. Ethnomusicology **24**(1), 1–60 (1980)
5. Sullivan, B.: Grammar and harmony: the written representation of musical sound in Carolingian treatises. Dissertation, University of California, Los Angeles (1994)
6. Chomsky, N.: Remarks on nominalization. In: Chomsky, N. (ed.) Studies on Semantics in Generative Grammar, 1st edn, pp. 11–61. The Hague, Mouton (1972)

7. X-Bar Theory. http://ai.ato.ms/MITECS/Entry/haegeman.html
8. Patel, A.: Music, Language, and the Brain. Oxford University Press, Oxford (2008)
9. Molholm, S., Martinez, A., Ritter, W., Javitt, D.C., Foxe, J.J.: The neural circuitry of pre-attentive auditory change-detection: an fMRI study of pitch and duration mismatch negativity generators. J. Cereb. Cortex 15(5), 545–551 (2005)
10. Carnie, A.: Syntax a Generative Introduction, 2nd edn. Wiley, New York (2011)
11. Foucault, M., Sheridan, A.: The Archaeology of Knowledge. Pantheon Books, New York (1972)
12. Phrase. http://0-www.oxfordmusiconline.com.divit.library.itu.edu.tr/subscriber/article/grove/music/21599?q=phrase&search=quick&pos=1&_start=1#firsthit
13. Radford, A.: Transformational Grammar: A First Course, Reprint edn. Cambridge University Press, Cambridge (1990). (Reprint ed.)
14. Bar. http://0-www.oxfordmusiconline.com.divit.library.itu.edu.tr/subscriber/article/opr/t114/e577?q=bar&search=quick&pos=2&_start=1#firsthit
15. Lerdahl, F., Jackendoff, R.: A Generative Theory of Tonal Music. MIT Press, Cambridge (1983)
16. Winkler, I., Háden, G.P., Ladinig, O., Sziller, I., Honing, H., Purves, D.: Newborn infants detect the beat in music. Proc. Nat. Acad. Sci. U.S.A. 106(7), 2468–2471 (2009)
17. Hexachord System. http://www2.siba.fi/muste1/index.php?id=72&la=enhexachords
18. Phonetics: The Sounds of American English. http://soundsofspeech.uiowa.edu/english/english.html
19. Katamba, F.: An Introduction to Phonology. Longman, London (1989)
20. Fuller, S.: Tendencies and resolutions: the directed progression in "ars nova" music. J. Music Theory 36(2), 229–258 (1992)
21. Godwin, J.: The Harmony of the Spheres: A Sourcebook of the Pythagorean Tradition in Music. Inner Traditions International, Rochester (1993)
22. Fuller, S.: Aquitanian polyphony of the eleventh and twelfth centuries. Dissertation, University of California at Berkeley (1969)
23. Treitler, L.: Musical syntax in the middle ages: background to an aesthetic problem. J. Perspect. New Music 4(1), 75–85 (1965)

Songs in African Tonal Languages: Contrasting the Tonal System and the Melody

Maria Konoshenko[1] and Olga Kuznetsova[2(✉)]

[1] Sholokhov Moscow State University for the Humanities, Moscow, Russia
`mb_konoshenko@il-rggu.ru`
[2] Institute for Linguistic Studies RAS, Saint-Petersburg, Russia
`siilille@yandex.ru`

Abstract. Over the past fifty years there has been a dramatic increase in studies investigating the rules of tone-tune correspondence in vocal music performed in tonal languages. In this paper we argue that considering structural properties of tonal systems is important for studying the interaction between tone and melody. Using songs in Guinean Kpelle and Guro as test cases, we prove that contour tones are less preserved in melody than level tones, and surface tones are reflected in melody rather than underlying tones. We also show that syllable structure as well as style, genre and structure of songs affect tone-tune correspondence.

Keywords: Tone · Phonology · Contour tones · Underlying tones · Surface tones · Syllable structure · Vocal music · Melody · Genre · Guinean Kpelle · Guro

1 Introduction

In recent years, there has been an increasing interest in the relationship between linguistic and musical structures in vocal music. Most studies assume that any song combines at least two independent tiers – a text and a tune, each of them conforming to its own set of well-formedness rules, cf. [1–6]. Questions have been raised as to whether there exists a correspondence between these tiers in vocal music, and (if there is any) how exactly text-to-tune mapping is organized in a given tradition. Rhythmical structures are usually explored for vocal music in stress languages, and melodic structures are examined in languages with phonemic pitch, i.e. tone languages.

Research on the relation between melody and speech tone has been carried out in a variety of languages including those spoken in Africa – see [7–14], also [6, 15] for an overview. However, given the total number of African languages, which amounts close to one third of the total number of living world languages [16], as well as the diversity of tone systems found across the areal, the total number of studies has been relatively few.

Various degrees of tone-tune correspondence have been reported in literature – from very weak (Ewe, [11]) to moderate (Shona, [13]) and rather strong (Mambila, [14]). Song genre has been proposed as a parameter governing the degree of correspondence within a given musical culture [8, 17, 18].

© Springer International Publishing Switzerland 2015
P. Eismont and N. Konstantinova (Eds.): LMAC 2015, CCIS 561, pp. 166–175, 2015.
DOI: 10.1007/978-3-319-27498-0_13

Studies investigating the correspondence between tones and tunes in African languages have devised various calculation methods such as general statistic assessment of absolute pitch values [12] or a detailed analysis of relative pitch transitions across adjacent syllables [13], for some discussion of the latter approach see also [6].

This paper discusses the relationship between tone and melody with a special focus on songs in Guinean Kpelle and Guro, two genetically related Mande languages spoken in West Africa which have considerably different tonal systems. We formulate a number of predictions regarding possible rules of tone-tune correspondence which mainly refer to the structural properties of tonal systems. Thus we predict that contour tones are less often reflected in melody than level tones; surface tones are mapped into the melody rather than underlying tones in languages with obligatory tonal rules; and some other morphophonological phenomena (i.e. syllable structure) may also affect tone-tune correspondence. We demonstrate that our data support these claims.

The paper is organized in the following way: In Sect. 2 we discuss methodological background of the present study as well as our crucial predictions. In Sects. 3 and 4 we analyze vocal music in Guinean Kpelle and Guro. Section 5 summarizes our findings.

2 Methodology

2.1 Background and Discussion

In most modern studies the melody of a song as performed by the subject(s) is compared to the spoken version of the same song. The speakers are thus recorded while singing and then reading a written text of the same song [12–14].

We believe that comparing musical melody with its written lyrics as read by the speaker may not provide safe results. When reading the text, the speaker may however be influenced by the melody – see Murray Schellenberg's note that he had to record one of the spoken texts twice as the speaker said the first version was "too much like singing" [13:143]. We encountered similar effects of "unnatural" text recording during our research. Such influence cannot always be ruled out, so it remains problematic.

Most studies cited above make statements such as "songs in language L ignore (or rather preserve) tones in the text", in some cases more complex rules are provided. We argue that, in order to make more insightful observations about the interaction between tone and melody, one needs to ground one's study on a profound understanding of language's tonal system and to consider its structural properties when exploring text-to-tune mapping rules[1]. Comparing just sung and spoken versions of the same song may be insufficient to fulfill this goal.

---

[1] On the other side, a number of musicological predictions can also be made. Apart from song genre briefly discussed in Sect. 1, various parameters may prove relevant, i.e. scale type, the use of instrumental accompaniment vs. *a capella* singing, polyphonic vs. monophonic texture etc. Future musicological research might investigate whether these factors influence tone-melody correspondence.

2.2 Our Approach and Predictions

This paper presents a study of tone-tune relationship in Guinean Kpelle, Guro, which are Mande languages spoken in Guinea and Ivory Coast respectively. We offer an approach to studying tone-tune relationship which may be considered a modification of Murray Schellenberg's [13] method.

In his study of three songs in Shona (Bantu, Zimbabwe), M. Schellenberg compares pitch transitions in melody and speech tone across pairs of adjacent syllables. The transitions are described as relative rather than absolute, and for any given syllable the pitch in speech as well as in melody can go up, down or remain the same. This yields nine possible combinations of pitch transition in language and music. They are then grouped into three categories: parallel transitions (direction of pitch change is the same for text and music), opposing (opposite direction of pitch change, e.g. musical melody going down whereas speech tone going up and vice versa), non-opposing (either of modes retain the same pitch level whereas the other one goes up or down). For example, if the speech tone goes up and the musical pitch remains the same, this counts as non-opposing transition – for details and results see [13:139–140]. Crucially, as many other researchers, Murray Schellenberg compares recorded sung and spoken versions of the same songs in his study.

In this paper we analyze the direction of pitch transitions across adjacent syllables in Kpelle and Guro vocal music following Schellenberg's classification of transition types as parallel, opposing and non-opposing. However, we don't use text reading as our main source of speech tones. Rather, we mark linguistic tones in texts using our knowledge of tonal systems in these languages as described in [19, 20] and [21, 22] for Guinean Kpelle and Guro respectively. We formulate and test the following predictions based on typological properties of tonal systems.

First, contour tones are more marked and more complex than level tones [23, 24]. This is why we predict that contour tones – phonemic or contextual – will be less often preserved in melody than level tones. This prediction is corroborated by our data from Guinean Kpelle as well as Guro.

Second, in some languages tones undergo obligatory changes in context, and so the distinction between underlying and surface[2] tones is crucial for such tonal systems. We predict that in these languages it is contextual tones that will be preserved in songs. The reason why this is possible is that in a language with obligatory tonal changes contextual tones are psycholinguistically relevant for the speakers, e.g. they can be separated from segmental structure in whistling. It seems quite natural that only psycholinguistically relevant tones will be preserved in vocal music. This prediction is crucially supported by Kpelle data. Unfortunately, it is not testable in Guro as there are no obligatory tone changes in this language.

Finally, some features of text-to-tune mapping correlation may depend on phonological and morphological phenomena, such as syllable structure, phonetic or

---

[2] Sometimes the terms *lexical* vs. *postlexical* are used to refer to underlying vs. surface representations in phonology. However, we prefer to speak about underlying vs. surface tones in this paper, because in African languages, including Guinean Kpelle and Guro, underlying tones are often assigned by grammar in which case they replace tones specified in lexicon.

morphemic boundaries. These phenomena proved to be relevant for text-to-tune correspondence in Guro.

3   Guinean Kpelle[3]

Guinean Kpelle is a Mande language spoken by ca 460 000 speakers [16] in the Republic of Guinea.

In this paper we follow African phonetic alphabet writing conventions for both Guinen Kpelle and Guro. We use the following notation and abbreviations: á – high tone; ã – mid tone; à – low tone; H – high tone; (H) – floating high; M – mid tone; L – low tone; C – consonant; V – vowel.

3.1   Tonal System

Each syllable in Guinean Kpelle bears H or L tone, but there are strong restrictions on possible combinations of these tones within a lexeme. The two tonal elements thus make up six fixed underlying patterns, or melodies: /H/, /L(H)/, /HL/, /LHL/, /L/ and marginal /LH/.

Contour tones are not phonemic, but phonetic [HL] contour may occur phrase-finally, otherwise contour simplification rule applies.

Crucially, the six underlying melodies given above are modified in context. Three basic rules apply: H tone spread, contour simplification with downstep and regressive (H) linking. There is also downdrift, but it was not considered in this study as it does not change tone contrasts. An example of H tone spread is shown in (1).

> (1) /bówá hèyě/ → [bówá héyé] 'take a knife'
>   align knife with same line above

In (1) the verb, which has underlying /L(H)/ melody, appears with surface H tones after word-final H tone on its direct object. These processes are described at length in [19, 20].

3.2   Data

In this study we analyze three songs performed and recorded a capella by a young female speaker of Guinean Kpelle in 2012. The recording took place in Guinean embassy in Moscow, five months after the consultant had left the country. The two songs are biblical hymns sung at catholic mass, the other one is a civil song about life in Guinea. The authors of these songs are not known, but another Kpelle consultant, a catholic priest, said that these songs might have been written in the beginning of 2000 s, and also that music and lyrics are likely to have been written by the same person.

[3] This research has been supported by the Russian Science Foundation, project 14-18-03270 "Word order typology, communication-syntax interface, and information structure in languages of the world".

The subject could not read in Kpelle, so she was also recorded reciting the texts by heart. These recordings were then used to check for surface speech tones – with caution though, as the speaker was obviously influenced by the melody (see discussion in Subsect. 2.1). All the three songs were annotated with surface as well as underlying tones deduced using our knowledge of the tonal system.

As discussed in Subsect. 2.2, in this study we compare pitch transitions across adjacent syllables. There were 119 transitions in total[4] (36, 49, 34 in the three songs respectively).

3.3   Results

As predicted in Subsect. 2.2, the melody corresponds to surface rather than underlying tones in our data. The scores for underlying vs. surface tones as compared with melody in the three songs are shown in Table 1.

Table 1. Tone-tune transitions for underlying and surface tones in Guinean Kpelle

Transition type	Parallel	Non-opposing	Opposing	Total
Underlying	72 (60.6 %)	32 (26.8 %)	15 (12.6 %)	119 (100 %)
Surface	93 (78.2 %)	26 (21.8 %)	0	119 (100 %)

Surface tones predict whether the melody will go up or down better than underlying tones; the difference between the two rows is statistically very significant (chi-square test, $p < 0.001$).

Overall percentage of parallel and non-opposing transitions turned out to be very high in the data, especially if surface tones are calculated. Interestingly, the percentages of transition types were similar across the three songs. This is shown in Table 2, only surface tones are given.

Table 2. Surface tones and melody in three songs in Guinean Kpelle

Transition type	Parallel	Non-opposing	Opposing	Total
Song 1 (religious)	28 (78 %)	8 (22 %)	0	36 (100 %)
Song 2 (religious)	27 (79.4 %)	7 (21.6 %)	0	34 (100 %)
Song 3 (civil)	38 (77.5 %)	11 (22.5 %)	0	49 (100 %)

Thus religious vs. civil songs show no difference in the degree of text-to-tune correspondence (chi-square test, $p = 0.98$). Certainly more data are needed to investigate various song genres properly.

There were 13 instances of surface [HL] contour tones in the data. In our calculation we regarded each contour tone as a combination of H and L attached to a single syllable and having falling pitch transition. It corresponded to a fall in the melody in

---

[4] Transitions across verses were not considered in this study.

just three cases, and this counted as parallel transition; in the remaining ten cases musical pitch remained the same (non-opposing transition). As predicted in Subsect. 2.2, the difference between the degree of tone-tune correspondence for level and contour surface tones turned out to be statistically very significant (Fisher exact probability test, $p < 0.001$).

4   Guro[5]

Guro is a South Mande language spoken in central part of Ivory Coast. The data analyzed in this paper was collected from speakers of Zuénoula dialect from Gohitafla subprefecture.

4.1   Tonal System

Guro has three level tones (high, mid, low) and two contour (falling, rising) tones, the tone-bearing unit is syllable [21, 22, 25][6]. No downstep is attested; co-articulation, especially in fast speech, affects tone realization to some degree (e.g. a high tone between two lower tones is pronounced with a lower pitch than in other sequences). Average F0 values can be ascribed to specific tones for individual speakers, and these tones are psycholinguistically relevant for the speakers (e.g. trained speakers can easily whistle or sing different tones as separate items, in isolation from any tone-bearing unit).

There are very few rules for contextual tone alternations and they are not obligatory. As a result, underlying and surface tones rarely differ from each other, and this distinction is negligible for the purposes of this research.

4.2   Data

Four musical pieces of different genres are analyzed in this work. Two of them are traditional children's songs performed as unaccompanied solos.

The example of second genre is a musical fragment from a fairy tale, also an unaccompanied solo. The child sings to a fruit tree three times, asking it first to blossom, then produce fruits and make them ripe. The three musical phrases are sang to the same tune, in spite of the fact that some fragments of the lyrics are changed.

The third genre is a modern religious song performed by choir with a leader and instrumental ensemble. We analyzed only a capella part of the composition. The song has the following structure: beginning of the phrase (recitative performed by the leader), end of the phrase (leader sings), repetition of the end of the phrase (choir sings).

[5] This research has been supported by Russian Humanitarian Scientific Foundation, project 13-34-01015 "Verbal systems of Mande languages in the context of typological and areal researches".
[6] Le Saout [26] describes Guro tonal system somewhat differently. But his description proved not to be applicable to contemporary Guro and it is rather a plausible historical reconstruction.

Melody varies from one textual phrase to another. Recited and sung fragments were analyzed separately.

As in Kpelle, we compared pitch transitions across adjacent syllables. The number of transitions for each genre was as follows: two children's songs (47), a song from fairy tale (43), modern recitative (56), modern song (37), 183 transitions in total. Transitions across verses were not taken into account and contour tones were analyzed as consisting of two level tones for the sake of comparability with Kpelle data.

4.3   Results

As predicted in Subsect. 2.2, contour tones are reflected in melody less often than level tones. There were 7 contour tones in our data. In just one case a parallel transition in language and music was attested. Comparative data for level and contour tones are shown in Table 3.

Table 3. Tone-tune transitions for level and contour tones in Guro

Transitions	Parallel	Non-opposing	Opposing	Total
Level	101 (57 %)	54 (31 %)	21 (12 %)	176 (100 %)
Contour	1 (14 %)	6 (86 %)	0	7 (100 %)

The difference between the degree of tone-tune correspondence for level and contour surface tones turned out to be statistically significant (Fisher exact probability test, $p < 0.05$).

Some cases of non-opposing and opposing transitions can be attributed to morphophonology. In morphemes with CVV structure, the tone of the second syllable has no influence on musical pitch. It is sung at the same level as the first syllable, cf. (2). This conforms to a general tendency to contract vowel sequences and simplify their tones, which is very prominent in Guro [25].

(2)   D   - - - - - - - ●-
      E   - ●○ - - - -

          mɛ̄ɛ̀   *klɛ́*
          ML   H

The degree of tone-tune correspondence turned out to be significantly different for transitions between the syllables of CVV morphemes as compared to other transitions (chi-square test, $p < 0.01$) (Table 4).

Table 4. Transitions within CVV stuctures compared to other transitions in Guro

Tranitions	Parallel	Non-opposing	Opposing	Total
CVV	3 (20 %)	12 (80 %)	0	15 (100 %)
Other	100 (60 %)	47 (28 %)	21 (12 %)	168 (100 %)

Table 5. Tone-tune transitions for different genres

Transitions	Parallel	Non-opposing	Opposing	Total
Children's	38 (81 %)	9 (19 %)	0	47 (100 %)
Modern (recitative)	35 (63 %)	18 (32 %)	3 (5 %)	56 (100 %)
Modern (singing)	13 (35 %)	20 (54 %)	4 (11 %)	37 (100 %)
Fairy tale	17 (40 %)	12 (28 %)	14 (32 %)	43 (100 %)

We also discovered that tone-tune correspondence was significantly different across the genres of songs represented in our data (chi-square test, $p < 0.01$ for four rows in Table 5).

Table 5 shows that the children's songs have the highest degree of correspondence between language tones and the melody. In fact in this genre has almost one-to-one correspondence, e.g. in one of the songs low tone is sang as C, middle as D and high as E. This finding is compatible with the hierarchy of song types as proposed for Mandarin [17], which predicts that the degree of correspondence increases along the scale: sing-song > recitative > tonal composition; similar hierarchies were suggested in [8, 27]. The singsong type corresponds to children's songs in our data, and tonal composition is represented by the modern song and the song from a fairy tale.

Naturally, the recitative has relatively high degree of correspondence. Modern singing has the lowest percentage of parallel transitions but no opposing transitions. The tune is very simple, with many sequences of repeated notes which often correspond to sequences of different tones. On the other hand, sequences of syllables with the same tone correspond to leaps in the melody. This antiphase relation between tones and melody explains the highest percentage of non-opposing transitions and is probably an essential feature of choir singing in Guro worth further investigation.

Fairy tale song has the highest percentage of opposing transitions. Most of them represent the fragments which have different lyrics sung to the same tune. Transitions in text fragments repeated in every line and those specific to different lines are shown in Table 6.

Table 6. Transitions in Guro fairy tale: repeated text vs. specific to different verses

Transitions	Parallel	Non-opposing	Opposing	Total
Repeated text	6 (37,5 %)	8 (50 %)	2 (12,5 %)	16 (100 %)
Specific text	11 (41 %)	4 (15 %)	12 (44 %)	27 (100 %)

The difference between the two rows is statistically significant (Fisher exact probability test, $p < 0.05$), which proves that the structure of musical piece is a factor that should also be taken into account in tone-tune correspondence studies.

5   Conclusion

In this paper we have argued that, in order to gather a more profound understanding of the interaction between tone and melody in vocal music, one needs to consider structural properties of tonal systems in languages under analysis. Using songs in

Guinean Kpelle and Guro as our two test cases, we have demonstrated that certain elements of tonal systems in these languages are less often reflected in melody. This pertains to contour tones – either phonemic or phonetic – as opposed to level tones, which holds for both languages. Underlying tones showed a significantly lower degree of tone-tune correspondence than surface tones in Guinean Kpelle, a language with obligatory rules of tone realization in context. Finally, tones on CVV structures proved to be less often reflected in melody as opposed to other morpheme types in Guro.

We have provided some statistics suggesting that certain properties of musical piece, i.e. style, genre and structure, also affect the degree of tone-tune correspondence in Guro data.

This study has a number of important limitations. First of all, while assessing pitch transitions in melody, we only looked at the direction of a transition (i.e. whether musical pitch goes up or down or remains the same). Considering exact intervals may prove equally important for studying tone-tune relationship, especially in languages with more contrasted tone levels (four or five). Second, we did not consider rhythmic structure which may certainly be relevant for text-to-tune mapping rules.

Obviously, further work needs to be done to establish the exact properties of tonal systems which are pertinent to the degree and the nature of tone-tune correspondence in a given musical tradition. More contrastive and typological studies of songs in languages with different tonal systems should be carried out.

References

1. Hayes, B., Kaun, A.: The role of phonological phrasing in sung and chanted verse. Linguistic Rev. **13**, 243–303 (1996)
2. Kiparsky, P.: A modular metrics for folk verse. In: Elan Dresher, B., Friedberg, N. (eds.) Formal approaches to poetry, pp. 7–49. Berling, Mouton (2006)
3. Dell, F., Halle J.: Comparing Musical Textsetting in French and in English Songs. In: Jean-Louis Aroui & Andy Arleo (a cura di.), Towards a typology of poetic forms, 63–78. Amsterdam (2009)
4. Rodríguez-Vázquez, R.: The rhythm of speech, verse and vocal music: a new theory. Linguistic Insights **110**, 394 (2010)
5. Halle, J. Text, Tune and Metrical Form. MS. http://www.johnhalle.com/musical.writing. technical/similarity.real.pdf
6. Ladd, R.: Singing in tone languages: an introduction to the kinds of things we might expect to find. In: Lechleitner, G., Liebl, C. (eds.) Jahrbuch des Phonogrammarchivs der Österreichischen Akademie der Wissenschaften, vol. 4, pp. 13–28. Cuvillier Verlag, Göttingen (2014)
7. Richards, P.: A quantitative analysis of the relationship between language tone and melody in a Hausa song. Afri. Lang. Stud. **13**, 137–161 (1972)
8. Rycroft, D.K.: The relationships between speech-tone and melody in Southern African music. In: Malan, J.P. (ed.) South African Music Encyclopedia, vol. 2, pp. 301–314. Oxford University Press, Capetown (1972)
9. Leben, W.R.: On the correspondence between linguistic tone and musical melody. In: Proceedings of the 9th Annual Meeting of the Berkley Lingusitics Society, pp. 148–157 (1983)

10. Ekwueme, L.N.: Linguistic determinants of some Igbo musical properties. J. African Stud. **1** (3), 335–353 (1974)
11. Agawu, K.: Tone and tune: the evidence for northern Ewe music. Africa **58**(2), 127–146 (1988)
12. Gibbon, D., Ahoua, F., Kipré, B.F., Griffiths, S.: Discrete level narrative, terraced music: insights from underdocumented Ivorian languages. In: Austin, P.K., Bond, O., Charette, M., Nathan, D., Sells, P. (eds.) Proceedings of Conference on Language Documentation and Linguistic Theory 2. SOAS, London (2009)
13. Schellenberg, M.: Singing in a tone language: Shona. In: Ojo, A., Moshi, L. (eds.) Selected Proceedings of the 39th Annual Conference on African Linguistics, pp. 137–144. Cascadilla Proceedings Project, Somerville, MA (2009)
14. Connell, B.: Tones in tunes: a preliminary look at speech and song melody in Mambila. Speech Lang. Technol. **14**(15), 137–146 (2012)
15. Schellenberg, M.: Does language determine music in tone languages? Ethnomusicology **56**(2), 266–278 (2014). (Spring/Summer 2012)
16. Lewis, M.P., Simons, G.F., Fennig, C.D. (eds.): Ethnologue: Languages of the World, Eighteenth edn. SIL International, Dallas (2015). http://www.ethnologue.com
17. Chao, Y.R.: Tone, intonation, singsong, chanting, recitative, tonal composition and atonal composition in Chinese. In: Halle, M., Lunt, H.G., McLean, H., van Schooneveld, C.H. (eds.) For Roman Jakobson: Essays on the occasion of his sixtieth birthday, 11th October 1956, pp. 52–59. Mouton and Co, The Hague (1956)
18. Schellenberg, M.: The realization of tone in singing in Cantonese and Mandarin. Ph.D., Dissertation. The University of British Columbia, Vancouver (2013)
19. Konoshenko, M.: Tonal systems in three dialects of the Kpelle language. Mandenkan **44**, 21–42 (2008)
20. Konoshenko, M.: The syntax of tone in Guinean Kpelle. In: Proceedings of the Fortieth Annual Meeting of the Berkeley Linguistics Society, pp. 233–252, 7–9 February (2014)
21. Kuznetsova, N., Kuznetsova, O., Vydrine, V.: Propositions pour une réforme de l'orthographe du gouro. Mandenkan **44**, 43–52 (2008)
22. Kuznetsova, O.: Tones in Guro and their indication in practical orthography. Qualification paper. Saint-Petersburg State University (2005) (In Russian)
23. Maddieson, I.: Universals of tone. In: Greenberg, J.H. (ed.) Universals of Human Language Phonology, vol. 2, pp. 335–363. Stanford University Press, Stanford (1978)
24. Zhang, J.: The effects of duration and sonority on contour tone distribution – typological survey and formal analysis. Ph.D. Dissertation, UCLA (2001)
25. Luznetsova, N.: Le statut fonctionnel du pied phonologique en gouro. Mandenkan **43**, 13–45 (2007)
26. Le Saout, J.: Notes sur la phonologie du Gouro (zone de Zuénoula). CEPLAN, Nice (1979)
27. List, G.: Speech melody and song melody in central Thailand. Ethnomusicology **5**(1), 16–32 (1961)

Author Index

Printed in the United States
By Bookmasters